RINGSIDE

A tale of music and mayhem from
the man behind rock and roll
superstars Cold Chisel

ALLEN&UNWIN
SYDNEY·MELBOURNE·AUCKLAND·LONDON

Allen & Unwin
Cammeraygal Country
83 Alexander Street
Crows Nest NSW 2065
Australia
Phone: (61 2) 8425 0100
Email: info@allenandunwin.com
Web: www.allenandunwin.com

Allen & Unwin acknowledges the Traditional Owners of the Country on which we live and work. We pay our respects to all Aboriginal and Torres Strait Islander Elders, past and present.

A catalogue record for this book is available from the National Library of Australia

ISBN 978 1 76106 924 6

Set in 12.5/17 pt Adobe Garamond by Post Pre-press Group, Australia
Printed and bound in Australia by the Opus Group

10 9 8 7 6 5 4 3 2 1

The paper in this book is FSC® certified. FSC® promotes environmentally responsible, socially beneficial and economically viable management of the world's forests.

CONTENTS

PROLOGUE

Dawn light breaks in the rear-view mirror as, ahead, a flock of emus strides across the wet bitumen dividing the boundless Hay Plain. Careening down the Sturt Highway to the City of Churches, I find myself the latest in a procession of managers to attempt to take on a bunch of wild lads from Adelaide. Three weeks earlier, at the insistence of my younger brother Ian, I had reluctantly ventured to a small club in Sydney's Chinatown to check out a band with a questionable name: Cold Chisel. Ian had sworn they were exceptional. I was intrigued, as I hadn't experienced anything exceptional since my return to Australia from the UK two months earlier.

Cold Chisel were on their way to a Thursday-night gig at their self-proclaimed home base, the Largs Pier Hotel. It was 19 May 1977, and it would be the band's first show in the venue in close to a year. I had decided to express my solidarity and a shared affinity for life on the road by sharing the fifteen-hour road trip with them. The car suggested to me that money was tight. I had been allotted the middle rear seat, wedged between drummer Steve Prestwich and bassist Phil Small, a position

1

disparagingly known as the 'bitch seat'. I realised why when my coccyx, perched precariously above the Holden's drive shaft, responded unkindly to every bump in the road. Despite many years of driving trucks throughout Europe and the US in all manner of conditions, I wasn't prepared for the state of Australian roads—or every young bloke's desire to emulate Peter Brock at Mount Panorama. With the exception of singer Jim Barnes, dozing, his feet on the dashboard, and keyboard player Don Walker, who usually had his nose buried in a book, everyone else in Cold Chisel seemed to believe that 'unless your foot is glued to the floor, then you're not serious'.

'What's the speed limit round here?' I asked as we roared down the highway.

Ian Moss, who was at the wheel, turned to me with a wry grin and pumped the pedal even harder. I guess the years of pulling all-nighters and driving shitty cars on routes that were less than roadworthy had taught them this: the right way was the quickest way.

Fuel and food stops were a blessing and a chance to offer a prayer to the rock gods for getting so far safely. But never once did I allow myself to express any fear or pain. I needed to show my mettle, that I was of old roadie stock, conditioned to way worse than whatever Australia could throw up at me. Yet upon reaching the sanctuary of Adelaide, remarkably in one piece, I must admit the thought of kissing the bitumen crossed my mind.

At first sight, the Largs Pier Hotel seemed totally out of place in the flat suburban landscape. Three storeys high, the 1882 Italianate structure sat on a vast corner block directly opposite the Largs Bay Pier, a wharf where over the years thousands of 'New Australians' had disembarked. The atmosphere outside the hotel was like a family reunion—Jim, Phil and Steve were locals, raised in suburban Adelaide. Punters were milling around, cheering and backslapping 'Chisel', the homecoming heroes. It appeared as if everyone—band and fans—was on first-name terms: 'Hey Jimmmmmy, hey Steve, Chisellllll!' Overwhelmingly the punters were working-class suburban kids, mad for loud rock and roll.

The gig was different to what I'd experienced over the past eleven years in the UK, where pub crowds listened in relative silence until a song ended. Here I found myself among a sea of drinkers—of beer, or bourbon and Coke, mainly—who just carried on talking and shouting throughout every song. Their arms were draped over their mates' shoulders, so close that they shared sweat in a strange act of wrestling and moving to the music. As I looked around the packed, smoke-filled room, its beer-soaked carpet smelling like a wet dog, the crowd noise seemed to be in direct competition with the band. The only interruptions to this ritual were the thunderous cheers and whistles that greeted the end of every song. Every so often the packed dance floor would part like a faultline as two punters, often women, teed off on each other. This would be quickly extinguished by burly bouncers, who'd hurl the offenders out the front door onto the Esplanade. I later learned that these evictions weren't always successful. On one memorable night, after being ejected, two highly intoxicated shearers re-entered the venue via the back wall at the wheel of their Holden ute.

Since the gig in Chinatown, I had seen two other Cold Chisel performances: one a lunchtime show at the University of Newcastle, the other a support at the Bondi Lifesaver. While I was impressed enough to move forward, the show at the Pier was something else altogether. Chisel already had that raw energy, that vital ingredient that made a band unique, but it was the enthusiasm from the packed crowd that seemed to lift them to new heights—and they fed off it. What also stood out were the originals poking through the obligatory covers, such songs as 'Home and Broken Hearted', 'One Long Day', 'Just How Many Times' and 'Juliet'.

Maybe they were responding to their rapturous hometown crowd or the feeling of finally having someone on board who believed in them—namely me, this jungle-green manager who'd blown smoke up their arses for near on 1400 kilometres. The truth was that I needed this to work too. My wife was pregnant and my future was as uncertain as the band's. I went away thinking that if they could produce this kind of energy in other blue-collar hubs then nothing could stop them. This would be our blueprint, a plan built on a solid base of working-class punters with a love for unapologetically loud rock music. I figured if I got this right, the mainstream would follow. I trusted my gut feeling. This novice prospector had finally struck the seam.

That night I learned that they were the real deal: the singer with the impish grin and dirty sneakers; the shy guitarist who hid beneath his tousled mane; the bass player who never ever looked untidy; the Scouser on drums, ever so contrary, with his oversized shoes; and the tall, erudite piano player, with a voice as dry as an outback watering hole and the songs to galvanise a generation.

This is my story of how I teamed up with a wild bunch of lads from Adelaide for 32 years. It's the story of who I was before, who I am now and what fell in between. I hope you enjoy the ride as much as I have.

1

NORTHERN BEACHES BOY

I'm standing in the garden of a palatial home in Mosman, a suburb that borders Sydney Harbour. I gaze across the manicured green of the Mosman Croquet Club and, in the background, a large two-storey stucco building accentuated by tall palm trees appears above the suburban red brick. Its iron spire is reminiscent of a church in Spain. It seems oddly out of place in this leafy, affluent area, a blend of deep-red Federation-era houses, Californian bungalows, modern townhouses and apartment buildings. This building was once the All Saints Church of England hospital, and that's where I made my raucous entrance in November 1947.

My grandparents, Brian and Dorothy, were married at London's Wandsworth Registers Office in December of 1911; my father, Graham, was born at the Croydon General Hospital in London in December 1912. Brian took a job as a commercial traveller for WD & HO Wills, the British tobacco company, and they moved into the middle-class suburb of Redlands in Bristol.

Dad's brother Stuart would arrive just as the First World War was breaking out in 1914. My grandfather enlisted in the

British Army's Dorset Regiment and only five days into battle was caught in a poison gas attack in France. He was hospitalised and sent back to England and ironically spent the remaining war years working as a gas instructor.

Growing tired of the postwar gloom in England, the Willis family decided to try their luck in Australia. Dad was ten when the family boarded the RFA *Largs Bay* on her maiden voyage in January 1922. Dad remembered being on deck to see the Rock of Gibraltar as they steamed through the straits, and marvelling at the alien tropical vista from the veranda of the Galle Face Hotel at sunset in Colombo. It was a world away from dreary grey Bristol.

The Willises reached Sydney in April, and within a week they had relocated to Mosman, where my dad and his brother Stuart were enrolled at Mosman Public School. It was a wonderland for Dad and Stuart, bashing cricket balls around in the quiet streets, or jumping on a tram to make the long, winding trip down the hill to Balmoral Beach on stinking-hot summer days. Most Saturday afternoons in winter, my dad, Stuart and my grandfather would jump on the tram to North Sydney Oval and barrack for local rugby team Northern Suburbs. Dad's dream of playing rugby were shattered when he was diagnosed with myopia at the age of twelve. Unfortunately for him, contact lenses were a thing of the future.

Despite poor marks at school—a trait I would inherit—Dad secured his first job in 1928 as a copy boy on the *Evening News* newspaper before moving to their rival, *The Sun*, as a cadet. *The Sun* had come up with a unique way of letting the passing public know the test cricket scores: on the outside of their office building, which faced Hyde Park, a large blackboard was affixed to the wall with the layout of a cricket oval painted on it. Large white chalk dots signified the players' positions. Dad's task was to monitor the live radio broadcast and shift the dots according to the state of play. Literally hundreds of people would gather as the game played out via the blackboard.

In the spring of 1933, Dad moved into a new vocation with the giant motion picture studio Metro-Goldwyn-Mayer (MGM). At first, he ran the radio movie club, which publicised the latest MGM movies on 2GB; eventually he was promoted to run the publicity department.

In 1939, as another war loomed, Dad rushed to enlist but his poor eyesight initially ruled him out. This was a stressful time for him as he watched all his mates enlist without any trouble. One morning he awoke to find a white feather—an accusation of cowardice—had been placed in the letterbox, an act of pure bastardry if ever there was one. Finally, in 1943 he was able to join the 2nd Coast Artillery Training Battery based at North Head. He was assigned to the Australian Army Amenities Service and sent to run radio station 9AD, on the island of Morotai, north-west of what was then Dutch New Guinea. As corporal-librarian he was excited to finally be among the action, albeit at the radio station. His hopes were shattered, however, as the Japanese surrendered on the day his ship landed; the war was over. He spent the next nine months on Morotai providing music and news, and staging live comedy shows similar to the hijinks seen in the famous 1970s British sitcom *It Ain't Half Hot Mum*.

Returning to civvy life, Dad rejoined MGM, where he produced the popular radio show *The Lion's Roar* for the Macquarie Network. At a Friday-night dance at the Congregational Hall in Mosman, he zeroed in on an attractive dancer named Peggy Presgrave They married in December 1946.

My mother was born in 1923 in the NSW country town of Scone, to Herbert and Laura Presgrave. When she was five the family moved to Bellevue Hill in Sydney's affluent Eastern Suburbs. Mum was enrolled at the prestigious Sydney Church of England Girls' Grammar School (now known as SCEGGS) and excelled at sport, particularly tennis, athletics and swimming. She spent her summers as a member of the North Bondi surf club, manning patrols. Her father Herbert was a commercial traveller—they were the only family in the street with a car.

Mum, like Dad, had been keen to join the forces but her parents argued that at seventeen she was far too young. Finally in 1942 she enlisted with the Australian Women's Army Service stationed at Sydney's Moore Park. To help flog war bonds, every Friday her company would march down George Street from Martin Place to Sydney Town Hall. On one occasion a *Woman's Day* photographer bailed up the company commander, inquiring whether he could photograph my mother in uniform. That photo went nationwide on the cover of *Woman's Day*, on the side of post delivery vans and in the advertising for an electrical company in cinemas across Australia.

At war's end, Peggy, like her older sister Glory, took up modelling. Glory was quite a star—her face had graced the cover of numerous women's magazines and she had become a famous pin-up with the Aussie troops during the war. Mum would go on to study drama. She appeared in various theatre shows and also became a regular on Australia's version of the popular *Lux Radio Theatre*, which was broadcast nationally over the Macquarie Network.

When I was born in 1947, Mum named me Rodney because, she told me, I think with her tongue firmly placed in her cheek, if I became a movie star I could be known as 'Rod', and if I became a knight, I could stay as Rodney, which was more appropriate.

★

By 1950 my parents were able to afford their first home, in the northern seaside suburb of Curl Curl, perched high on a ridge that looked due south. I can recall lots of Sunday journeys in Dad's 1937 Morris Eight exploring Terrey Hills and Ingleside—mainly scrubby bush and rural plots where we picked wildflowers and searched for blackberries. Within a couple of years our family had expanded to include my younger siblings Vicki and Ian, and we moved to a bigger house a few miles north in Dee Why. Inspired by an ocean liner, our house—with its rounded Art Deco white-stucco facade and flat roof—was in an architectural mode colloquially known as the 'P&O style'. In the late afternoon the smell of salt water would drift our way on the north-easterly wind.

I was an adventurous kid. At the age of three, while supposedly in the care of the two elderly ladies who ran Lakeman's Kindergarten, I quietly slipped out an unlocked side gate with my buddy Tony Raper and we set off on an adventure. The main obstacle between us and our intended destination—the local golf course—was a major road. The mind boggles at the thought of us making it across those four lanes without getting run over, let alone the chaos erupting simultaneously at Lakeman's.

After a couple of hours we grew hungry and headed back. Our reception on return was less than what we expected. Frogmarched, we were secured in a large cupboard under the stairs, bound with stockings and locked away until our frantic parents arrived. I was duly expelled from kindergarten—quite an achievement. In later years, my dear mother loved to relate this tale to my children, the inference being that I was a 'juvenile delinquent' from a very early age. I saw it differently. To me it represented a desire to seek adventure and throw off constraints, a trait that would develop as I grew older.

Our back garden in Dee Why was big, or so it seemed to me. It featured an old weeping willow, which was easy to climb and also produced thin, pliable branches that could be fashioned into whips and wrapped around some unsuspecting mate's legs or arse. (I often wondered why we didn't have many visitors.) At the bottom of the garden was a chook pen, home to a number of highly inquisitive bantams. We discovered that by holding a bantam's tiny beak to the ground and drawing a straight line in the dirt, the helpless fowl would be left in a hypnotised state, a trick our mates found hilarious.

Over our back fence, the dense bush was the domain of ticks, snakes, spiders and other undesirables. It wasn't unusual to come out in the morning to discover a headless brown snake left with loving care by our cat Blackie. The Northern Beaches were opening up to an influx of young postwar families, and growing up there offered many wonderful activities to occupy my time: the beach, the bush, the lagoon, and endless places to ride bikes and billycarts.

*

In 1956, my father landed the plum role of publicity manager at the newly opened Channel 7 station in Sydney. As part of his remuneration he received a brand-new black-and-white TV.

It was a major status symbol. Up until then we had travelled to Brookvale on special occasions to join the crowds on the footpath outside the local electrical store, where a black-and-white set projected images for everyone to see.

Now we all sat together in the lounge room, transfixed by this magical contraption. This was the new world and we wanted it. *Ramar of the Jungle, Hopalong Cassidy, The Lone Ranger*—it was like nothing we had ever experienced before. Even the test pattern at the end of the day's transmission was fascinating, if I could manage to stay up that late. When sent to bed under protest, I still found a way to quietly sneak from my bed and peer through a crack in the lounge room's sliding doors. More than once this was interrupted by my mother's stern question: 'Are you out of bed, Rodney?'

The 1956 Melbourne Olympics had all the pomp and ceremony of a royal visit. Athletes from across the globe descended on Melbourne; we watched in awe as the spectacle played out on our seventeen-inch black-and-white box. Dawn Fraser, Betty Cuthbert, Shirley Strickland and John Landy wove their magic over competition from the rest of the world, while the fiery water polo final between Russia and Hungary developed into a slugfest—it had an unsettling effect on me, a nine-year-old raised in the innocent tranquillity of postwar Australian suburbia.

One day in September 1960, I went into the city with Mum. As we entered the Paramount Pictures office in the Haymarket, Dad was descending the stairs towards us among a large group focused on an older bald man. 'Alfred,' my Dad said, 'this is my wife Peggy and our son Rodney.' Alfred Hitchcock was in Australia for the premiere of *Psycho*. I'd just met my first famous person.

★

The beach was my summer world. Every weekend, from early morning until late afternoon, my family would be at Long Reef beach until the onshore breeze chilled our bones and sent us scurrying home for a hot shower. The beach was a playground for swimming, playing and kicking the footy about. The waves were both enticing and scary, more than capable of snatching you up like a piece of flotsam and depositing you with interest hard into the sand. This resulted in either a face full of grit so abrasive it could strip off layers of your skin, or the far more humiliating experience of stumbling back to your feet, your costume distended with wet sand, giving the impression you'd taken a dump in your Speedos. By far my biggest buzz was to cling to my Dad's neck as he bodysurfed. Yes, we did go under, and yes, I was scared, but I never let go of his bronzed neck. No way.

I came from solid Anglo-Celtic stock, which meant that as the hours marched on, I would develop a bright pinkish glow. The sun-bronzed Aussie look was a badge of honour. Skin cancer—what was that? As night closed in, the consequences of the day would become apparent. I could tough it out on top of cool sheets, a damp cloth held to my face, or try an old family remedy: Robin starch, which gave Dad's shirts that crisp and fresh look, was also a trusted sunburn treatment in our house. The starch did what starch was designed to do—that is, go hard—and in no time at all I'd closely resemble an Egyptian mummy and feel like an embalmed pharaoh. Of course the starch would crack and flake and slowly crumble and by morning I'd be lying in a pile of chalky dust. One warm shower later and, as amazing as it may sound, I'd be free of pain. It did work, but I'm not sure how.

My dad was fairly conservative by nature, apart from his nightly routine of pissing on the passionfruit vine, insisting it fertilised the plant and helped with its abundant crop. The only time I ever recall him really loosening up was when performing his party trick—an impressive Hitler impersonation. Brushing his hair down onto his forehead, he would produce a black comb from his back pocket and, with it poised under his nose, would let fly with a torrent of mock German. Mum was loving, warm and kind, but was also the chief disciplinarian at home. A wooden spoon across my knuckles at the dinner table wasn't out of the ordinary if I left any food on my plate.

Four lanes of bitumen lay between our home and the Dee Why lagoon, known to locals as the 'Lugga' and famous as the nesting ground of the migrating black swan. Its dense bush and reeds became the backdrop for plenty of childhood adventures. My mates and I cobbled together a primitive boat from discarded corrugated iron and pieces of timber. Unstable, sure, but good enough to traverse the lagoon while we played out childhood fantasies from *Treasure Island* or *The Famous Five*. Unfortunately, our boat trips came with about a 50 per cent success rate; we'd either glide elegantly through the water like the majestic black swan or plunge straight to the murky depths like Captain Nemo.

Shadowing our neighbourhood and running adjacent to the coastline was a jagged rocky plateau. Its caves and rocky outcrops provided secret hideaways, while the giant ancient gums were the perfect haven for cubbyhouses. If anyone tried to invade our hidden world, we armed ourselves with slingshots, which were better known as 'Shanghais'. They could be deadly in the wrong hands.

Steve 'Stompy' Cummings was a couple of years older than most of us, and a future surf stomp Hall of Famer. Steve frequented the caves and cliffs of the plateau. For some odd reason, he liked to stand buck naked on a cliff ledge hundreds of feet above sea level, emitting a bloodcurdling roar that would have made Johnny Weissmuller cower. War cry aside, Steve possessed a much-desired weapon, a slug gun/air rifle, standard issue along with the 'Shanghai' if you could afford one.

One scorching summer day, I somehow persuaded Steve to let me look after the gun while he went about his naked ritual. I loved the feel of the metal, the shiny barrel, its lacquered wooden stock. A great sense of power came over me. Steve, meanwhile, had assumed his favourite position—naked, with arms stretched to the heavens, a Tarzan call bursting from his lungs. For some inane reason I drew a bead on his round white buttocks. Soon enough came the stark realisation that the gun had fired, and the projectile had travelled in a straight line to Steve's arse. The look of pain on his face said it all. To cut a long story short, I fucking ran! I fled through the bush like a gazelle, with a naked, wounded rhino hot on my heels. At one stage I managed to glance behind me; thankfully, Steve was nowhere to be seen. I guess a slug in the arse was painful enough without ripping your naked body to pieces on the unforgiving flora.

From an early age, I was rebellious, inquisitive and constantly looking for adventure. When I was about eleven, a mate and I cooked up a plan to steal a car and drive to Broken Hill—the furthest point on the Golden Fleece map in the glovebox of Dad's Morris Minor. It was a great idea, apart from the fact that neither of us knew how to drive, let alone hotwire a car.

2

THE PRIMAL BEAT

Music had been around our home for as long as I can recall, whether it was Doris Day, Bing Crosby, Perry Como, Harry Belafonte, or Johnnie Ray (my mum's favourite). I don't recall exactly when I was first introduced to the new phenomenon known as rock and roll, but I do remember my parents returning from witnessing Bill Haley & His Comets—creators of the huge hit 'Rock Around the Clock'—at the Sydney Stadium in 1957, along with The Platters, LaVern Baker, Big Joe Turner, and Freddie Bell and the Bellboys. From memory, they weren't impressed.

Rock-and-roll music gave the postwar youth its own battle cry. Parents hated it; kids loved it. At first, radio reacted in a predictably conservative manner but it didn't take long for DJs to realise that there was an audience out there, especially with Elvis's arrival in the mid-1950s. We were initially force-fed squeaky-clean versions of rock songs by Pat Boone and Connie Francis, and vocal groups like The Diamonds and The Crew Cuts. But nothing was ever going to stop the visceral power that drove Chuck Berry, Little Richard, Jerry Lee Lewis, Buddy

Holly, Fats Domino, Gene Vincent, Eddie Cochran, The Everly Brothers and the white prince of darkness himself, Elvis Presley. Suddenly all around me, I was aware of a change—older guys, their hair now Spruso-pomaded, wore skin-tight sky-blue jeans, 'Presley purple' shirts, and 'Sinatra red' or 'Mitchell blue' socks. This was the new teenage uniform.

In the late 1950s, my father, while employed at Channel 7, moonlighted for the magazine *TV Week*. His role was to review the latest pop releases in a column called 'Record Round Up'. His pseudonym was Ian Rodney, a melding of the names of his two sons. Other than having a musical cousin—Roger, the original bass player for Dig Richards and the R'Jays—this was my first serious association with 'rock music'. One night, Dad walked into my bedroom with a selection of vinyl 45s under his arm. Among them was Lloyd Price's 'Personality' and The Isley Brothers' 'Shout', plus releases from Dicky Doo & the Don'ts, and Santo & Johnny.

'Can you have a listen to this lot,' Dad asked, 'and let me know what you think?'

Dad was fine writing about crooners like Perry Como and Bing Crosby, but with rock and roll he was a lost soul in the desert. Every week he'd arrive home with a stash of singles, pop them onto the radiogram and solicit my opinion. I loved Fats Domino, The Coasters and Bobby Freeman, but Connie Francis and Pat Boone's vanilla pop left me cold. I still have my first LP—Jerry Lee Lewis's 1958 debut album.

Until around late 1957, the only way that I could listen to rock music was via the family radiogram, which, along with the TV set, was the entertainment hub in the Willis household. This would fundamentally change for me with the advent of the portable transistor radio. At last I had the freedom to listen

16

to my favourite DJs, like 2UE's Bob Rogers, playing the latest Top 40 hits. I could have music anytime, anywhere, for as long as the batteries lasted.

In late 1958 Sydney TV station Channel 9 replicated the highly successful US music show *American Bandstand* with their own *Bandstand*, featuring all the top family-friendly pop performers of the era, such as Col Joye and Little Pattie. By February 1959 the ABC had launched their own music weekly, *Six O'Clock Rock*, hosted by the king of Australian rock, Johnny O'Keefe. I still recall my excitement as the *Six O'Clock Rock* theme began and JOK sang, 'Well come on, everybody, it's six o'clock, huh-huh, uh-huh-huh.'

I was also a big fan of the midday movies on Channel 7, which might be *Casablanca,* or the Marx Brothers, or Audie Murphy mowing down the enemy with a blast of his machine gun. It's also where I first saw what were called 'jump blues' films, such as *Stormy Weather* and *Cabin in the Sky*, with amazing performers like Lena Horne and Cab Calloway and Fats Waller, which I loved. The predominantly Black casts were part of a genre known in America as 'race films'—it was my first exposure to any kind of racial divide.

*

Surfing was now an integral part of Australian culture. After growing up at Long Reef, I gravitated just north to Collaroy where the real scene was. Along with the other grommets and hangers-on, I could usually be found slumped against the sandstone wall between the surf club and the pool. That sandstone wall provided us with the perfect vantage point to observe the small waves that wrapped gently around the pool, and the young, nubile babes sunbaking. The Collaroy grommet crew at that time included a skinny kid named Nat Young. While we desperately tried to emulate our Hawaiian surfing heroes, he actually did it. He was a constant annoyance to the older guys but with his unique ability they just had to accept him. He would of course go on to become one of the true legends of the sport.

During 1962, a unique by-product of the surf culture emerged. Barry Farrell was a sixteen-year-old entrepreneur from Harbord who convinced the local Avalon surf club to let him stage weekly dances with his band The Sundowners. The dance—or, more accurately, 'the Stomp'—attracted local teenagers in droves across the nation. An obvious benefit for a surf club was the revenue; the downside was 1000 pairs of feet stomping simultaneously, which placed the building's foundations under major stress. Clubs quickly closed down venues, ending a phenomenon never before seen and never repeated.

The Art Deco picture theatre in Collaroy was directly opposite the beach, and the arrival of surf movies in the early 1960s led to locals (me included) queuing for hours along Pittwater Road. Lounging on the maroon velveteen, we'd be thoroughly immersed in the action on the giant screen; each wave was met with hoots, every wipeout with 'ahhhs'. The action on the screen was interspersed with bottle tops flying through the air and Jaffas down the aisle—it was all part of the surf-movie experience.

★

Before sewerage was connected to the Northern Beaches, we had the 'dunny man', a title given to the poor sod whose job was to empty the outside toilet. Exactly how much they paid this guy I have no idea, but it couldn't have been enough. Thankfully, around the mid-1950s, the septic tank business started booming in newly developing suburbs such as ours.

My parents commissioned a local builder, William Reeve Parker—known simply as Mal—to do the excavation and installation. Mal was a colourful character, short and stocky, with dark pomaded hair brushed straight back like a gangster's. He also swore like a sailor: 'Fuck this, fuck that,' he'd say, as I spent hours listening to stories of his boxing career, and the rough-and-tough world of living in the outback, shearing sheep. I liked that he swore in my company; it made me feel less like a kid. I soon started dropping the odd F-bomb while in Mal's company.

'I suggest you don't say that when your mother's around,' he warned me.

One of the many yarns Mal told me was how he often worked for Lee Gordon, the famous 1950s concert promoter, doing security at the Sydney Stadium Big Shows, as they were called. He recalled being with the outrageous Little Richard, crossing the Hunter River on the Stockton ferry in Newcastle, when he denounced rock and roll for God. 'The mad bastard threw his jewellery into the drink,' Mal said, shaking his head.

Mal was an orphan who'd grown up in foster homes. His surname was, I believe, a combination of two of his foster parents' names. He learned the building trade during his years in the bush and eventually married and settled in Dee Why, raising three sons.

I was somewhat surprised to see Mal at our house on regular occasions, even after he finished installing the tank. I put it down to his friendly disposition—it never entered my mind that he had something to do with the glint in my mother's eye. I don't recall how my parents dealt with this, although my sister has since reminded me of a huge argument between my parents over Mal, which ended when Dad shoved a broom through the back door. And yet life rolled on, and Mal remained a fixture in the landscape. In retrospect, it was all very bizarre, but then a situation arose that helped Dad deal with the issue.

★

It was 1960, and my high school choices were either the newly opened Narrabeen High or a private school. I'm not sure exactly why, but I showed an interest in going to the bush. Maybe I was influenced by the popular 'Smiley' films of the mid-1950s, but whatever my motivation, the nearest agricultural school was James Ruse Agricultural High School at Carlingford in Sydney's north-western suburbs. It was a fair hike from my beloved Northern Beaches, a journey of three hours each way. Dad worked at Channel 7 in Epping, which was not far from the school, so it was agreed that he and I would stay at West Ryde during the week and return to Dee Why on the weekends.

I think the move gave Dad some respite from the 'Mal situation'. I really don't know how Dad felt; I never asked him. I was too busy enjoying the freedom I now had between arriving home from school and Dad's return from work several hours later. Our host was Mrs Allebone, a lovely English lady who ran a guesthouse with her husband. They had a daughter; a son, Roger; and a foster son, Dennis. Roger and Dennis were around my age, so we quickly bonded. Roger would later become a well-known journalist for the ABC and 2JJ.

At James Ruse, I immediately bonded with Peter Warner who, like me, was more focused on sport and girls than academia. Unfortunately our lotus-eater lifestyle drew a fair degree of retribution from the teaching staff. A thin bamboo cane was the teachers' weapon of choice and this painful punishment was normally administered in full view of my fellow students. The only upside was that the more strokes I received, the more kudos and respect I collected from my classmates. A few of us devised a simple and effective method to return serve—we'd shove a potato up the exhaust pipe of the caner's car, which led to either an extremely loud backfire or, better still, the exhaust unit being blown clear off the car. By the time this happened, of course, we would be long gone. It was the perfect revenge.

★

By my third year in high school, we'd moved to a Victorian-era terrace in McMahons Point, overlooking Luna Park and the Sydney Harbour Bridge. The move meant I could travel by train to Carlingford, but I was despondent about leaving my beloved Northern Beaches. The upside was that I was closer to schoolmates like Peter Warner, who lived in Crows Nest.

Winter was footy time. My team, North Sydney, was a gun junior rugby side and in July 1963 we won a prestigious under-sixteen premiership, which led to a six-game tour of New Zealand. The pinnacle of our Long White Cloud visit was playing the curtain-raiser to a Ranfurly Shield match at Eden Park, one of the holiest rugby grounds in the world. We ran out onto the ground in front of a large crowd; it was spine tingling. Our adversaries were a local Auckland team, Eastern Suburbs. I recall the crowd, the manicured turf and the massive arena, but it didn't seem real. I caught the ball from the kick-off and took off down the sideline—I could see the tryline beckoning, I was going to score with my first touch! But no, I was drilled, blindsided by a large Māori player whose tackle drove me into touch. I can't recall if we won, but it was a great experience.

Although we were some 20–40 minutes from the coast, I was normally able to persuade Mum to drive me up to Collaroy or Manly beach on most summer weekends. On my thirteenth birthday I received a second-hand surfboard, built by legendary board maker Scott Dillon. It was a 2.9 metre malibu sprayed white; a large red-and-blue diamond pattern adorned the deck. The surfing phenomenon was sweeping Oz, but it came with a perilous downside: riding a long missile that speared through the foam at high velocity. (This was before the introduction of leg ropes.) Councils issued registration stickers that were to be affixed to surfboards, and they were banned between the surf lifesavers' flags.

One sunny Saturday, while I surfed a nice little break at Manly's North Steyne, I lost my board and it drifted into the no-surf zone. On my arrival at the water's edge I was greeted by a large bronzed chap who looked like the Chesty Bonds man; the words 'Beach Inspector' were emblazoned on his singlet.

'What are you doing surfing in the flags, you mug?' he spat out of the side of his sun-damaged lips.

My board was impounded for a week—and I was fined. My parents weren't thrilled.

*

When not installing septic tanks, Mal sometimes worked for Australia's largest private investigation agency, Websters. He decided to open his own agency, Parkers, with my uncle Ron, a solicitor by trade, and my mum, who became Australia's first female private investigator. They specialised in divorce and insurance scams. Mainly people falsely claiming inability to work due to a work-related injury.

In 1962, the ground floor of our newly acquired home in McMahons Point was transformed into an office for their business. Dad moved into a bedroom at the rear of the ground floor while Mum and we kids lived upstairs in our own rooms. To add to this bizarre storyline, Mal now began to sleep on a pull-out bed in the TV room on the ground floor. When people asked about him, we'd simply reply, 'Oh, that's Uncle Mal.'

I had just turned fourteen when Mal asked if I wanted to earn some pocket money over the school holidays monitoring an insurance case. Of course I did. Seated in an old lounge chair in the back of a battered Ford van with my transistor radio tuned to 2UE, I spent a couple of days logging our suspect's movements. It was mostly innocent everyday activities, until 'Suspect X' with a supposed injured back fired up his Victa lawnmower. Red alert! I went to a nearby phone box and called Mal, who arrived with his Kodak Zoom 8 as the guy was still mowing his lawn. Busted. I got my pocket money.

There were definitely perks associated with having the agency located at home. By far the best—and most dangerous—was Mal's collection of guns, which he kept in a filing cabinet that was rarely locked. God knows how my mother would have reacted if she had walked in and found me grasping a .45 snub-nose revolver. Another perk for a curious kid like me was the selection of racy photos that Mal kept stored in the same cabinet, the proof of adultery crucial to the divorce cases he was hired to investigate.

In late 1963, Mal sold the agency and bought a 50-acre dairy farm in Mogo, four hours south of Sydney, a sleepy backwater blip on the Princes Highway. Mal's move was a relief for my siblings and me; we no longer had to say 'Oh, that's Uncle Mal' when asked about his place in our lives. The relationship between Mum and Mal continued, but his visits were less frequent.

I did visit Mogo on school holidays and fondly remember spending time at the farm, arising at daybreak to call the cows from the lower pasture, watching them slowly amble up the muddy corrugated track to the milking shed. It was so cold in winter that my hands just about froze as I washed the cows' swollen udders clean before applying the vacuum cups. The aroma of mud and cow shit still resonates with me after all these years. Milking was a tough chore, but the upside was driving a tractor around the paddocks and tracks. I quickly learned that by hitting the turning brake of the old Massey Ferguson's rear wheels, I could drift through corners as if I was on Parramatta Speedway. Being a teenager and thinking I was bulletproof, the possibility of the tractor rolling never entered my mind.

One Saturday night during the Christmas break, when I was sixteen, Mal's oldest son Kim and I travelled into Batemans Bay to a dance at the local surf club. Hanging out in the car park was a group of local surfers, a few years older than us, drinking longnecks and shooting the breeze. Not long after our arrival a carload of young Indigenous kids of a similar age arrived and did the same—drank and hung about. Kim and I, being suburban kids, were intrigued by the dynamic between the two cultures. Soon enough, trouble began brewing. A member of each group headed for a point midway between the two mobs. They circled each other in a slow, combative dance until one threw a punch. When one of them went down, the other would stand back, allowing time for his rival to decide whether he wanted to continue. Two more combatants would then take centrestage and punch on in the same fashion. Most of them probably knew each other, went to school together, played footy together, but the cultural divide dictated that it was necessary to compete in this manner.

'Boy,' Kim said to me as the scene unfolded. 'This is even better than watching the band.'

3

THE LEAFY NORTH SHORE

By the end of 1963, we'd moved from McMahons Point to the leafy Upper North Shore suburb of Roseville. The unconventional was still the norm: my parents slept in separate rooms, Mum's relationship with Mal continued and we kids maintained a 'nothing to see here' attitude.

The Hamiltons, a larger-than-life family, lived across the street. The tribe consisted of Big John and his wife Nola; four boys—Tony, Kim, Gavin and Jamie; and a daughter, Leilani. Big John was a bit-part actor, entrepreneur, raconteur and brick cleaner; his great love was Cadillacs. A familiar sight was Big John in his bright-red Cadillac convertible, Nola by his side dressed bohemian style, her long blonde hair flying in the wind. The rear seat was occupied by two formidable white German shepherds. Two palomino horses resided in their backyard, much to the displeasure of snooty neighbours.

From a very early age, the boys had been involved in modelling; they'd often sing and perform on Desmond Tester's *Cabbage Quiz* and other kids' TV shows. Jamie, the youngest son, was the original Australian Milky Bar Kid, decked out in white cowboy gear. Being of a similar age, Tony and I immediately buddied up and I became a regular at the Hamilton house, perhaps in part because I was subconsciously avoiding the 'Mal situation' at home. It wasn't that our house was devoid of love, or particularly unhappy, but the elephant in the room was ever-present. I loved the Hamiltons' chaotic, loving family life, their openness, their acceptance of both my sister and me. What exactly they knew, or thought, about life at the Willises, I never discovered.

Roseville was home to many young families, so there were lots of other teenagers to hang out with. The streets were wide, providing abundant space for us to ride our bikes and engage in the new craze of 'sidewalk surfing'—skateboarding. Constructed from wooden boards to which roller skate wheels had been attached, our crude boards were designed for one purpose only: maximum velocity. 'No fear' was our sworn motto, but it should have been 'no fear, no brains'. Many a brave pilot ended their journey in a crumpled mess on the nature strip.

My close circle of friends included Ian 'Four Eyes' Lewis and Roger 'Dogsbody' Marshall. Roger had left school early to become a mechanic. This meant he had money and, more importantly, he had wheels—a black 1951 Ford Prefect. With this pride of British engineering, we were able to travel to the beach, parties, dances and, of course, the pub. The fact that we were all underage was a minor detail.

Jammed in the Prefect, we would cruise through the drive-in bottle-o of the Greengate Hotel in Killara trying to look as grown-up as possible. We'd stock up on a couple of cartons of Reschs Dinner Ale—known to us as 'Dirty Annie'—and head off to wreak havoc. High on our agenda was gatecrashing parties. Word would get around and, like clockwork, the hordes—generally fuelled by too many beers—would descend to intrude on the night's festivities. The reaction was mixed: sometimes it added that spark that was missing from an otherwise boring evening; at other times it just spelled chaos. As the mass would grow and the noise and chaos increase, the constabulary would be called, their arrival accompanied by the sound of jeers and cheers from the rowdy mob. I don't recall any wanton damage; it was more like some sort of a game being played out, a mixture of youthful exuberance and rebellion.

*

Tony had taken up guitar at an early age and, while at Chatswood High, he formed his first band with schoolmates Craig Collinge on drums (Craig would later play with Manfred Mann) and Chris Kennedy on bass. With the surf-music craze in full swing, they called themselves The Stompedes. They immediately became a popular attraction at such events as the St Ives Stomp at the community hall, which was always packed. Naturally there would be lots of girls, so I tagged along helping to carry their gear, taking my first baby steps on a road that would carry me for the best part of the next 50 years.

Things were changing in popular music. It was 1963 and word of a new phenomenon started filtering Down Under— The Beatles. Their first Australian single, 'Please Please Me', was released in February. Their sound was different, refreshing and exciting, a new and distinct style that was miles away from surf music. Youth culture had stagnated since Elvis had become safe and acceptable, but The Beatles seemed poised to shake it up once again. We teenagers began to grow our hair and embrace the new fashion. In August 1963 a fan magazine, *The Beatles Book*, was available locally, providing us with photos that we could imitate. We were able to track down a couple of shops in the city that sold the same high-collared shirts and black, pointed-toe, Cuban-heeled boots.

The year 1964 was going to be a big one for me: it was my final year at high school, and I could get my driver's licence. Music, too, was beginning to have a major impact on my life. What I was going to do when I left school was still up in the air, but music, surfing and generally having fun were my main priorities. I had survived so far through my quick wits and sporting prowess, so what could go wrong?

*

The British Invasion hit radio, the media and the fans like a tsunami. Radio became obsessed with the 'Mersey Sound' and The Beatles hijacked the charts, while Peter and Gordon, The Honeycombs, Cilla Black, Freddie and the Dreamers, The Searchers, Gerry and the Pacemakers, and The Dave Clark Five followed in their wake. Australian groups ditched the surf look and jumped aboard the Mersey bandwagon.

On 11 June 1964, I skipped school and joined the thousands of screaming fans at Kingsford Smith Airport to witness the arrival of the Fab Four. At 7.43 am, as the BOAC jet taxied towards the terminal, we all craned our scrawny necks to get a glimpse. The rain was torrential, the screams were deafening—and then suddenly they appeared at the top of the stairs. An adrenaline buzz rushed through my body; I didn't care about the rain and the wind, because The Beatles were actually here. Armed with flimsy TAA umbrellas, John, Paul, George and stand-in drummer Jimmie Nicol boarded a flatbed truck, fighting against the gale-force wind and rain as they greeted the huge crowd.

I was soaked to the skin but was on a mission and headed to the Sheraton Hotel in Kings Cross where the band was staying. I was among thousands of screaming fans and 'rubberneckers' who blocked the road outside. I will never forget that roar when The Beatles appeared smiling and waving on the balcony—it was as if a jet had taken off in Macleay Street.

Thanks to his position at Channel 7, my dad had managed to snaffle four ringside tickets for their first show on Thursday, 18 June at 6 p.m. Dad dropped me, my younger brother, my sister and her friend at the Sydney Stadium, where we mingled with thousands of teenagers milling outside, most of us in awe of the fact that we were actually, *yes really*, going to see The Beatles. Ticket touts were ignored by the police, who appeared more intent on keeping a watchful eye on the 12,000 fans being funnelled through a doorway that read 'RINGSIDE'.

We were in Row 7, amid mainly industry and media types looking embarrassingly out of place. The show opened with compere/comedian Alan Field, then British group Sounds Incorporated, followed by Johnny Chester, The Phantoms and rock-and-roller Johnny Devlin. I felt a bit sorry for the supports, who had to battle with the screaming and incessant chanting of 'Beatles! Beatles!'

All of a sudden, the heat in the old shed rose; the atmosphere was electric. Surrounded by a guard of honour of New South Wales' finest, the 'Fab Three Plus One' made their way towards the starkly lit stage. The noise was deafening. They launched straight into 'I Want to Hold Your Hand' and the place erupted in a cacophony of gyrating bodies, tears, screams and a constant shower of jelly babies directed at the band. Like everyone else I leapt to my feet; the only people still seated were those around us in the industry section. The sound system was primitive, so the best we could do was to stand on our tiptoes and lip-read, watching those movements that we had down pat. It wasn't just a musical experience—it was a moment in history.

While The Beatles presented a revolutionary shift in music, The Rolling Stones, who had emerged in late 1963, were seen as downright anarchic. Long-haired and androgynous, they were the antithesis of the postwar man—heaven knows what your man in the street in Dallas or Goondiwindi made of them. After my flirtation with Beatles songs and their pop contemporaries, the Stones had introduced a more earthy sound, harvested from US blues and R&B. Many of the young bands that had sprung up in the wake of The Beatles now turned their attention to the Stones. By late 1964, groups like The Missing Links in Sydney, Brisbane's The Impacts and Melbourne's Spinning Wheels were following their lead.

My mate Tony and fellow 'Stompeder' Peter Ellison decided to take a similar course. With a new rhythm section, drummer Baden Hutchins and bass player Ian Thomas, they formed The Showmen, a less than contemporary name compared to other groups of the time. As with The Stompedes, I tagged along in a quasi-roadie role. Although 'on the road' meant little more than a run to the inner city, it was a step up from lugging a mike stand into the community hall in St Ives. I felt a part of something, giving me a taste of what was to come.

★

Finally, aged sixteen years and ten months, I was old enough to apply for my driver's licence. It was the school holidays and I was in Mogo. The desk sergeant at nearby Moruya was a large, ruddy-faced bloke.

'You have a car here?' he asked me.

'Yes, Mum's,' I replied, nervously pointing towards her shiny 'Woomera red' Ford Falcon XL parked out front.

Leaning across the railing, his ample stomach acting like a bumper bar, he said: 'Son, drive down to the corner, turn around, come back and park.'

I followed his instructions and returned to the desk. 'Well, you can drive,' he said, 'so let's get you a licence.'

I named my first car 'The Beast'. It was a black 1938 Plymouth V8, built like a Sherman tank, which I bought from a Mogo farmer who swore his father had it from new. I didn't feel overly confident driving it back to Sydney solo, so 'Dogsbody' Marshall came to the rescue. With him at the wheel, his foot pressed firmly to the floor, The Beast growled like a Serengeti lion and surged northwards. There were no seatbelts, just our two feet firmly braced against the firewall. Back in Sydney, I now had wheels able to accommodate six or more, and with our boards strapped to the roof, my mates and I had the means to surf whenever we wished.

One particularly hot summer's day, as my mates and I cruised up the very steep Oliver Street in Harbord, the radio tuned to Chuck Berry's 'No Particular Place to Go', The Beast began to cough and splutter, and then ground to a halt. The line of angry beachgoers behind us burst into a chorus of horns and angry gestures, as Dogsbody straddled the huge wheel arch and threw open the side bonnet, a bottle filled with Shell Regular in hand. The carby gulped like a thirsty man in the Sahara and with a jolt sprang to life. Cheers of encouragement rang from the back seat but suddenly, without so much as a 'pardon me', The Beast backfired, producing a spark that leapt into the air. I screeched to a halt and we evacuated through windows and doors as flames higher than the Plymouth's roof line shot into the air. Chaos broke out all around us.

'Quick,' screamed Dogsbody, 'let the brake off and roll the fucker back!'

Thankfully, most of the petrol had trickled away from the car and the fire was swiftly extinguished. Potential disaster averted, we clambered back aboard The Beast and resumed our journey in search of the perfect wave.

*

I was not a particularly good student, and as the year end approached, so did my final exams. My academic career had seemed to be more about how to get around work than actually doing it. I excelled at finding ways to get through exams by whatever means I could come up with. If I had put as much effort into homework and study as I did circumventing the system I would have done a lot better academically, but I had survived up to now. Sitting for my Leaving Certificate would leave me totally exposed. I grew so anxious that I began to suffer severe migraines and nervous indigestion so fierce I could hardly read the papers let alone answer the questions. While I managed to pass some subjects, I failed others and flunked the Leaving Certificate. My parents weren't thrilled and neither was I. We agreed that I would redo the subjects I had failed by corre-spondence, and complete a sheep husbandry and wool science certificate at the Sydney Technical College the following year.

All this was momentarily forgotten when The Rolling Stones toured Australia. I saw them on 22 January 1965 at the Manufacturer's Auditorium at the old Sydney Showground, a venue typically associated with the Royal Easter Show. Also on the bill that night, but a bit lost in the moment, were the legendary Roy Orbison and US vocal trio The Newbeats. The falsetto sound of The Newbeats was mere cannon fodder, brutally mauled by baying Stones fans. Roy, however, got a good reaction—who could fault that voice?

Then the lights faded, the crowd went berserk and from behind the velvet drapes emerged flaxen-haired Brian Jones playing a white, teardrop-shaped Vox guitar, laying down the Bo Diddley beat of Buddy Holly's 'Not Fade Away'. As with The Beatles the year before, the screams all but drowned out the music. But compared to The Beatles, the Stones were wilder; they rocked with a primal beat that just oozed sex. The gig was truly electric and proof that something was changing culturally. The Stones were the bad boys and that's who I wanted to be.

By then my interest in music was expanding. One Saturday night at a party in Paddington, as we sat around drinking and puffing on the occasional joint, a guy with long hair and a corduroy jacket, an art student at Sydney University, produced a trove of vinyl LPs from blues artists Bukka White, Jimmy Reed, Muddy Waters, Brownie McGhee, Howlin' Wolf and John Lee Hooker. I experienced a light bulb moment; it became clear how big an influence these bluesmen were on bands like the Stones.

In a basement below the busy thoroughfare of Oxford Street was a small unlicensed club called Beatle Village. Descending the old stairs past a jukebox blaring 'Like a Rolling Stone', my mates and I entered a cellar whose walls were adorned in fluorescent swirls, and where the luminescent glow highlighted every bit of dandruff and lint. Gathered there was a mix of newly arrived British immigrants from the hostels and suburban kids like us, all of us sipping bad orange cordial while witnessing an underground revolution. The Showmen, The Throb, The Missing Links and The Easybeats belted out their sounds in this dungeon as we sat, cocooned and secure from the outside world that didn't take too kindly to long-haired teenagers.

Tony the doorman—a wrestler, we were told—stood sentry, welcoming people like us in and keeping the trash out. As the venue was unlicensed, the Oxford Hotel on the corner of Oxford and Bourke streets, Taylor Square, was our watering hole and meeting place. Although the dash from the pub to Beatle Village only covered a few metres, it could be risky. The local street gangs, predominantly Maltese kids from the area, didn't take too kindly to these 'pooftas' being on their turf. But many of the migrant kids at Beatle Village came from tough working-class cities—Liverpool, Glasgow and the suburbs of London—and were used to fighting. They had perfected the use of the 'Liverpool kiss' and the 'slipper'—a headbutt swiftly followed by a kick to the balls. On numerous occasions I witnessed the quick demise of a foe at the hands of a smaller kid from Glasgow's Gorbals. The good thing was that the migrant kids were our mates and often our protectors—and our mentors in fashion and music.

As Beatle Village regulars, The Showmen were signed by Leedon Records, the label established by promoter Lee Gordon, who'd mysteriously died in 1963 in a London hotel room. In May 1965, they cut a single, 'Don't Deceive' produced by fifties rocker Lonnie Lee, but radio ignored it. But there was still hope. *Everybody's* was a magazine aimed at the young-adult market and, along with radio stations 2SM in Sydney and 3UZ in Melbourne, it decided to run a national competition called the Battle of the Sounds. The Sydney event was staged at the Sydney Stadium, where The Showmen—now sporting Kinks-inspired lace-fronted shirts—stole the show. Along with the other Sydney finalist, Jimmy Crockett and the Shanes, they travelled to Melbourne for the national final at Festival Hall. Brisbane's sole representative was The Embers, while Melbourne had three contenders: The Pink Finks, featuring young Ross Wilson and Ross Hannaford (later to form Daddy Cool); The Rising Sons, with Keith Glass, future country artist and Nick Cave manager, on vocals; and The Crickets, an obscure covers band. I couldn't make the trip and was stuck in Roseville anxiously awaiting the results. The Crickets were surprise winners, but after one forgettable single, they disappeared into obscurity.

As a result of winning the Sydney final, The Showmen snagged a support for the upcoming Dave Clark Five tour. The British band had had a number of major hits in Australia, including 'Glad All Over'. Covering the gig, Sydney's *Daily Telegraph* described The Showmen's music as 'pulsating noise'. As for The Dave Clark Five, they wrote: 'Although one couldn't hear the words of their songs above the screaming, stamping and whistling of thousands of teenagers, it didn't seem to matter.'

The Showmen chose Chuck Berry's classic 'Too Much Monkey Business' as their second single but not long after, drummer Baden Hutchins and bassist Ian Thomas defected to the wild and unpredictable Missing Links, one of the most original acts ever to emerge in Australia. Their shows were a combination of chaos and mayhem, pure aggression and excitement; many will claim they were the world's first punk band. Inside Beatle Village, swinging from the water pipes and dripping sweat, Andy James screamed his lyrics over a pulsating beat accompanied by ear-splitting feedback. They were way ahead of their time—so far ahead! In later life Andy would venture into the TV world as Andy Anderson, taking on the role of Jim Sullivan in the highly successful series *The Sullivans*.

By 1965, Sydney's inner-city circuit had expanded to venues like the Hawaiian Eye, The Bowl and Suzie Wong's. Most Sunday afternoons I would venture down to Suzie Wong's, by day a Chinese restaurant in an arcade where the MLC Building now stands. This is where Stevie Wright had met Harry Vanda and Dick Diamonde in late 1964, leading to the formation of The Easybeats. As more venues opened up, interstate groups like Brisbane's Purple Hearts and Melbourne's Loved Ones often appeared in Sydney. I was a big fan of the Hearts' frontman Mick Hadley; I loved watching him stalk the stage. They were one of the first bands to 'go mod', a look my mates and I adopted, wearing our hair shorter and brighter clothes.

I also caught American P.J. Proby in action at the Sydney Stadium. Renowned for his outrageous clothes, ponytailed and bowl-cut hairstyle, and trousers that always seemed to split, he'd been banned by the BBC. The then-powerful British morals campaigner Mary Whitehouse had declared his act obscene, and the controversy guaranteed full houses during his Australian tour in September 1965. Backed by a ten-piece orchestra and surrounded by police, Proby entered the arena dragging 30 metres of mic cable behind him; the place erupted. Proby prowled the stage, his pants so tight they might have been glued on, and he teased the audience into hysterics. Midway through the gig, the Reverend Roger Bush suddenly appeared on stage, microphone in hand, and began to denounce Proby as the devil, 'a merchant of obscenity'. After copping a barrage of heckles and jeers, Rev. Roger quickly departed. I recall wondering later if Rev. Roger was a real preacher or just a part of the act. I would never know.

Our anticipation grew as we awaited Proby's pants-splitting party trick, but his painfully tight strides remained intact. Finally, soaked to the skin, he left the stage and ran the gauntlet of weeping teenage girls trying to get a piece of him. It was a hell of a show.

★

Towards the end of 1965, Mal won a building contract in Darwin and offered me a job. It sounded like fun, a real adventure in the Top End. To get there I rode in one of the trucks taking materials overland from Sydney. Steve, a 35-year-old truckie from Blacktown, welcomed me aboard his bright-red rig; it resembled a small house on wheels. With two blasts of the air horn we headed north, almost 4000 kilometres of road ahead of us.

At night we slept on top of the load, the southern sky's constellation above us. As we entered the Northern Territory, wildlife was in abundance: kangaroos, emus and pigs, many far too close for their own wellbeing, destined to join the ever-present roadkill at the edge of the bitumen. It was dry, bloody hot and so dusty you couldn't open the window.

Darwin in 1965 was as close to a frontier town as you could find in Oz. It had the highest consumption of alcohol per capita in the world. Our base was two exhibition halls at the local showgrounds. The place was clad in corrugated iron, the roofing asbestos for sure, and not ideal in the oppressive heat. My lodgings were spartan, but I had a bed, a shower, and a toilet with a resident huntsman spider. It was luxury after the long road trip.

The tropical heat sapped my energy and beer was the coolant of choice. There wasn't much else to spend my hard-earned on. Kev, one of my co-workers, told me, 'You need some knee-length socks if you want to go to the pub', which came as a surprise. Shorts were allowed, mandatory in fact, but thongs—'Japanese riding boots' to the locals—no way. With my new hosiery pulled high like a *Schuhplattler* dancer during Oktoberfest, I jumped into the back of Kev's ute and headed for the pub. To describe it as a barn would be to do a disservice to barns. More than a thousand drinkers, many looking like they were on day leave from prison—and all wearing knee-high white socks, of course—were jammed into one large room, the overflow spilling out into the adjoining beer garden.

Into the unknown we charged, Kev tracking a course, with me trailing in his wake. The noise was deafening; the only way to communicate was by shouting louder than everyone else. Apart from the bar staff, there weren't any other women in the place, and the dominant complexion was sunbaked white. The local Indigenous population, it seemed, drank elsewhere.

After a few months, the job came to an end. Mum came up for a holiday, and we flew back to Sydney with Keith, a local croc shooter we'd met, aboard his 'squeezy' Beechcraft Bonanza. The journey was spectacular. We soared above the desolate countryside and slowly made our way south, our route guided by towns far below, or cattle stations with their names conveniently emblazoned on their homesteads' roofs.

Sometimes identifying these landmarks at 7000 feet proved tricky and became a point of conjecture between Mal and Keith. At one stage in the flight, Keith put the plane into a Stuka-like dive to prove a point as Mum and I gripped our seats so tightly our knuckles turned white.

'There, I told you so,' Keith declared as we resumed normal altitude, and Mum and I exhaled with relief.

★

I arrived back in Sydney in early 1966 with £550 in my pocket, and was straight back into checking out the new bands and clubs that had sprung up in my absence. Mum and Dad were a little concerned that I'd fritter away my nest egg so they suggested that I get a job. With my recently attained certificate in wool science and sheep husbandry, I was able to secure a position sorting wool at a mill in Botany. It was fairly easy work, and my hands became soft as a baby's bum from the lanolin in the wool, but it was repetitive and boring.

Weekends were still about surfing, parties, hanging with mates at the Chatswood bowling alley and seeing bands on Friday, Saturday and Sunday. My flame at the time was Carol, who wasn't quite five feet tall. I was about a foot taller, maybe a little more, so we made an interesting couple.

Tony Hamilton, meanwhile, had left The Showmen and teamed up with a band based in Newcastle that went by the incredibly imaginative name of Barry Cousins and the Citizens (which I soon encouraged them to change to Barry and the Steam Packet). They were managed by Phil Clarke, a local boutique owner who also ran Shindig Village, a popular music venue, situated above a shop on Hunter Street. As most of the band lived in Sydney, I would often travel up with Tony. Every weekend the place would be packed with music-starved teenagers.

Newcastle was your classic working-class town, rough and tough. Long-haired weirdos wore a proverbial target on their backs. It was unwise to venture too far from the safety of the club, as beltings from local heavies were fairly commonplace. Two young locals, Wayne 'Swampy' Jarvis and Mick Cox, were regulars at Shindig Village. They both worked at the meat-works and took it upon themselves to ensure that those inside the venue didn't get hassled by any local yobs. Many an unfortunate protagonist would find themselves rolling backwards down to Hunter Street after crossing paths with these two. Swampy and Mick would go on to carve their own legends as roadies in the Australian music scene.

Back in Sydney, two new clubs had opened: Here disco in North Sydney and Rhubarbs in the city. 2UW's star DJ, Ward 'Pally' Austin, and his business partner, August Maranesi, had opened Here; the awesome Jeff St John and the Id, and Max Merritt & the Meteors played there a lot. Horst Leipolt, a legend of the jazz scene, ran Rhubarbs. It was definitely the coolest place in town. In this dark cavern of a club I'd hear the best soul music around. Regulars Python Lee Jackson, their repertoire drawn from the catalogues of Wilson Pickett, Otis Redding and James Brown, were a five-piece fronted by the charismatic Mal McGee.

I was eighteen and a big problem loomed for me: national service. Being called up to fight in Vietnam when I turned twenty had become a very real possibility. The mainstream view at the time was that the war was a good thing, a way of stopping the 'Red menace' and the 'Yellow peril'. In reality we had followed the US like lapdogs into a war that would achieve nothing apart from sending thousands of young men to their deaths. But I had an entirely different journey in mind.

4

MUSIC MECCA

For a music-mad teenager like me, England was Mecca. I had managed to save money from Darwin, and London was constantly on my radar. It was where everything was happening, not only in music but in fashion and lifestyle. It was the world of The Beatles and the Stones and The Who and The Kinks and the King's Road and so much more. I couldn't realistically see myself disappearing into the outback for a career in the woolsheds, and I dreaded the possibility of Vietnam. As much as I was terrified to step outside of my comfort zone, I sat down with my parents and they somewhat reluctantly gave me their blessing. England was my father's birthplace, so I had a British passport which proved incredibly handy.

My return ticket on the SS *Castel Felice* cost me the grand sum of $288 in the new decimal currency. The boat would take me to Naples in Italy, where I would disembark to travel by train through Italy and France, eventually arriving in England.

As I stood on the dock in Pyrmont on a beautiful spring day, with Mum and Dad staring up at the giant vessel, I knew there was no turning back. I guess they must have wondered

43

whether they would ever see me again. I was caught up in my own world—but not so much that I didn't stand on the rear deck as we set off and wave to them for a long, long time.

As I reached the top of the gangway, I was surprised to see Glenn Shorrock, Paddy McCartney and Laurie Pryor, members of The Twilights, casually leaning against the railing. I found out that they were travelling to London after winning the 1966 Hoadley's Battle of the Sounds. I also learned to my delight, soon after beginning our journey, that they played every couple of nights in the main ballroom, their audience predominately younger passengers like me, all amply fuelled by cheap booze. This was a much more exciting option than the normal cruise-ship offering with a name like La Trio Roma blasting out 'O Sole Mio' and bad Beatles covers. With no real reason to get up in the morning, it was a common sight to find a party animal cocooned snugly in a deckchair, squinting in the morning glare.

Approximately twenty days in, we entered the bustling port of Singapore and I looked on as tugs, punts and sampans went about their business as our larger vessel slowly docked. My nostrils registered a unique smell, an exotic mixture of food and spices and tropical heat. Ashore we were immediately converged upon by taxi drivers, vendors and street hustlers. Weaving through the scrum, my cabinmate John and I headed out to wander the busy streets, carefully dodging every known mode of vehicle, all rushing to get somewhere fast.

Aside from checking out the tourist attractions, we had an important mission—to obtain supplies of the local herb for the long voyage ahead. With no thoughts of what horror awaited us if we got busted, John and I hailed a Morris Oxford taxi, armed with clear instructions on what to do. We arrived at a large colonial house set among tropical gardens. At the front door we were met by an overenthusiastic Malay and as soon as we entered, we were immediately surrounded by a bevy of Asian beauties, offering exotic pleasures of the flesh. Though tempted, we had a different type of pleasure in mind.

Back in the taxi, we again made clear our intentions and the driver nodded in agreement. A few miles further down the road we veered into a narrow lane and entered the gates of another colonial-era house. The driver turned to us with a wicked grin, but John let him know that our only interest was herb, not women.

'Okay,' the driver sheepishly replied, and we set off again.

When we did finally find the gold, John gave it the once-over.

'Looks good, smells good, it's good,' he declared with a wink.

Knowing now the implications of being caught with drugs in Singapore, I shudder to think what the consequences could have been. But this was another time and young luck was on our side.

The ship sailed for Colombo and then Aden in Yemen, a port close to the eastern entrance of the Red Sea. As we strolled through streets and tight alleyways, men in white flowing robes and women in black burqas warily observed us, these strange long-haired individuals in strange Western clothes.

With the deserts of Egypt on our left and Saudi Arabia on the right, we began a twelve-hour journey along the famous Suez Canal. Along with Twilights Glenn and Peter Brideoake, I decided on the Cairo day-trip option. As we approached the city, I was surprised to see a massive army camp that seemed to stretch along both sides of the highway for miles. It was a warning of what lay ahead—the Six-Day War between

Israel and several Arab states, which broke out in June of the following year.

Our first stop was the pyramids at Giza. Sidestepping the camel rides and postcard sellers, Glenn, Peter and I decided to have a closer look at the King's Chamber in the largest of the three pyramids, the Great Pyramid. Once inside the stone passage, at times the only method of forward progress was crawling on our hands and knees, and the deeper we went the more claustrophobic I became. But it was still worth the effort.

Naples was my final destination on the good ship *Castel Felice*. A day out from port, the conditions began to change: heavy winds and an increasing swell tossed our vessel about as if we were in a scene from a disaster movie. The deck was off limits due to the blinding wind and spray, while the more adventurous among us headed towards the front of the ship to watch the display of nature's immense power in action. I succumbed to seasickness and retreated to my bunk. We had run headfirst into a massive storm that, when it finally reached Italy, would cause widespread destruction and the loss of more than 100 lives.

As the lights of Naples came into view, a wave of anxiety and apprehension washed over me. After five weeks of being cocooned onboard I was about to leave all my new friends for a journey through countries that I knew very little about, and whose languages were unfamiliar to me. In my heart I wanted to stay, but my head told me I needed to take the next big step.

Stepping out from my digs at the Naples Youth Hostel, the sounds and smells of the city seemed so alien: scooters and strange-looking cars with funny horns honking incessantly whizzed around me. I kept walking, taking in the sights, the people, the cafes, the unfamiliar smells. Even cigarettes smelled different. I found a tiny restaurant in a quiet back alley and sat down to peruse the menu—written in Italian. I couldn't find a single word I recognised: where was the 'spag bol'?

As I continued to ponder the menu, the waiter—an Italian version of Alain Delon—arrived at my table. He said something in Italian, his pen poised, his dark eyes looking for some form of response. I looked at the menu, at him, and again at the menu. My mind was racing when suddenly, two tables away, I spied what looked like spaghetti. I pointed, and then the waiter fired back another question. The seconds ticked away until I heard a voice from a nearby table.

'He wants to know what sauce you want.'

'Ahhh . . . tomato,' I replied in a grovelling manner.

My saviour rattled off an order; the waiter nodded, turned and headed for the kitchen. I felt as though I was in the middle of the restaurant without my pants.

After Naples, my journey took me via Rome and Florence, through the Swiss Alps and onto Paris. From Paris I travelled by train to Calais and crossed the English Channel by ferry, landing at the famous white cliffs of Dover.

My trip was over, but my journey had only just begun.

*

November 1966. London was the hippest city on the planet, and I was finally there. England was in a state of euphoria having won the soccer World Cup in July. The Beatles, meanwhile, had just dropped *Revolver*, while in the 'straight' world, Harold Wilson was the prime minister and *The Avengers*, *Coronation Street* and *Till Death Do Us Part* were essential TV viewing. My plan was to stay a couple of years and then head back to

Oz. I ended up staying for almost eleven years. Who could blame me?

Music was everywhere. Pirate radio stations Radio Caroline, Radio London and Radio Luxembourg, staffed by hip young DJs Emperor Rosko, John Peel and Tony Prince, were stealing the airwaves away from old 'Auntie', the BBC. TV music shows *Ready Steady Go!* and *Top of the Pops* featured the hottest bands, while music mags *Melody Maker* and *New Musical Express* (*NME*) helped define the latest trends. The Beach Boys were the cover stars of the *NME* when I arrived in London; their single 'Good Vibrations' sat at number 2 on the charts, just behind the Four Tops' 'Reach Out I'll Be There'.

A youth-driven cultural revolution was upon us; it was a magical time to be in London. My digs were the youth hostel in Kensington. It wasn't quite London at its hippest, but I was there and that's all that mattered.

Staring at my reflection in a shop window, I realised that my dated Australian attire was out of step with the current look of London. As Shakespeare so rightly put it, 'The apparel oft proclaims the man.' Clothes were not cheap, but I knew that this was an emergency, and had to tap into my limited resources. After a few hours of hitting the stores around Carnaby Street, I felt like I looked very *now*. Using the Manchester mod band St. Louis Union as my template, I bought a purple-and-white-striped button-down shirt, which I matched with a pair of white straight-legged pants.

In the back of the *NME* was the gig guide, listing all the clubs and acts for the following week. Scrolling down I stopped at the line-up for the Flamingo Club in Soho. Jimmy James and the Vagabonds, one of UK's finest soul/ska acts, were on the bill. That would do me. As I approached the Flamingo's entrance,

I noticed a dozen or so black teens chatting on the pavement, looking very sharp in mohair suits and pork-pie hats. They paid little attention as I slipped past. The venue was packed with a mixture of mods, West Indians, spivs, ladies of the night and suburban kids. The seven-piece band were crammed on stage and when the Vagabonds fired up, I felt I had entered soul heaven. The room came alive; the floor was a sea of innovative moves. This was my first taste of genuine soul music, and my love of it has never faded.

The next band I caught was The Move, a psychedelic rock/pop act from Birmingham that incorporated theatrics—smashing TVs, burning effigies of Hitler, and pyrotechnics—into its live show. Joining a queue outside the famous Marquee Club that stretched over a block towards Shaftesbury Avenue, I felt so cool to be at the cutting edge of what was happening instead of just reading about it after the event in a dated edition of the *NME*. Dressed like 1920s gangsters, The Move tore through a set of tight harmonies and wonderful Roy Wood–penned pop songs. Their final song featured sirens and smoke machines that rapidly engulfed the venue in acrid smoke, leading to a mass evacuation. I was among the coughing and choking patrons who stumbled out onto Wardour Street to be met by firefighters, hoses drawn.

About a week into my trip, I asked myself the burning question: 'What am I going to do to get by?' London was pretty daunting. I didn't know anyone other than The Twilights, who were off doing their own thing. I was alone—perhaps not entirely, though. I recalled a conversation with Jeff Abram, a fellow traveller on the *Castel Felice*. He was a brickie from Adelaide who was living with his wife and young son in Preston, a town north of Liverpool.

'If you ever need anything, just call me,' Jeff had said as we parted ways on the ship, and right now it sounded like a good option.

'Hang on, I'll get Jeff,' replied someone with a broad accent when they answered the phone. Jeff came on the line and seemed to be blown away to hear another Aussie voice.

'Does your offer still stand?' I asked him after rambling on for a bit.

'Yes,' he said hesitantly. Jeff went on to tell me that things weren't great, work was tough to find and his family was bunking down at his mother-in-law's place.

Even though my prospects were unclear, I had nothing really to lose. I boarded a train at Victoria station heading north, totally unaware of what awaited me at the other end.

I left the train at Preston station and followed Jeff's directions, catching an ivory-and-cherry-red Ribble bus. Making its slow journey down cobbled streets, it passed rows of houses seemingly straight out of *Coronation Street*, while thick accents surrounded me.

'This'll be your stop, then,' the conductor told me.

'Thanks,' I replied in my Aussie drawl, which attracted inquisitive stares from those seated nearby. The passengers on Route X40 were now aware that there had been an alien on board.

I soon reached a row of identical-looking terraced houses only distinguishable by the numbers on the front doors. Jeff had organised a room for me in a boarding house directly across from his mother-in-law's. It was comfortable enough, although I had to share a room with a guy who worked night shift.

My first dinner was a sight to behold: a large plate of mashed potato with sausages poking out at odd angles like the quills of a hedgehog, all smothered in HP Sauce, accompanied by lashings of bread and butter and washed down with a 'cuppa'. The next night's banquet was fish and chips with plenty of bread and butter. Method: pile chips onto a slice of bread, cover with salt and tomato sauce, roll it up and away you go with a 'chip butty', downed with yet another 'nice cuppa tea'. This, I would later confirm with Cold Chisel's Liverpudlian drummer Steve Prestwich, was a long-held northern tradition.

My next cultural experience was a pub crawl with Jeff and his brother-in-law. I figured I was a pretty good drinker, well trained in the art back home, so the local beverage presented me with little fear. English beer was served at room temperature (not warm, as per the urban myth), and it had a strong taste and the uncanny ability of creeping up on you. I stuck with the local brews: Tetley's, Boddingtons Bitter, Whitbread, Double Diamond, Newcastle Brown, Tennent's. All tried, all consumed. As a consequence, I found myself slumped against a wall, 'yodelling' my guts out as my two companions struggled to keep me from meeting the cobblestones face-first. I guess this seasoned beer drinker from Down Under had met his match.

As fond as I was of 'hedgehog-quilled mash', I knew I couldn't stay doubled up in a single room much longer and found new lodgings at Mrs Lee's Guesthouse in St Marks Place. Mrs Lee was a jovial Scottish lady who lived with her beautiful teenage daughter Laura. This was a much better option than sharing a room with some bloke working the night shift.

I got work as a yardman at Kellett's Transport in Penwortham, about 5 kilometres from downtown Preston. My salary was the princely sum of £12 per week—which, after board, left me enough to hit Preston's nightlife. The best-looking girls would pack into the Fox and Grapes and Exchange pubs every Friday and Saturday night to enjoy the latest soul music blasting from speakers above the bar.

Laura, Mrs Lee's daughter, promptly introduced me to her friends, and it didn't take long for word to spread that I was from Australia, so I became a bit of a local curiosity. The only recognisable names associated with Australia at that time were Frank Ifield and Rolf Harris, or tennis great Rod Laver. Girls loved to hear my accent.

'Say something,' they'd ask me, giggling. 'I luv the way ya talk!'

At the same time, the local accent presented issues for me; people could have been speaking Swahili for all I knew. Luckily, I had Laura as my interpreter.

★

I was watching *Ready Steady Go!* on a Friday night in early December 1966 when a rock-and-roll gypsy exploded onto the screen. His electrifying performance of the Billy Roberts song 'Hey Joe' would announce the emergence of Jimi Hendrix. Music wasn't just exploding in London—it was exploding everywhere: Liverpool, Blackpool and Manchester, all just a ride away from Preston. Laura and I caught a bus to the Tower Ballroom at Blackpool to see The Easybeats, whose single 'Friday on My Mind' was in the UK Top 10. The band Cream played at Southport, just 30 kilometres down the road, in January 1967. They'd only been together for six months, yet their debut album *Fresh Cream* was sitting at number 6 in the UK and had cracked the US Top 40. We headed for the seaside to check out what the music press had labelled a 'supergroup'. They were loud and exciting, a three-piece without any pretence, just pure energy driven by Ginger Baker and Jack Bruce, with Eric Clapton leading the way. The hype was vindicated: this was something special. With The Jimi Hendrix Experience on the rise, it was clear that the power trio had been born.

Laura and I were hanging out regularly, checking out bands or hitting the pubs. The looks between us made it clear we were becoming more than just friends.

Floral Hall in Southport quickly became our go-to place for seeing live music. In May 1967, The Pink Floyd, who'd just released their debut single 'Arnold Layne', appeared. Their charismatic singer and guitarist Syd Barrett was resplendent in a lurid orange shirt, while the liquid light show projected fluid abstract shapes and colours across the walls of the old seaside auditorium. This was my first exposure to 'psychedelia', which was slowly making its mark on the mainstream. The hippie revolution had firmly touched down by 25 June 1967, with a live TV global broadcast of The Beatles performing 'All You Need Is Love' to over 400 million people worldwide.

Unfortunately my tenure at Mrs Lees' came to an abrupt ending when I got into an ugly altercation with Laura's large and imposing elder brother. A mate from the Exchange pub, Peter Williamson, alerted me to a tiny attic flat in a large three-storey house in a quiet neighbourhood close to the city centre. It was there that Laura and I spent our weeknights, listening to Big Brother and the Holding Company on my newly acquired record player, which I had bought on the tick—£5 down and £1 a week. During the cold winter we huddled in front of a small electric heater, feeding coins into a meter one flight down. The problem was that there was no warning of when the feed would stop. I'd stumble about in the pitch-black dark, searching for change to feed the greedy contraption.

With the northern winter setting in, outdoor work with the trucking company wasn't so appealing. Luckily, I managed to find a new job packing orders at a grocery warehouse; not only was it warmer but every Friday we could purchase damaged stock on the cheap. I confess to sometimes 'accidentally' dropping cans of ham to snag a discount.

*

Ray Holder was the leading mod in Preston, the 'ace face'. Ray had the look and the moves, and he was also a treasure trove of the hippest soul and R&B. I had met Ray at the Exchange Pub one Friday night, and he became my guide to the northern soul scene of 1967. Unlike most mods, who wore grey mohair suits, Ray opted for a mulberry-toned outfit. We scoured second-hand clothing stores for the much-desired pinstriped grandad shirts, which we complemented with stiff paper collars and cool skinny ties. We wore our hair short. Stylishly attired in our mohair suits and brogues, each clutching an airline bag containing spare collars and a fresh shirt, we were ready for a weekend trek to Manchester and The Twisted Wheel, *the* spot for soul and R&B in the north, and the club eternally hailed as the origin of Northern Soul.

The walk from Manchester Central station to the Wheel was a big part of our night: it was there that we scored the pills for an amphetamine-fuelled night of dancing. Blue-and-greens, black bombers, dexies—they came in all shapes, sizes, names and colours, their toxicity unknown. It was a common occurrence to stumble upon a body sprawled on the pavement, ambulance officers frantically pumping someone's chest. Yes, it was dangerous, but being young, foolish and apparently bulletproof, all we cared about was getting 'blocked' and having a good time.

Access to The Twisted Wheel was via an old warehouse entrance before a descent to the cellars below, their dark walls adorned with old wagon wheels. A throbbing, sweaty gathering of gyrating bodies awaited us, fuelled by the soul and R&B sounds of Detroit, Philadelphia and Chicago. Legendary DJ Roger Eagle spun such classics as Darrell Banks's 'Open the Door to Your Heart', Bob & Earl's 'Harlem Shuffle', Marv Johnson's 'You Got the Love I Love' and Tony Clarke's 'The Entertainer'.

Live music began at 2 am sharp. I saw US legends Edwin Starr, Junior Walker, Eddie Floyd and Oscar Toney Jr perform on the tiny stage, as well as the top UK soul groups. Everyone danced, whether partnered or not; the vibe was infectious, and our sole purpose was to have an amazing, fuelled night of dancing. Around 7.30 the following morning we'd finally exit, exhausted, our eyes squinting in the bright morning light.

5

THE HAZE

I knew Paul Varley well from the Preston pub scene. He was the drummer for local favourites Purple Haze, a three-piece that played a mixture of Hendrix, Cream, The Who and The Creation covers. Frank Newbold played bass, while Peter Illingworth was on guitar. Peter had been in Preston's most successful rock band of the early 1960s, David John and the Mood. They'd released three singles, all overseen by two legendary producers: Shel Talmy, of Kinks/Who/Easybeats renown, and the innovative genius Joe Meek. Unfortunately, even with all this juice, their records never fired and they broke up in 1965.

In January 1968, Paul asked if I wanted to tag along as Purple Haze's roadie on a trip to Belgium. This was the band's second foray into a market that was starved of good British rock. I'd been ably trained during my days with The Showmen and agreed to help out.

Accompanying us for the ride was Clive Kelly, a larger-than-life Prestonian. A few years earlier, 22-year-old Clive, along with ex-Beatles manager Allan Williams, had opened a string of

R&B clubs across the north of England. Later on Clive would pioneer 'fly pitching' (illegal street trading) in London before heading to Brazil in the late 1970s, opening clubs in Sao Paolo, eventually emerging as 'Captain Kelly', a fearsome ecowarrior who convinced Sting to get involved in protecting Brazilian forests and indigenous communities. He was an interesting rogue whose life story would make a great movie.

Winter in Belgium was a real eye-opener for me; my only previous exposure to snow had been minuscule drifts on the side of the road in the Blue Mountains of New South Wales. Purple Haze's run of shows was largely centred around Liège in Wallonia, the French-speaking region of Belgium. The crowds were super responsive and treated this unknown band like returning heroes. The local kids were stylish, heavily influenced by French culture and fashion: they were modish, flamboyant and androgynous.

One night, in a popular Liège club, I encountered my first unisex toilet. I tried to appear as inconspicuous as possible at the urinal as members of both sexes argued over the use of the lone mirror.

★

I think there's no question that my burgeoning association with Purple Haze put a strain on my relationship with Laura. I was spending more time touring with the band around the north of England, and when Laura decided to move to Edinburgh where she had family, I knew that it was definitely over. We still remained friends and would catch up whenever she visited Preston. Years later she would resurface in Sydney with her husband and child, and we renewed our friendship all over again.

Although I was enjoying my rock-and-roll times with Purple Haze, I hung onto my love of soul music and remained a regular at The Twisted Wheel. In March 1968, the Philadelphian soul group The Showstoppers, featuring two of the younger brothers of R&B legend Solomon Burke, appeared at the Preston Public Hall. 'Ain't Nothing but a House Party' was a big hit that year, and soul devotees travelled from all over to see the show. The different factions—kids from Manchester and Liverpool and elsewhere—congregated in their groups on the perimeter of the dance floor, initially keeping a safe distance from one another.

'Peace, love and mung beans' meant little here; it was more about a pint of Boddingtons Bitter and a 'bit of a bovver'. Burly bouncers in scarlet jackets and bow ties stood at the ready. As the night rolled on, the vibe among the Preston locals became unsettled; snide looks and comments were coming their way from across the dance floor. Suddenly a disturbance near the Liverpool camp was met by a surge of scarlet jackets. More heated words were exchanged and the protagonists finally came together. It was, as they say, 'on for young and old'.

I leapt over the shoulder of a bouncer and exchanged a pleasantry with an enemy. Where he was from I was unsure, but he wasn't one of us. Boom! Fists and boots flew on the dance floor. All of sudden, a large hand grabbed my collar and flung me like a rag doll to the floor. Thankfully, I evaded arrest as the shrill whistles of the constabulary sounded their arrival.

All the while, The Showstoppers didn't miss a beat or a step, as the Burke brothers sang, 'They're dancin' on the ceiling / They're dancin' on the floor / People everywhere comin' through the door / They know it's a party goin' on.'

*

Although secreted away in my northern mod world, I wasn't immune to 1967's 'summer of love' sweeping the world. Most groups seemed to be affecting the hippie/psychedelic look, and talk of LSD was in the air. Our poison of choice up to then had been pills and grass—pills to get you up, grass to come down. Ray Holder and I agreed that we needed to try this 'acid' thing out for ourselves. We were told that if we wanted the good stuff, we needed to try a club in Covent Garden called the Middle Earth. That was London's hippie haven.

So we two mods from Preston boarded a bus for London. Six hours later we were on the tube. Middle Earth was located below King Street in a large cellar. Once inside, we were immersed in a whole new world, light years away from the sweaty, testosterone-fuelled Twisted Wheel. Our clothes and short hair confirmed we were out of place as we explored this bizarre new universe. The sweet smell of incense blended with the odd whiff of pot. Eastern rhythms flowed from the sound system as the locals, with wild hair and multicoloured clothing, swirled and weaved to the music. Colourful liquid projections, similar to what I had witnessed at the Pink Floyd show, brought the walls of the venue to life.

In an alcove, I recognised Alexis Korner, whose picture I'd seen in the music papers, a man often referred to as 'the god-father of British blues', deep in conversation with Mick Farren, singer, activist and prominent figure in the British counter-culture. On a small stage, Sam Gopal's Dream, a four-piece featuring a tabla player from Malaysia, played a mixture of raga and psychedelia.

We started asking around about illicit substances. 'No, sorry, man,' was the recurring response.

Finally, after what seemed like a couple of hours, a bearded guy in a patterned Indian shirt approached us.

'What are you looking for?'

'Acid,' we replied.

'Wait here.'

With that he scurried off into the smoky haze. Eventually he returned and, in a dark corner, the deal was done. I held a small sheet of what appeared to be blotting paper. Seeing that I was puzzled, our new friend explained that it contained a number of trips.

'The best stuff in all of London,' he assured us. It probably came with a fancy name like 'Electric Sunshine', but I can't remember for sure.

The next night, back in Preston, following the clear instructions from our Covent Garden guru, we cut two sections and swallowed.

'Mmmm—tastes just like blotting paper,' quipped Ray.

One hour later, nothing.

'Fook,' said Ray, 'we've been ripped off.'

We were bummed out: a long journey for no result, and good money wasted.

'Maybe we haven't taken enough?' Ray piped up.

'You're probably right,' I replied.

We swallowed another two sections but still nothing. Convinced we had been dudded, we headed over to a mate's place to lament our 'lost expedition'. Miffy had been the lead singer of David John and the Mood, and his house was a hub for music and drugs. Beer in hand, I settled back on his comfy lounge and tried to put our disappointment behind us. Staring deep into the embers of the open fireplace, I began to notice that strange patterns were forming in the coals.

I glanced up at Ray. His toothy grin confirmed it—we were 'on'. Someone suggested we go for a drink, which seemed like a grand idea. But this changed the moment we entered the pub; I got the sense that everyone in the room was fixated on us. Voices seemed louder and more aggressive, and a wave of paranoia washed over me. I retreated back to the sanctuary of Miffy's lounge.

Suddenly I had an overwhelming urge to pee and headed for the outside toilet, but only managed to reach the back door when necessity took over. As I peed, to my astonishment my flow morphed into a torrent of beautiful flowers woven into cascading patterns in the freezing Lancashire night air.

*

The hippie world brought with it a fascination for the exotic cultures of Morocco, India, Afghanistan, Pakistan and all points east. Paddy Jones was a few years older than us and had been visiting these hotspots since the early 1960s. We saw him as a bit of a guru, a guide, whose tales of adventure and illicit delights in these far-off lands fuelled our desire to experience it for ourselves.

So it was, in the summer of 1968, that Ray and I headed off to the hippie utopia of Morocco. As Jimi Hendrix sang, we needed to find our 'castles made of sand'. With thumbs extended, Ray and I hitched through France and into Spain, eventually arriving in San Sebastián, a seaside town on the Bay of Biscay. Spain was still under the rule of the fascist leader Franco. A magnificent full moon vividly reflected off the waters of the Atlantic like a great arc light, and we agreed that the beach at Playa de la Concha was the ideal spot to camp.

Nobody hassled us, no one seemed to care, food was cheap and the locals seemed friendly. Life couldn't get much better.

Metres from the shoreline, we unrolled our sleeping bags and, after a bottle or two of the local drop Txakoli, we called it a day. Under the bright moonlight, my eyes were drawn to movement on the cliff twenty metres away. It was the unmistakable silhouette of *Rattus norvegicus*, in this case the common Spanish rat. Now, let me tell you: snakes, spiders, sharks—no problem. But a rat? Well, that's a different story. I shook Ray awake.

'Don't worry,' he mumbled, 'they won't come anywhere near us.'

Eventually tiredness won and I fell into a deep sleep, but was later roused by loud curses.

'Fookin' rats!' Ray wailed.

It seemed that these marauding bastards had made off with our provisions. While Ray bemoaned the loss of his breakfast, I was more concerned with how near those yellow-toothed devils had come to me as I slept.

We were hungry and in a foul mood as we headed into the old town to replenish our supplies. In a small alleyway, plastered to a wall, was a large, colourful poster featuring a bull and a matador in close combat. It read: 'Plaza de Toros, San Sebastián, Thursday 15th August'. Our knowledge of bullfighting began and ended with El Cordobés, the 'rock star' 1960s matador dubbed 'the bullfighting Beatle', so we decided to check out the action.

The day was scorching hot. A dry wind fanned the multi-tiered (and not very well shaded) Plaza de Toros, which was packed. Cold beer was our only coolant. The matadors appeared in a dazzling display of embroidered satin waistcoats and knee-length skin-tight pants. (Move over, P.J. Proby.) They sauntered about the ring as they acknowledged the crowd, who waved white handkerchiefs. The arena quickly filled up with their underlings, as well as mules and a horse with a heavy blanket on its back (which we later learned was to stop the bull from goring the poor steed to death). The action that followed was lost on us until an affable bearded American seated behind us offered a tutorial in the significance of the ritual. For years I thought he was noted bullfighting tragic Ernest Hemingway, only to learn that Hemingway had been dead for seven years.

My takeaway from the bull ring was this: the poor old bull didn't stand a chance. The thickening stain in the sand would be my strongest memory.

★

We had plenty of company during that summer of '68. A stream of fellow travellers was also heading south, all of us on a similar journey. The more experienced were happy to give directions and suggestions on where to go and what to expect on the road ahead. One thing that cropped up frequently was that Morocco was now old hat—the island of Formentera was the place to be. I heard rumours that Bob Dylan had convalesced there after his motorcycle crash in 1966, while Pink Floyd had also been known to visit the island.

'How do we get there?' I asked a Belgian hippie.

'You need to travel to Barcelona and then get the ferry to the island,' he told me. 'Oh, and while you are in Barcelona you can make some money.'

'How's that?' I asked, hoping he wasn't going to suggest I sell my body.

'They will buy your blood!' he replied.

I dislike needles as much as rats. But Ray was up for it and promised to catch me should I pass out. We managed to find the blood bank in Barcelona easily—it was legit, it was clean and there wasn't a vampire in sight. Thankfully I made it through and, with our newly acquired funds, minus a pint of my type O, we headed off to find our mystery island.

The bow of the small ferry gently broke the Balearic's aqua-blue water and a small island came slowly into view. I could make out a cluster of whitewashed buildings, seemingly uninhabited white-sand beaches, and a rocky coastline that went on and on.

The dilapidated wooden wharf in the small harbour of La Savina seemed to have been around since Christopher Columbus was a boy. I had other concerns, though: I was immediately drawn to a beautiful Scandinavian-looking girl among the crowd on the dock. Her translucent white dress flowed gently to her bare feet, and her golden curls cascaded onto tanned shoulders.

'I think we have come to the right place,' I mumbled to Ray, more than a little bedazzled. Sadly our Nordic dream girl was leaving but we were convinced that she was an omen: we had made the right choice.

Formentera's population was around 3000, comprising mainly locals plus a few resident artists and writers with holiday homes. But that summer about 1300 hippies descended on the place; clearly, word had spread. Every ferry deposited another boatload of young travellers, who then took the five-minute stroll up the dusty track to the largest town on the island, aptly named Sant Francesc (San Francisco).

A kilometre further on was Sant Ferran, whose cheap food and lodging attracted most of us young travellers. The Fonde

Pepe restaurant/hostel was the meeting point for hanging out, singing and playing guitars, the sweet smells of incense and hash wafting through the warm evening air. During the day we could usually be found lazing in the hot sun on one of the numerous beaches circling the island, consuming cheap local cheese, bread and wine. Occasionally a nude hippie would amble past, flashing a peace sign. I don't think anyone read a newspaper, wore a watch or knew what was happening in the rest of the world. This was our time, Formentera time.

But after a blissful few months, I realised I wasn't quite ready to embrace the full hippie transformation. It was time to make our way back to the grey-sky reality of Preston.

Ray, however, would later claim we left Preston as mods and came back as hippies. Unfortunately for me that wasn't completely true, although Ray did end up later living in a gypsy caravan with a herd of goats in an English forest.

*

On my return to Preston from my hippie adventure, I learned that Purple Haze was considering making a move to the big smoke: London. Now writing and performing their own material, they had attracted the interest of local art student/ fashion designer Eddie Sandham, who offered to manage them. They'd also attracted a bit of interest from an indie label, Transatlantic Records, whose roster included The Humblebums, featuring Gerry Rafferty and Billy Connolly; The Dubliners; Bert Jansch; Ralph McTell; Pentangle; and a duo named The Sallyangie, comprising Mike Oldfield and his sister Sally.

A name change was top priority if they were to be taken seriously. A book about the meaning of names provided inspiration:

'Paul' meant little, 'Frank' meant free and 'Peter' meant rock, so they became Little Free Rock. Preparing to say goodbye to Preston in June 1969, they asked if I wanted to tag along as their roadie—they didn't have to ask twice.

In early July our new home was the ground floor of a large house on Newlands Park in Sydenham, south-east London. It quickly became a hub for drop-ins from the north: child actors, circus performers, hustlers, itinerant musicians, drug dealers and a stream of young beauties.

Within days of us moving into Newlands Park, news broke that Brian Jones of The Rolling Stones had drowned. Two days later, I joined a crowd estimated at 500,000 that converged on Hyde Park for a free Stones concert. Anybody and everybody was there, from rock stars to royalty—William Jellett (aka Jesus), the famous hippie dancer, was front of stage, weaving his naked dance in the warm summer rays.

I circumnavigated the vast crowd and reached the back-stage entrance where a number of Hells Angels zealously stood guard. So much for a sneak peek behind the scenes.

Arriving to a thunderous roar that must have been heard all over London, the Stones took the stage with newly recruited guitarist Mick Taylor. Wearing a Michael Fish–designed white blouse, Mick Jagger read Shelley's poem 'Adonais' as 3000 white butterflies were released into the bright sunlight. The familiar opening chords of 'Jumpin' Jack Flash' were all that was required to lift the massive crowd to their feet. Their fourteen-song set concluded with an eighteen-minute version of 'Sympathy for the Devil', powered by the percussive rhythms of Ginger Johnson and His African Drummers, led by Nigeria's 'Prince of the Talking Drum'. Ginger would soon play his part in Little Free Rock's musical journey.

Led Zeppelin, however, was the buzz band of 1969. I headed for London's Lyceum in early October to see what all the fuss was about. The room was packed with a who's who of the music industry and media. When they opened with an earth-shaking version of 'Good Times Bad Times', I was blown away. I had witnessed Cream in early '67, but this was louder, heavier, more intense. Their sound all but nailed me to the back wall of the venue. They closed with 'How Many More Times' and I still recall how Jimmy Page's primal riff made me feel. Rock-and-roll history was being made.

★

Morgan Studios in north-west London was one of the most famous recording studios in the UK: Led Zeppelin, Blind Faith, Pink Floyd and Free had all recorded there. In the late summer of 1969, Little Free Rock (aka LFR) commenced work there on their debut album. Unfortunately, this was engineer Mike Bobak's first solo venture as a producer, and the band became his crash test dummy.

LFR were studio novices and it didn't help when their manager, Eddie Sandham, decided to take over as producer. The meagre budget meant the album had to be recorded and mixed in nine days, a timeline that was fine for the folk artists on Transatlantic but not for a rock band trying to capture their powerful live sound in the studio. Meanwhile as LFR were going through their studio traumas in leafy Willesden, across the Atlantic in Woodstock, New York, 250,000 people revelled in the mud, while on the west coast, Charles Manson and his followers were bringing Helter Skelter to Los Angeles and the world, and with it the end of peace, love and happiness came crashing down.

With their debut album recorded—sort of—and scheduled for release in November, LFR headed north, playing shows at their old stomping grounds of Blackpool, Preston and Liverpool's famous Cavern Club, the birthplace of Merseybeat and The Beatles.

In mid-October we headed to Germany for a five-night run at Hamburg's legendary Star-Club, where The Beatles had once had a residency. We arrived late on a Wednesday evening and headed straight to the club to catch the last set of Irish three-piece Taste, featuring the extraordinary guitarist Rory Gallagher. I knew Rory's brother Donal, who was also his road manager, from nights at The Ship pub on Wardour Street, a regular drinking hole a few doors up the street from the Marquee Club.

The Star-Club was situated in the heart of red-light St. Pauli, and was surrounded by discos, nightclubs, sex cabarets, bars and strip joints. We shared a large room on the top floor of a sleazy hotel on the Reeperbahn, our fellow guests mostly ladies of the night. Adjacent to the Star-Club was a popular drag venue named Monika's, a haven for many of our nocturnal neighbours.

As we got in the van after our first show, we were quickly set upon by three exotic creatures dressed—undressed, really—in micro-miniskirts and high heels, their pouting lips rouged to the max. They headed straight for pretty-boy drummer Paul, caressing his face, murmuring 'darling', 'sexy' and 'baby' in a gabble of German and broken English. Paul was lapping up the attention like a labrador, seemingly unaware of the genetics at play. The blonde of the trio suddenly launched herself through the open van door and planted a huge sloppy kiss on Paul. I'm not entirely sure if it was the large hand cupping his head, or the husky voice in his ear, but Paul recoiled as if he'd been electrocuted as we roared off into the night.

Monday was our final show and, as was the tradition, club manager Horst Fascher farewelled us with boozy delights into the small hours. We somehow managed to navigate our way back to the hotel to catch some sleep before the return journey to London.

I'm not quite sure who woke first, but I came to and saw plumes of black smoke streaming under our door. 'Fire!' I yelled and, in a synchronised movement, five bodies shot bolt upright in bed. We began to panic as smoke came belching under the door, shutting down our escape route. We were on the third floor, so jumping wasn't an option. I managed to prise open one of the large bay windows to the street, as the eerie sound of sirens grew louder. With suitcases in hand, we squeezed outside onto a narrow ledge as down on the Reeperbahn the Hamburg fire brigade got to work. Just then the windows of an adjacent room were flung wide open and out climbed a number of barely dressed young ladies.

We watched anxiously from our perch as an extension ladder slowly made its way in our direction—or so we thought. But then suddenly the ladder changed direction and was steered towards our neighbours. One by one the ladies descended into the safe arms of their brave rescuers, whose lascivious grins said it all. As for us, we expected to be consumed by flames at any second, leaving us like overcooked snags on a barbie. But suddenly the door to our room was flung open and a fireman in breathing apparatus barked muffled orders in German. We read it as 'get the fuck out' and we did just that.

*

Transatlantic's distribution manager, Keith Bleasby, was an avid percussionist who'd sometimes jam with LFR on congas. Word soon filtered through to the pick of the percussion world, and players like Speedy Acquaye from Georgie Fame's band, Gasper Lawal from Ginger Baker's Air Force, and Remi Salaka, a future Stones percussionist, would often drop by to jam. Although this went down well with audiences, it was a bit confusing—the band's debut album, which had been released in late November to good reviews, presented them as a classic heavy-rock three-piece.

LFR's appearance at Christmas Moonrock, staged at St Pancras Town Hall in December 1969, was a seminal moment. Also playing were Caravan and Hawkwind. Word of LFR's dabbling with players like Speedy and Gasper had clearly reached the ears of the Prince of the Talking Drum, Nigerian Ginger Johnson, who was also on the bill. That night, Ginger and his drummers joined LFR for a jam that many saw as an early incarnation of afro rock. (Little Free Rock's use of percussion had also been noted by top music journalists like Roy Carr, Chris Welch and John Peel, who wrote glowingly of the band.)

In the spring of 1970, it was festival time in Europe. Little Free Rock were booked on The Essen Pop & Blues Festival in Germany, which attracted more than 60,000 people; the bill also included Black Sabbath, It's a Beautiful Day, Johnny Winter, Kraftwerk and Taj Mahal. While the audience was all about 'peace, love and reefer', the police in attendance gave a starkly different impression. They were in full riot gear, with balaclavas covering their faces, and wielding water cannons—it looked like they were preparing for war.

In late June, LFR appeared at the Open Air Rock Circus at the Radstadion in Frankfurt. The massive line-up included Deep Purple, Black Sabbath, Chuck Berry, The Byrds, Bo Diddley,

Chicken Shack, Badfinger, Jackie Lomax and Screaming Lord Sutch. For some strange reason the stage had been constructed high in the stands; as a result the acts peered down at the audience below, who had to crane their necks to see them play.

Percussive jamming had now become a regular aspect of Little Free Rock's live shows, and it was setting them apart from other bands. Guitarist Peter Green, who had recently departed Fleetwood Mac, turned up in May for a jam at the Eel Pie Island club in Twickenham. Soon after, a bill declaring 'Peter Green meets Little Free Rock and Ginger Johnson' assured a sold-out Marquee Club in June. Blown away by the crowd's response, Peter invited LFR and Ginger's drummers to appear on the solo album he was recording. The session was an unscripted free-form jam, with the tape left running. Unfortunately, Ginger Johnson managed to piss Peter off by demanding more money than the other drummers. I'm guessing Green had had his fill of dramas in Fleetwood Mac and promptly canned the session.

On most Sundays, The Roundhouse in London's Chalk Farm was transformed into what could best be described as a hippie circus. The pot haze hung like a rain cloud in the reflections of the spotlights. The walls of what was once a steam-engine shed, built in the mid-nineteenth century, were a canvas of coloured liquid light as a crowd of 3000 whirling dervishes danced into the night.

By July 1970, afro rock had truly arrived with the staging of the three-day Afro Rock Carnival at The Roundhouse. Little Free Rock (with Ginger's drummers) were the special guests, along with fourteen African bands, among them an early version of Osibisa. The closing night's finale in front of an ecstatic full house featured LFR, Ginger—plus no fewer than 26 drummers—and an African witchdoctor resplendent in a feathered headdress, white face and flowing robes. It was euphoric.

★

A roadie mate of mine named Jed Clampett—yes, really—asked me in August if I was interested in giving him a hand with a new band that was currently in rehearsal. It was all very hush-hush. LFR was off the road, so I was more than happy to earn some extra coin.

Emerson, Lake & Palmer was a prog-rock supergroup in the making, comprising Keith Emerson on Hammond organ, bassist and singer Greg Lake, and Carl Palmer on drums. They'd come from highly rated bands King Crimson, The Nice and Atomic Rooster. With a very high-profile debut scheduled on the Saturday night of August's Isle of Wight Festival, as part of a line-up that included The Doors and Jimi Hendrix, they began rehearsing in a large studio in south London. Secrecy was paramount.

Carl lived in London's East End, Greg lived in Chelsea, while Keith was in Kensington. Collecting Carl and Greg's gear was fairly straightforward, but Keith's Hammond organ was something else altogether. A Hammond weighs about 160 kilograms, while two Leslie speakers add an extra 120 kilos. It's a fair old hump.

Keith lived on the third floor of a beautiful heritage building opposite Earls Court Exhibition Centre. The ornate stairs and doors were so magnificently polished you could see your image reflected in them. As Jed and I struggled with the organ and speakers, Keith casually mentioned, 'Guys, be careful with the stairs, I don't need a bill for their remodelling.' Keith smiled but we knew he was deadly serious. The mostly elderly residents were shocked to see two long-hairs struggling down the stairs with an old, battered wooden box. Judging by their mutterings and stares I figured that if the speaker boxes hadn't been so dilapidated, they might have called the constabulary.

Setting up was just as tricky. Greg Lake, the least friendly of the trio, insisted that his vast array of foot pedals was displayed on a lavish Indian rug. Taking centrestage was a massive gong, situated behind Carl, almost dwarfing his enormous drum kit. Keith's impressive Hammond L100 and synthesiser set-up was stage right and he played loudly. Really loudly.

Jed and I roadied for the trio at their warm-up show at the 3000-seat Plymouth Guildhall in Devon, six days before the Isle of Wight. Keith took to the stage shirtless, wearing an iridescent satin jacket and trousers that sparkled like a Christmas tree. At one point he climbed onto his Hammond organ, stabbing the keys with a large dagger, which the crowd loved. Emerson, Lake & Palmer would go onto huge success internationally with their fusion of classical music, blues-rock and jazz, and they became a massive stadium act in Europe and the US. I was lucky enough to have been there at their very beginning.

La Chasse club in Soho was a preferred private drinking hole for the music luminaries of London. It was owned by Jack Barrie, the legendary manager of the Marquee. Although small, with just a bar, jukebox and an old couch, it became one of the key meeting places for rock stars, record company execs, journos, promoters, groupies and roadies, who rubbed shoulders freely without the scrutiny of Joe Public.

I'd had a hectic drinking session at the nearby Ship with my mate Jed and he decided it was time for me to experience La Chasse. We stumbled up a creaky flight of stairs and Jed banged on a plain-looking door. We could hear music and loud voices inside.

'Hey Jed,' someone asked from inside. 'He's with you?'

We were in. The tiny smoke-filled room was packed. The faces were very familiar, with members of Yes and Supertramp jostling at the bar, while burly roadies were in deep conversation, leaning against a wall.

Bang!

All of a sudden, the front door flew wide open and in stumbled Keith Moon, The Who's manic drummer. His eyes were like saucers as he made his way towards the bar. He had an empty plastic crate in his extended arm and he demanded, loudly, 'Barman, fill this up!'

A few people looked his way but most in the room continued talking and schmoozing. I would learn that this was standard Moon behaviour. On subsequent occasions, he would greet me effusively, but I doubt that he actually remembered me.

Along with the Ship, La Chasse and the Marquee, the superfecta of social venues included the Speakeasy, another popular drop-in. Strictly members only, it was the watering hole for the A-listers. On any given night, tables would be frequented by the rock elite—Hendrix, the Stones, a Beatle or two—as well as the B-listers, who were the roadies, record-company suits, models, wannabe models, rich kids and bands looking for a break. A lot of up-and-coming acts played there for shitty money in the hope of being noticed.

Luck was with me when a friendly Australian, Wayne de Gruchy, turned up working the door. Wayne had managed the band Zoot back in Australia before heading to London, like me, to seek his fortune. Wayne's advantageous post at the front door meant I could just sail through the entrance.

Old mate Jed came up with the goods again in October 1971 when he got me work on a Fleetwood Mac tour of the UK and Ireland. Christine McVie from Chicken Shack had been added to the line-up of Jeremy Spencer, Danny Kirwan, Mick Fleetwood and Christine's husband John McVie.

The tour kicked off in Newcastle and then moved to Ireland. The National Stadium in Dublin was the first purpose-built boxing stadium in the world. When bands like Fleetwood Mac played there, half of the venue had to be curtained because the boxing ring sat in the centre of the room. That night the support act was Thin Lizzy, a young Irish band with a charismatic singer/bass player, Phil Lynott. 'This guy looks a bit like Hendrix,' I thought to myself as I watched him play. 'He's going to be a star.'

This was my first visit to Ireland and I loved its lush greenery, quaint villages, ancient churches, narrow country lanes and friendly people. However, I couldn't help but notice the quizzical looks I'd get from locals whenever we stopped for fuel or food. Maybe it was our long hair, or perhaps it was my multi-coloured leather patchwork jeans, a fashion statement best seen through sunglasses.

Belfast was part of a very different Ireland. This was the height of the sectarian unrest, the 'Troubles'. Armed soldiers occupied street corners, the windows of their Land Rovers encased in steel mesh. This was a war zone, an unsettling place. I was standing outside our hotel with Mick Fleetwood, awaiting transport, when we felt a shockwave followed by an unmistakable boom that seemed far too close. The look on Mick's face said it all: 'What the fuck was that?' I couldn't wait to get the hell out and back to the safety of England.

I continued working with Little Free Rock until late 1971, when things went stale for the band. Their manager Eddie had picked a fight with the record label, which left them in recording limbo. To add to their woes, they sacked Frank Newbold, their original bass player.

But my good fortune continued and I managed to pick up

the odd gig with touring acts The Byrds, Grand Funk Railroad and the newly formed Roxy Music. I'd been overseas for five years and had discovered a new life and friends in a northern English town, while my role with Little Free Rock had opened the doors to a bigger world of opportunity.

I flashed back to that Sydney dock in 1966, as I had bid goodbye to my tearful parents. I would never have dreamed that this journey would take me so far in such a short time.

6

UNIDENTIFIED FLYING THING

Formed in 1970 in north-east London, UFO was a young hard-rock band, brash and wild. Mick Bolton, Pete Way, Andy Parker and Phil Mogg began gigging around London and would soon gain a solid following. I knew the band and crew well as our paths had often crossed during my time with LFR. In late 1971, UFO offered me a position on their crew, and although I was sad to leave LFR, I knew I needed to make a move.

UFO had been regularly packing out the Marquee. A proposed show at the end of January 1972 was intended to eclipse anything that had gone before. We organised a monster PA, smoke machines and large industrial fans. Punters stretched all the way down Wardour Street and the 'house full' sign was up within minutes.

After ripping through their set to a near-hysterical response, during their finale—'Boogie for George', a seven-minute epic—UFO unleashed the wind and smoke machines. Handfuls of glitter were tossed in the air, spraying the throng as if a million disco balls had exploded. Reminiscent of the Move in 1966, smoke swept through the venue. The band powered on to a mighty climax, sending their instruments crashing to the floor. They raised their arms in triumph and strode off to the sanctuary of the dressing room.

Left in their wake was chaos. Fire doors were flung open in a futile attempt to clear the air, while most of the crowd had been forced out onto the street. Outside seven fire engines blocked Wardour Street. Inside, the smog slowly cleared to reveal a handful of diehards in front of the stage looking like abandoned orphans, their faces and hair plastered with glitter, tears running down their cheeks. Somehow, they had survived the assault.

I needed new accommodation. I met 'Hippie Ray' Bielaczyc, who was visiting London from Detroit. He was your archetypical hippie, wearing John Lennon glasses and a beard, his long mane pulled back behind his ears. Ray was permanently stoned. He lived in a squat in the basement of a beautiful old Victorian three-storey house just off the Kensington high street. It was rent free, clean and comfortable, so I moved in.

A short while after joining up with UFO, I was at a party when a dark-haired beauty quietly sitting in a corner caught my eye. Every so often I'd catch a casual glance and a cheeky smile from across the room; by the end of the night, Sharon Sly and I were an item. Sharon and her sister Carol—who would later marry Les Gray of the band Mud—lived in Enfield in north London. Their father was a bookmaker; he drove a Jaguar, wore a Crombie camel coat and resembled the stereotypical East End underworld character. I hoped the resemblance was purely physical.

Sharon and I spent one of our first dates at The Wake Arms in north-east London, a frequent gig for Deep Purple and Black Sabbath. Status Quo's road manager Bob Young had suggested

I come and see the band, who'd moved on from their glam 'Pictures of Matchstick Men' past to become a hard-rocking force, decked out in faded denim. The room was so packed, bouncing in unison to the music, that I thought the floor might collapse. No doubt about it, Status Quo had been reborn and were soon ready to take on the world.

Back in Kensington, meanwhile, my dream world was growing precarious. Worried about property values, owners were resorting to heavy-handed tactics to evict squatters like me. It was time to find a safer abode.

Mark Hanau was an intriguing character: Jewish, with a trendy afro. He managed the prog rock band Curved Air and was credited with designing and creating the first picture disc in the UK for their album 'Air Conditioning'. Mark became UFO's manager in early 1972 and I took up the offer of a room in his apartment in Hampstead, which he shared with his American girlfriend Sunny. I soon learned that they had a predilection for sex in unusual locations, such as Westminster Abbey or when riding public transport. While I never observed them in action, it did make for entertaining discussions around the dinner table.

Working for UFO was a step up from my days with Little Free Rock—they played more shows, in larger venues, sharing bills with bigger acts like Chicken Shack, Barclay James Harvest, Hawkwind, Brinsley Schwarz and one that really stood out, the magnificent Free. I was with UFO when they supported Free at a stadium in Liverpool and the opening chords of 'All Right Now' sent the place wild. There were no fancy clothes, no razzamatazz, just loud, bullshit-free rock. Free was undoubtedly one of the most influential rock bands of the time—I couldn't help but notice their impact when I finally returned to Australia in the late 1970s.

For ages, my Detroit connection 'Hippie Ray' had extolled the virtues of the Motor City's rock powerhouses: MC5, and Iggy and the Stooges. In early March 1972, both bands played Camden's Roundhouse. Iggy didn't disappoint, throwing himself around wildly, stage diving, spitting, gyrating and leaving his mark on everyone in the room. Then a massive Stars and Stripes was unfurled and MC5 took the stage, with Wayne Kramer cranking out Detroit rock at its most intense as singer Rob Tyner screamed 'Kick out the jams, motherfuckers!' to an adoring crowd. I still love them.

Trouble was brewing, however, within the ranks of UFO; the band was dissatisfied with guitarist Mick Bolton's playing. It was sad because Mick was a really lovely guy and had started the band with bassist Pete Way. Auditions were held and Larry Wallis, who'd played with underground stalwarts the Pink Fairies, clinched his with his take on an obscure Jimi Hendrix cover, 'Drivin' South', an old song by Curtis Knight. With Larry's injection the band were upbeat that the change in guitarist was a positive move forward. Image wise, Larry's wild afro hair fitted better, not to mention he came with a fair amount of underground credibility, which was certainly an asset.

★

In early spring 1972, I headed to Italy and Germany with UFO for a run of shows. They'd invested their £8000 publishing advance in a huge PA system and, bizarrely, a 1960s Bentley that they insisted on taking on tour. It was certainly a step up from your bog-standard Ford Transit van. Arriving in Italy, they stumbled, and I mean *stumbled*, out of this classic of British engineering.

In the 1970s Italy was pretty much starved of heavy rock, which might explain why UFO's first show in the seaside town of Rimini ended in a full-scale riot. Likewise show number two: the promoter, fearing the worst, panicked and tried to kill the sound system, which resulted in a punch-up with us, the road crew, who were sworn to the mantra 'The show must go on'. When manager Mark tried to quell things, he was flattened by a punch from the promoter. As chaos reigned backstage, the punters went about tearing the joint apart as the band played on.

We headed north in our Hertz truck to Frankfurt, where we discovered that the Zoom Club's main clientele were GIs from the local US Army base. Eight more shows in Germany followed before trouble struck. Let's just say a man with strong Sicilian heritage brought the tour to an abrupt end and took ownership of the Bentley. We escaped home to London.

★

In early June, MC5 returned for some summer gigs, which included a large outdoor show in the grounds of Clitheroe Castle, a twelfth-century medieval fortress in Lancashire. UFO was one of the support acts. It was around this time that Mark was relieved of his management role, in the fallout from the German tour's disastrous end. Wilf Wright, the brother of Chrysalis Records co-founder Chris Wright, took over and live work picked up significantly. This meant I had to move house again, which was a shame because Mark and Sunny were entertaining hosts.

Lynda Cowgill was an old friend from Preston, and she offered me a room in a large apartment on the top floor of a two-storey place in Willesden Green. The house was divided into three apartments; nine of us lived there. As I recall, only Lynda, who was a waitress at the newly opened Hard Rock Cafe, and I had regular jobs; everyone else was on the hustle in one way or the other. Among the other residents were John, who dealt in second-hand cars, and his girlfriend Jan, who had a talent for entertaining wealthy Arab sheikhs. Another house-mate, Roy, would often disappear for long periods to exotic locations.

More 'grape and pasta' madness was scheduled for early August with a run of seven shows in Italy. The dates this time were better produced; the venues were great, as were the audiences. But there were problems ahead.

On 22 August 1972, at the Hive in Bournemouth, I got into a heated argument with Phil Mogg after the show. The vibe in and around the band had become unpleasant. The overriding view was that new guitarist Larry wasn't cutting it, leading to a great deal of tension within the band. As I was the low man on the totem pole, I knew it was time for me to move on.

UFO would help to define what would be referred to as the 'new wave of British heavy metal' (NWOBHM) of the late 1970s and '80s, and were revered by the likes of Def Leppard, Iron Maiden and Metallica. As for Pete Way's legendary excesses, Ozzy Osbourne once stated, 'They call me a madman but compared to Pete Way, I am out of my league.' My induction into that crazy world would serve me well in the future.

*

Some of my old Preston friends had made the big move to London, many selling hippie trinkets, belts and bags to tourists.

The upside? Easy money. The downside? It was illegal. In the early 1970s, Martin Burnie, a colourful East Ender, established 'fly pitching' on a large scale, illegally trading on Oxford Street, the heart of West End shopping. Traders peddled a range of jewellery, belts, bags and beads that were extremely popular with both hippies and tourists. Burnie's business model was simple: he supplied the stock and the barrow, and would cover any fines incurred. In return he pocketed 60 per cent of the takings.

Known as 'grafters' or 'fly pitchers', Burnie's traders were usually hippies or young travellers who set up portable A-frame barrows on wheels. They quickly became a common sight dotted along both sides of Oxford Street, from Marble Arch to Bond Street.

A week or so after leaving UFO, I approached a hippie 'fly pitcher' on Oxford Street. He had a Guru Maharaj Ji badge pinned to his tie-dyed shirt.

'How do I get a start here?' I asked.

'You need to speak to a Mr Martin,' he replied, telling me where he could be found every evening around 6 p.m.

That evening a burgundy Jaguar slid into a narrow lane near Oxford Street. One tinted window slowly rolled down, revealing a burly, dark-haired man. As he stepped out of his Jag, dressed in his Crombie camel overcoat—as worn by most East End 'wide boys'—I watched closely as 'Mr Martin' collected and then divvied up money, handing it to the maybe ten traders gathered around him. He didn't have a wallet, just a wad of notes as thick as your fist, rolled tight.

'Anyone get nicked today?' he asked, looking over his troops.

I fronted up and asked if I could get a start.

'No problem, son,' he bluntly replied. 'Be here at 7 a.m.'

Working Oxford Street opened up my eyes to another world. Pretty soon I was rubbing shoulders with an underbelly of characters from the shady side of London, the kind of people I'd only ever seen in old movies. I was quickly on nodding terms with most of them: the pickpockets, shoplifters, dealers, pimps and rent boys.

The perfume lads had a good hustle, touting expensive French perfume at bargain prices. To help flog their wares, they had a newspaper named *The Knightsbridge Courier* lying open, displaying a full-page ad that showed how expensive this same brand of perfume was at high-end stores. Of course, there was no such newspaper, and probably no such perfume.

Three-card Monte was a guaranteed crowd draw. Three cards were displayed on a cardboard box on the footpath: Jack of Spades, Jack of Clubs and the Queen. The dealer placed the three cards facedown and rearranged them. He then challenged a punter to find the Queen. If successful, the punter won an amount equal to his bet.

Then came the sting. The dealer would allow the gullible punter to win a few times, tempting him to bet more and more. Greed kicked in. Standing beside the punter was a 'shill', playing the role of an innocent bystander encouraging the poor sucker: 'Mate, you're killing it!'

At a certain point, the 'shill' grabbed all the cash from the punter's wallet and threw it onto the table; the cards were played and the punter lost. Then a shout rang out—'Police!'—and everyone scarpered. I watched the many gullible tourists, who were left wondering what the fuck had just happened.

If you were on the hunt for a new suit or sports jacket, 'the Pole' was your man. He was a middle-aged Polish gent, reputably the best shoplifter in London. He'd take an order in the morning and by early afternoon return with said item for a good price. It was as if you'd visited a bespoke tailor in Bond Street yourself.

★

One day, a young bobby approached me.

'Have you been nicked this week?'

'Nope.'

'Come with me then.'

This was an unfortunate part of the business. I lugged my barrow to Marylebone Police Station, where my charge read: 'Without Lawful Authority or Excuse Wilfully Obstructing the Free Passage Along a Highway'. I was bailed to appear before the magistrate the following day at Marylebone Magistrates Court.

The holding cells below the courthouse contained an intriguing array of characters: pickpockets, shoplifters, rent boys, drunks. Congregated in their own corner of the cell were the elite—the three-card tricksters and perfume boys, all sharp-dressed lads.

'Oi!' they called out to me. 'What are you doing over there?' And with that, I had the privilege of joining them in their corner of the cell.

I was fined £10 and got straight back to work. Over my period of working the streets I'd spend more than twenty mornings at the Marylebone courthouse. I've kept some of my bail slips as mementos.

Eventually I found more legitimate work with Martin Burnie's wife, running a licensed barrow on the corner of Old Cavendish and Oxford streets. We sold the usual tourist crap:

toy figurines of bobbies and Queen's Guards; model London taxis and buses; postcards, badges, pendants and flags. The irony was that most of the stuff was made in China.

Drugs were a regular part of my life and I found out pretty quickly that my licensed barrow provided the perfect cover to sell a few pills to other traders. It was 'a nice little earner', in the Cockney vernacular. After about six months, however, I concluded that drug dealing was a mug's game. I really didn't want to see the inside of Wandsworth prison; its exterior walls were daunting enough.

*

Music was still my obsession. In late 1973, the much-hyped New York Dolls arrived in London, touted as America's Rolling Stones. Their one-off London performance was at a most unlikely venue: the Biba store, a fashion icon of the sixties on the Kensington high street. The crowd was a mixture of curious media, hardened music industry types, and the likes of Malcolm McLaren and his then-girlfriend, fashion designer Vivienne Westwood. The Dolls' music was a patchwork of hard rock and glam that would be a major influence on future groups KISS, Sex Pistols, Ramones and Guns N' Roses, as well as the soon-to-explode punk scene. There was something new and exciting about them.

Sharon and I, meanwhile, were doing so well that we even discussed getting married and moving to Australia. This all come crashing down when she learned she had underlying health issues that would require a major operation, followed by months of rehabilitation in a wheelchair. Our plans were now very much on hold.

Around this time, Paul Varley from LFR called and said he was joining a new band called Arrows. They would go on to have numerous hits, plus their own TV show, and would write the classic 'I Love Rock 'n' Roll'—a worldwide hit for Joan Jett & the Blackhearts. Paul's call brought on a flashback to Preston and the journey we had taken in the summer of 1969, which had fundamentally changed the direction of my life. My heart went out to Pete Illingworth, the last man standing—the real rock of LFR.

★

Roy from Preston lived below me in the ground-floor flat in Willesden Green. He'd recently returned from a visit to South America. While gazing out my bedroom window, I noticed an eviscerated surfboard lying on the lawn below. As a surfer I was intrigued, totally unaware that Roy had taken up the sport. (Not a lot of surf in Preston.) I ventured downstairs.

In the kitchen, Roy and a friend named John sat around a table, grinning like Cheshire cats. Piled high on the table was a huge mound of Colombia's finest cocaine. Over the next couple of weeks, my nightly ritual was to plunge a porcelain teacup into the coke mountain and head back upstairs to enjoy. Roy's bounty was enjoyable while it lasted.

Willesden Green remained the do-drop-in for old friends from Preston, old friends from anywhere—our beanbags were always available. One interesting visitor who passed through was Tim Hardin, the writer of such classics as 'If I Were a Carpenter' and 'Reason to Believe'. Sitting around one night, he candidly opened up about his heroin addiction and the toll it had taken on his life and career.

'Down and out, broke, ripped off, sad,' I wrote in my diary.

Tim would die of a heroin overdose in 1980, a tragic end for a truly gifted singer and songwriter.

★

By the summer of 1974, Sharon and I had begun to drift apart. Although we saw each other often, something was missing, and her illness had complicated things further. One day she told me she was seeing someone else. I took it very badly. I anguished over what I could have done better, but it was too late.

I was stirred from my self-pity by a call from my old roadie mate Jed. He was working for folk-rocker Jonathan Kelly and they needed help. I jumped at the opportunity for a change of scenery and to get back on the road. Jonathan was from Drogheda in County Louth, Ireland, and had been in a band with ex–Bee Gees drummer and former Australian child star 'Smiley' Colin Peterson before becoming a guitar-strumming troubadour, now with three albums on RCA.

In 1973, Jonathan 'went electric', forming Jonathan Kelly's Outside. This line-up comprised A-list players: guitarists Snowy White and Chas Jankel, along with drummer Dave Sheen and bassist Kuma Harada. Between them, they'd later play with Pink Floyd, Ian Dury, Kate Bush, Roger Waters and Thin Lizzy.

My first gig with Jonathan was at Scunthorpe in the north-east of England (known as 'the town with cunt in its name'). On the way back to London, we hit atrocious weather just outside of Luton. While I was driving, either my attention waned or I dropped into a microsleep and I lost control of the truck. We aquaplaned across three lanes and slammed into an embankment. Jed and I were shot out of the van (seatbelts weren't yet compulsory in the UK) and the back doors burst open, spewing gear onto the motorway like a drunk throwing up on a Friday night.

I lay there in the rain, in a state of shock. Two days in Luton hospital followed; Jed's collarbone was broken, while I escaped with just a few stitches. Jonathan, thankfully, didn't fire me; he accepted it was an unfortunate accident, nothing more.

7

LAND OF THE FREE
WITH SAVOY

The band Savoy Brown was one of the earliest innovators in the British blues/rock scene. In late 1974, I got a tip they were looking for another roadie. Knowing full well that they spent most of their time touring the US, I wanted that job. America was the birthplace of my true musical loves—soul, R&B, blues and rock—and while I'd seen a bit of the world, the USA had so far evaded me.

I put in a call to their manager, Harry Simmonds, and got the job. Harry had been a blues aficionado since his days at art school with his mates Brian Jones and Mick Jagger. The three were members of the Tamla Motown Appreciation Society that met regularly at The Ealing Club, the first recognised R&B venue in London. An avid collector of blues and R&B records, Harry would inspire his younger brother Kim to take up the guitar. By 1969, although barely eighteen, Kim had formed the Savoy Brown Blues Band, which originally had two black members—unusual for bands in those days. By the time I hooked up with them, there had been thirteen line-up changes.

Savoy Brown of 1975 comprised Kim on guitar, Dave Bidwell playing drums, bassist Andy Rae and Paul Raymond on keyboards. Paul and Dave had played with Chicken Shack, who'd had a hit in 1969 with singer Christine Perfect (aka Christine McVie) covering the Etta James classic 'I'd Rather Go Blind'. The road crew was tour manager John Knowles plus roadies Pete Bennett, Michael Jessup and me.

John was a seasoned road warrior from Liverpool, Pete a tough nugget from Wallasey on the other side of the River Mersey. John supported Liverpool, Pete backed Everton and they butted heads in a tribal way. Little did I know it at the time, but this would prepare me for the similar kind of volatility between Jim Barnes and Steve Prestwich when I worked with Cold Chisel. Michael, being the youngest of the crew, was the fall guy, the victim of band and crew jokes.

My first tour with Savoy was a run of campuses and clubs through the UK, Germany, Switzerland and France. It was winter—cold, wet and snowing—which made handling a five-tonne truck on icy roads in snowy conditions hazardous. No crashes this time, fortunately.

Back in London in early 1975, Savoy Brown set up in Olympic Studios to record their twelfth album, *Wire Fire*. But there was a problem. Dave Bidwell was an excellent drummer and a lovely person but had a major heroin habit. I often hung out with him at his flat in Notting Hill Gate; sometimes he'd be upbeat, at other times nodding off. He knew he had a problem but couldn't overcome it. Eventually, recording with him became too difficult and Tommy Farnell, from folk-rockers Fairport Convention, replaced him.

★

Wire Fire was released in the US and Canada on London Records in July, and a North American tour kicked off in Vancouver in August. Fifteen shows later, we crossed the US border at Buffalo. My American dream was becoming a reality.

Compared to the more reserved Canadian metropolis, New York City was a sensory overload. Cars jostled for position in the traffic, horns blaring, sirens wailing, while yellow cabs weaved through the mad congestion. With a white-knuckled grip, I managed to navigate our truck through the chaos to Central Park, the green oasis smack in the middle of Manhattan.

The Schaefer Music Festival on 8 September was part of an annual event sponsored by the famous brewing company. The stage was set up in the south-east corner of Central Park at the Wollman Skating Rink Theater, which could handle up to 7000 patrons. Savoy Brown went down well, their signature songs being ten-minute epics of 'Hellbound Train' and 'Tell Mama', both featuring Kim Simmonds' slide-guitar attack.

On my day off I decided to do the tourist thing. I observed people going about their business with no eye contact or smiles. The hustlers on 42nd Street, meanwhile, were on the lookout for easy targets. Black hookers in outrageously short skirts gestured at me, promising this boy from the Antipodes pleasures I could only dream of (and most likely couldn't afford). Cops, guns holstered at their hip, chatted on street corners, monitoring the human circus. While New York felt unpredictable to me, I also found it intoxicating. I was seduced.

We left the crazy intensity of 'Gotham City', heading south on the I-95 to the relative sanity of Florida, the 'Sunshine State'. West Palm Beach Auditorium was a 5000-seater, a regular stop for rock acts. Savoy Brown were special guests of Steppenwolf, while Montrose, featuring a younger Sammy Hagar, would open the show.

As I reversed the truck up to the auditorium's rear loading bay, I was met by half a dozen burly dudes in black satin bomber jackets, 'Teamsters 769' emblazoned on their backs. They seemed to be in a surly mood. Up to then, my only involvement with unions had been during a brief stint working in the wool mill in Botany, and later on at Leyland Motors in the UK. But I was about to learn how powerful unions such as the Teamsters were in America.

At first, I put their black mood down to the heat—it was 30-plus degrees—and didn't think any more of it. As I had done at thousands of prior gigs, I opened the roller door and got to work. I grabbed a stencilled flight case marked 'Savoy Brown Guitars' and proceeded to wheel it towards the edge of the ramp. The Teamster crew started murmuring among themselves. Within seconds, a T-shirted long-hair came scurrying out of the bowels of the venue.

'Whoa, whoa, stop!' he yelled. 'What the fuck are you doing?'

'I'm unloading the truck,' I replied, stating the bleeding obvious.

'Fuck, buddy,' he shot back, 'this is a union shed—*they* unload the truck. Are you trying to get us shut down?'

The Steppenwolf stage manager pulled me to one side and explained that I was transgressing venue rules and endangering the show.

'This is a Teamsters room,' he told me. 'You don't know the Teamsters?'

I told him that I didn't.

He looked at me, shook his head and muttered one word:

'Fuck.' He then turned to the Teamsters and said, 'Sorry guys, they're English.' In response, they mumbled a few words which I took to mean 'fuckwit'.

I later learned that this was right around the time that former Teamsters president Jimmy Hoffa disappeared without trace. Many believed he was murdered by the Mafia.

*

We headed north to the University of Indiana in Bloomington for a big outdoor show with Aerosmith, Blue Öyster Cult and Joe Cocker. Ross Todd, the concert's promoter, spent much of his time whizzing around backstage in his golf cart. By late afternoon, whispers had spread among the stage crew that the gate takings weren't great and there were real fears that people might not get paid. I observed a very animated conversation between the stage manager and promoter. I was perched on a road case and watched as the promoter and his golf cart made a final sweep backstage, then disappeared out the rear gate and off down the road.

It didn't take long for this news to filter back to the stage crew. Their response was to start dismantling the stage flooring, section by section, which also happened to coincide with Blue Öyster Cult's soundcheck. All credit to Eric Bloom, the band's singer, for vainly trying to tread a stage that was disappearing beneath his feet. To add to the chaos, Aerosmith's tour manager was gesturing wildly at the promoter's lone representative. This one poor sod left holding the fort could clearly be heard trying to reassure everyone that the promoter would return at any second to clear everything up. To his great relief, Ross and his trusty golf cart reappeared, carrying what I could only assume was a bag of cash, and the show was back on.

Something I took away from my first American adventure was the size of things: the excess astounded me. The food servings were huge, as were the cars, while TV and radio catered for every taste. Everything seemed to be bigger and better—and it was all right there at my fingertips.

*

Tour manager John Knowles was a rough and rude character who'd address hotel managers as 'Bozo' in a thick Liverpudlian accent, and he knew every groupie and topless bar in the US. When it came to matters carnal, he told me, Atlanta was the place to be. 'Even the fookin' ugliest roadie gets laid there!' he assured me.

He told me that Atlanta was the home of the 'Georgia Peach'—not fruit, but groupies—and the most famous was Sweet Connie, who hailed from Little Rock, Arkansas, and had been immortalised in the Grand Funk Railroad song 'We're an American Band'. John insisted that he'd marry her one day. The most delectable 'peaches' could be found in the bar at Alex Cooley's Electric Ballroom, which was situated in the historic Georgian Terrace Hotel. It was the major rock hall in the city where you were guaranteed to spot locals like the Atlanta Rhythm Section and Grinderswitch, as well as bands passing through town.

After the Savoy Brown show at the Electric Ballroom, as we left by the backstage exit, we were greeted by the diehard fans, clutching autograph books and albums; equally appealing was a throng of young beauties. My eyes were drawn to Mona, a tall, slim blonde in cut-off shorts, midriff top and a smile that said, 'Hi, I want you!' Hell, I had to oblige.

Over the next three rest days I barely saw daylight, let alone the rest of the band. Mona had moved from Jacksonville, Florida, where she had attended Robert E. Lee High School with Ronnie Van Zant and Gary Rossington from Lynyrd Skynyrd, who'd later record 'Georgia Peaches', their own salute to ladies such as Mona. Mona loved to party, knew all the bands and introduced me to the delights of Quaaludes— 'ludes'—a very useful sexual stimulant.

While travelling through the South, we'd often use the rural back roads rather than the highways. Although it took longer, we were able to experience the real South—small towns with curious names like Sparta and Panther Burn, Old Glory flying proudly from the porches, Black kids playing in the streets while their parents watched with some suspicion as a bunch of white strangers crawled by in a U-Haul. They were still unsettling times; desegregation was only a decade old, and the Ku Klux Klan was still casting a dark shadow.

*

Louisiana Tech was located in the college town of Ruston. Savoy were there for two nights with the 'Godfather of Southern Rock', multi-instrumentalist Charlie Daniels. Charlie was a southern icon who would later become known internationally for his 1979 hit 'The Devil Went Down to Georgia'.

After our first night, a little weary, we set off at around 1 am to make our way back to our hotel, a quick journey on Highway 20. I turned the Ryder down the ramp towards the highway only to encounter a large sign that informed me STOP TURN BACK WRONG WAY! The road was deserted so I decided that instead of reversing back up the ramp, it would be far easier to do a quick U-turn. I executed a copybook four-lane U-turn and headed back up the ramp.

What I didn't notice was a police vehicle at the top of the ramp with its lights flashing. Standing alongside the vehicle, beckoning me to stop, was one of Louisiana's finest. He was a dead ringer for Rod Steiger in the movie *In the Heat of the Night*.

I pulled over and wound down the window, conscious of the silver revolver holstered at his hip.

'What the hell are you doing, boy?' he barked at me.

'Sorry. Err, we're English,' I blurted, like a child caught stealing lollies.

'You didn't see the sign?'

'I panicked,' was my lame reply, as an image of a night in a Louisiana jail cell with 'Bubba' and his buddies flashed through my mind.

His inquisition continued. Why were we there? What were we doing? When I told him we'd played a show with Charlie Daniels, his tone changed.

'I should throw you boys in jail for the night, but I am going to let you go with a warning,' he said. 'Now you English guys have a good night and say hi to Charlie for me.'

★

It was 4 October 1975 and the Capitol Theatre in Passaic, New Jersey, shook as if it was under nuclear attack. Smoke engulfed the crowd, as the band on stage launched into the anthemic 'Rock and Roll All Nite', their first Top 40 hit. Savoy Brown were co-headlining a show with KISS, the New Yorkers who had just released their breakthrough album *Alive!*.

To the more serious muso, KISS was seen as a novelty, but this would soon change. When they arrived at the theatre, they looked like your average rockers in jeans and T-shirts. Within an hour the band was transformed; bassist Gene Simmons looked like the devil incarnate.

Their pyrotechnics were still fairly primitive, little more than flash pots placed around the rim of the stage and detonated by a trusty roadie. UFO had experimented with flash pots during my time with them, but KISS possessed a much larger arsenal. It took several hours for my hearing to return to Earth.

*

Buddy ran a popular music shop in Chicago, *the* place for drum supplies. Buddy and his best mate Steve became constant fixtures backstage when we were in Chicago, the 'Windy City'.

After Savoy played the Aragon Ballroom on 19 October, Steve invited the band and crew for dinner at his uncle's Italian restaurant. Seated along a large communal table, we stuffed ourselves silly on an endless supply of delicious Sicilian cuisine. Adorning the walls were photos of the owner with VIPs and celebrities like Frank Sinatra, Vic Damone and Tony Bennett.

'Does Frank come here often?' I asked Steve.

'Whenever he's in town,' he replied. I was impressed.

After dinner we headed to Steve's house for drinks. From the street, the house looked like a traditional brownstone but once inside I discovered that it was actually two houses opened up into one palatial spread. A large marble staircase led upstairs, while ornate furniture and a huge open-plan kitchen filled the marble-tiled ground floor. Outside was an expansive sunken patio.

'What does Steve do for a living?' I asked Buddy, taking in all this luxury.

A wry smile came over his face. 'He works on the water-front,' said Buddy, explaining that he was what they called a 'ghost worker'. 'Someone clocks on and off for him, but he doesn't actually work. Let's just say he is well connected.'

I couldn't help myself, and leaned forward to whisper in Buddy's ear. 'Mafia?'

Buddy raised his eyebrows, smiled and asked if I wanted another drink. Enough said.

★

The Armadillo World Headquarters, once a National Guard armoury building, was at the time the major rock venue in Austin, Texas. I loved this venue from my very first visit—there was always a receptive crowd, while ice-cold Lone Star beer and tasty burritos made the long, hot drive across the Texas prairies worthwhile. A full house of 1500 crowded in on 22 October to see Savoy Brown, who were ably supported by the legendary Texan guitar player Bugs Henderson.

Texas was full of wide-open spaces, longhorn cattle, pickup trucks and steaks so big they often required two plates. Although the film *Easy Rider* was set in the late 1960s, the rural areas it depicted were still redneck heartland even in 1975. After the gig, needing to fuel up our Ryder rental, I pulled into a dusty Texaco station in the middle of nowhere.

A battered red pickup was parked at the bowser, displaying a Confederate flag bumper sticker, with a Winchester rifle slung across the rear window. Wearing grubby overalls and a stetson, the driver was deep in conversation with the attendant. The golden gallons flowed into the Ford's massive tank and, once full, the attendant and driver continued talking, seemingly oblivious to us.

Michael Jessup was a private school–educated guy from Surrey; like me, he had never been to the US before. He leaned across and pumped the horn twice. I don't recall who hit him first or whether it was all of us in unison.

'Fuck!' I screamed. 'Do you want to get us killed?'

The pair at the pump slowly turned, and for what seemed an eternity they fixed their eyes on us. After a time, they resumed their conversation. Lesson learned: this was Texas time, not real time—and certainly not our time.

While in the South, a rock band named Baby were Savoy's support. They were a hot young four-piece out of Amarillo, Texas. We quickly grew tight. I loved touring with these 'good ol' southern boys'—both band and crew were such fun on the road. Johnny Lee Schell was their lead guitarist; he'd later record with Renée Geyer and Bonnie Raitt, and tour with Jimmy Barnes.

Baby's drum roadie went by the name of Spook. One night, as we sat around shooting the shit, he shared an interesting story. Spook's father was a photographer and on 3 February 1959 he had been in the first of the news crews to arrive at the scene of the plane crash that killed Buddy Holly, Ritchie Valens and the Big Bopper. He took the eerie black-and-white photos that were seen all over the world.

Sadly, Baby broke up after a couple of albums, but I still

keep in touch with members of the crew today. Once you're part of the roadie brotherhood, you're in forever.

★

Los Angeles was the last stop on our five-month tour. LA was a great place for a few days off. It was the hub of the west coast music scene, most of the record labels were there and it had the best clubs. We stayed at the Hyatt on Sunset, better known as the 'Riot House'. Many of the scenes from the movie *Almost Famous* were filmed there, and it was at the Riot House that Keith Richards dropped a TV off the balcony of room 1015, where John Bonham rode his motorcycle along the halls, and where Lemmy wrote 'Motorhead'. At times it resembled a circus, with musicians, roadies, groupies and hangers-on jamming its fourteen floors.

From the Riot House, it was a leisurely stroll west along Sunset to the epicentre of Hollywood rock and roll: the Whisky a Go Go, the Roxy, and the Rainbow Bar and Grill. The Rainbow was the place to hang out at night. As a visiting roadie, the door was always open—in fact, the door was open at every place on the strip, often with a free bar tab attached. Upstairs at the Rainbow was where the roadies, drug dealers, A-list groupies, gangsters, movie stars and rock stars would converge.

Mario, the owner, respectfully known as 'the Godfather of Sunset Strip', knew everyone: who to let in, who to turn away. And he never forgot a face. When he recognised you, he greeted you like a long-lost brother. He also owned the Whisky a few doors down the Strip.

The Starwood was a few blocks east of the Riot House. Bands performed downstairs, while upstairs was the exclusive bar where lots of young groupies—some very young—tried to outdo each other. Coke flowed in abundance, while such scenesters as DJ Rodney Bingenheimer and manager/producer/ Svengali Kim Fowley were regular faces, as were the dealers, pimps, and general flotsam and jetsam of the 1970s LA rock-and-roll world.

The Starwood was owned by the notorious Eddie Nash, a scary guy with major Mafia connections (he was linked to 1981's gruesome Wonderland murders). It was always fun to hang out upstairs at the Starwood, where drink and drugs were readily consumed. One night I hooked up with a dark-haired damsel, ending up at her place near Laurel Canyon. She told me she was the daughter of George Reeves, the original Superman. Many years later I discovered Reeves never had children. Still, it was Hollyweird; everyone had a story.

I returned to the relative sanity of London for Christmas. It was around this time that I began a relationship with Lynda, my flatmate. We had known each other since my days in Preston, and we had lived in the same apartment for the previous few years. She was fun to be with, and she loved music and partying.

*

Jay Surf Shop was one of only two such institutions in London, a welcome respite for the lonely surfer in me. It was in Wandsworth, a working-class suburb better known for its high-security prison than its surf culture. The shop was owned by Phil Jay. Upstairs were the shaping and glassing bays—Eric Muchmore was the shaper and John Povey glassed—while downstairs was the retail shop with racks of freshly minted Corky Carroll 'Space Sticks' surfboards.

John, with his tangled, sun-bleached mane, manned the shop downstairs. Quite the enigma, he was a member of the legendary 1960s band The Pretty Things, who were heroes of mine as a teenager, from 1967 to 2007. John co-wrote several tracks on their acclaimed fourth album *S.F. Sorrow*, recognised as the first rock opera album.

I'd often drop by the shop to talk music with John and check out the imported surf magazines. I'd eventually shell out my hard-earned pounds to buy a board but regrettably left it in the attic of my Willesden Green flat when I returned to Oz. I sometimes wonder if it's still up there.

By the early spring of 1976, I was back in Germany with Savoy Brown. They had a new album *Skin 'N' Bone*, and a new bassist, Ian Ellis from the Scottish outfit Clouds. Germany was mainly clubs and small concert halls and I loved touring there. I loved the beer and I loved the food, and as most people spoke or understood English, it was relatively easy to get around.

Although we never did a show east of the Berlin Wall, we would travel the autobahn through East Germany from West Berlin on our way to Stuttgart or Munich. Miles of barbed wire enclosed the autobahn and guard towers kept watch for any defectors. Border guards, armed with submachine guns, checked beneath every vehicle for stowaways. Their dogs looked ready to rip your throat out. We were always careful, but that terrible sick feeling—'Did I forget something?'—hung in our minds.

Although young East Germans could listen to Western music on the American Forces radio network, they couldn't purchase it. Often, in some East German autobahn diner, we would be discreetly approached by young guys asking about Western magazines, books, music or a highly prized pair of jeans—Lees or Levis, ideally.

Come April 1976 and I was back in La La Land for a five-month run of shows that stretched from one coast to the other. It gradually became a blur: another auditorium, another hall, another club, another town, another city. We'd usually end up in a Holiday Inn or a Best Western—or the Paradise Motor Lodge in Dothan, Alabama, where crackhead hookers slept in deckchairs beside the pool. As long as there were fresh sheets, a shower and a TV, it was home for the night. The only novelty was seeing on which side of the bed the drawer holding the Gideon bible was. The routine: walk in, dump bags, turn on television and check for the Gideon.

When required, we'd fly between gigs—it wasn't unusual for us to drive our truck onto the tarmac and load the gear straight into the baggage hold. There were times when we were even able to convince a taxiing plane to turn back for us. Pissed-off passengers would glare as eight smirking, long-haired rock-and-rollers scrambled aboard.

Savoy Brown played with some amazing people. We did two nights with blues legend Muddy Waters at a 250-seater club in Denver named Ebbets Field—after the famed Brooklyn Dodgers' baseball stadium in Flatbush, New York. The place was a shrine to bad taste, with walls, floors and seating all covered in orange-and-brown shagpile carpet. Muddy's band at the time featured legends Pinetop Perkins, Jerry Portnoy, Luther Johnson, Bob Margolin, Calvin Jones and Willie Smith. Sharing a dressing room with the great man remains one of my most cherished memories. I was also lucky enough in my time with Savoy to work alongside other blues giants such as Albert Collins, Freddie King, Buddy Guy and Albert King.

★

Toronto became another favourite stop on the rock-and-roll road. The El Mocambo Tavern was the city's premier venue. Known as the 'El Mo', it was where The Rolling Stones would later record four of the tracks for their double live album *Love You Live* in 1977.

Backstage at the El Mo would be crammed with friends of the band, including Burton Cummings of The Guess Who, as well as record reps, radio jocks, assorted friends and local musos, all there to party and plunder.

During the first Savoy Brown show at the El Mo in 1976, while I was wedged uncomfortably beside the bass bins, an attractive redhead in the front row drew my attention. Enter Barbara Collins of Kitchener, Ontario. Later on, during a break in touring, I flew back up to Canada, and Barbara and I spent a week at a cabin by a beautiful lake in the Algonquin Provincial Park in rural Ontario. I am sure Lynda back in London had a fair idea of what happened on the road, but my relationship with Barbara fast developed into more than a casual fling.

The tour rolled on. CB radio was a new toy to keep us amused over long journeys. We quickly learned the lingo: 'Bears in the air' referred to police in planes or helicopters, 'bears in the woods' meant highway patrol were hiding nearby, while 'bears in a plain wrapper' referred to unmarked police cars. Every truck/operator had a handle, an identifying name; ours was 'London Bridge'. We were quizzed about where we were from and where we were going—and what for? Fellow truckers soon identified our rig and would toot a friendly blast on their air horns as they passed.

In late May, Savoy Brown was booked to do a big outdoor show with Scottish band Nazareth and my old mates UFO at Saginaw, north of Detroit in the Great Lakes area. I had repaired my friendship with Phil Mogg over a bottle of Southern Comfort. The gruesome consequence was waking up with my face glued to the pillow by my own vomit. Interestingly, within months of the Saginaw show, Savoy's longstanding guitarist/keyboardist Paul Raymond would leave to join UFO and play a huge role in their future success.

All the time my relationship with Barbara continued to build. I knew this was not going to end well but at the time that stupidly didn't seem to deter me.

The shady Kim Fowley, who I'd first met in LA, had put together an all-female group named The Runaways. In August we shared an outdoor bill in Michigan with them and 1960s legends Spirit. It was a peculiar mix: Spirit were jazz-influenced hippies, Savoy played blues-based rock, while The Runaways were teen glam rockers. We were all staying at the same motel and some of us ventured over to The Runaways' rooms for a few drinks. The scene was like a Valley Girls slumber party: they jumped about in their pyjamas, bouncing on their beds while listening to Slade. It felt a little bizarre to us, and we drifted back to the comfort of our rooms and Mr Jack Daniels.

I was starting to understand how the romance of the road could quickly lose its appeal. It became an endless grind of brain-numbing freeways, all-night diners, rental trucks, airport check-ins and lookalike hotels with shows like *Sesame Street*; *Happy Days*; *Welcome Back, Kotter* and reruns of *The Lone Ranger* seemingly on an endless loop on the TV.

Back in London for a few weeks before embarking on another tour of Germany, Belgium and France, I had the very unpleasant task of telling Lynda about Barbara. The news did not go down well. I made things worse by telling Lynda that I was planning to bring Barbara to London to live with me, an unbelievably selfish move on my part. It took quite a while, but Lynda and I moved on and became—and remain—good friends.

Before we set off for our European dates, tour manager John Knowles announced that he was leaving Savoy to take up a similar role with UFO. This now left the role of tour manager open for me, and I gladly accepted. Travelling with the band was a much more comfortable proposition than in the equipment truck.

For a while in London I had been aware of the emergence of punk. My local record store was run by an obsessive 35-year-old Little Feat fan, complete with beard, long hair and Lowell George overalls. In November I watched him put on the Sex Pistols' new record, 'Anarchy in the UK', as his eyes rolled in derision. I found the music abrasive, confronting, divisive and unlike anything else around at the time. My gut told me that something was happening. I went to the 100 Club to see what all the fuss was about; it was packed with young suburban kids going apeshit. I was 29 and felt old.

In November 1976, we learned that Barbara was pregnant and we married at Willesden Green registry on 29 December. Facing the stark reality of becoming a father, the lifestyle and career that I had enjoyed for more than ten years seemed unviable to me. I decided that it was time to head back to Australia.

8

SYDNEY TOWN

I'd spent more than ten years overseas learning my trade—as a roadie, a sound and lighting guy, and eventually a tour manager. I had earned my stripes. I would not necessarily return in triumph, but with the skills I'd learned over the past decade I was determined to further my way in the business of music—I was moving into management.

I landed on 15 March 1977 with no money and a heavily pregnant wife, and we agreed that it was best for Barbara to stay with my mother and Mal, who now had a sheep and cattle property at Gulgong in country New South Wales. I would travel there on weekends, returning to Sydney each Monday. Dad had an apartment in Cremorne where I'd stay; I was also able to use his office in North Sydney.

I needed to circulate in Sydney and do some networking, spreading the word that I was looking for acts to manage.

As I settled in, I was struck by how much Sydney had changed. The fashions were modern and there seemed to be a flourishing pop-music scene, with Sherbet, Hush, Dragon, Skyhooks, John Paul Young and Marcia Hines dominating the charts. ABBA had just toured, breaking all records, while 2SM in Sydney and 3XY in Melbourne were the taste setters. *Countdown* was must-see TV. *Go-Set* had been replaced by *RAM* in Sydney and *Juke* in Melbourne.

The key AM radio stations in the capitals sponsored free outdoor concerts for the likes of Sherbet, Dragon and the Ted Mulry Gang, which drew huge crowds of enthusiastic teenagers. I was soon to discover that lying just beneath the surface, in the small pubs and clubs across the country, was a burgeoning rock scene just waiting to emerge.

My younger brother Ian was playing guitar in a band called Toons that had a small but credible following, and I decided to give them a hand. Then one day, as I sat in my office counting paperclips, I received a call from Gene Pierson. He ran Living Sound, a small label that had been set up by the Nine Network and had distribution through RCA. Gene had a new band called Australia and was searching for someone to look after them. Initially I thought it was a joke, but no—that was really their name. Although apprehensive, I discovered that they were actually good players, and they had a record deal, so at least this was a start. They released an album on Living Sound but it went nowhere and I would eventually move on. I was keeping an eye out for something unique, a band with whom I could build a career.

★

On most weeknights, Ian and I would visit the clubs and pubs around Sydney, looking for something or someone that would blow me away. I found most acts underwhelming, their influences too obvious. But Ian was particularly excited about a young band from Adelaide. Although they were raw, he said, at least they were doing their own thing.

'So what are they called?' I asked.

'Cold Chisel.'

Oh no, I thought. *First 'Australia' and now 'Cold Chisel'.* What was it about these lousy names?

Ian persisted. 'Forget the name,' he said. 'Just come and see them play.'

One mid-week night, I tagged along with Ian to a party in Kings Cross for a member of the Mangrove Boogie Kings, a rockabilly band from the north coast of New South Wales. It was a typical musos get-together, fuelled by alcohol, weed and lively banter. A few drinks loosened my tongue and I began to inform anyone in earshot what was wrong with the local music scene—all this, mind you, from a guy who'd only been back a few months and currently managed a band called Australia. The vibe in the room was unmistakable: they thought I was a wanker. What I didn't know was that Don Walker, from the band Cold Chisel, was among the gathering that night.

*

In May, Ian and I traipsed down to a dingy club called Chequers in Sydney's Chinatown to check out this Cold Chisel. Once the Chequers stage had been graced by the likes of Liza Minnelli, Sammy Davis Jr and Shirley Bassey, but the club's star had faded and the owners had attempted to revive it as a rock venue. A few years earlier, AC/DC had made their live debut there.

The room was all but deserted; it was dark and dingy, a mirror ball pretty much the only sign of life. I once said that there were three men and a dog in attendance that night, but that's not true: there was no dog. Disco music blared from the sound system; the smell of stale Chinese food hung in the air.

Crammed on the tiny stage were drums, bass, guitar and keyboards; a few lights dangled precariously from a steel bar. The band ambled on stage, and the wild-haired singer grasped the microphone and turned his back towards what little audience there was. He held the mike so close to his lips it looked as though he wanted to eat it. The rhythm section laid down a driving beat that was super tight, the piano player pounded like Jerry Lee Lewis and the curly-maned guitarist ripped effortlessly between rhythm and lead, on a par with anyone I had seen overseas. When the singer kicked in, I had to pinch myself: his voice was awesome, unique. It startled me, reminiscent of the first time I heard Steve Winwood.

As I watched Cold Chisel, I started asking myself questions. Was I fooling myself that they were that good? Where were the music aficionados, the trainspotters, the suits? There were just half a dozen girls on the dance floor, seemingly more intent on each other than the five guys on stage. I went away that night convinced that they were exceptional and had the potential to be huge all around the world, not only in Oz. But soon I started to question myself again. Maybe they weren't as good as I'd thought. And they did have a shitty name.

A couple of days after the gig, my phone rang. It was Don Walker. He spoke slowly, sounding more like a cattle farmer from Longreach than the keyboard player of the young band I'd seen in Chinatown. He asked if we could meet for a drink at the Hilton and I agreed. Perhaps Don had liked my diatribe at that party in the Cross—or perhaps he just didn't have other options. It was also quite possible that he was at the end of his tether, having navigated the band through tough times over the past four years. I think Don really needed someone who could help steer the ship.

I liked Don's sense of occasion: the Hilton was the premier hotel in Sydney. He walked in with a dog-eared folder tucked under his arm and, without missing a beat, gave me the rundown of the band's sorry circumstances. They survived on what gigs they could scrape together, lived in two rooms at a hotel in Kings Cross (and the occasional couch), and had gone through more managers than he could count. And to top it off, their lead singer, Jim Barnes, said he was leaving to join his brother John in a band named Feather.

'Mate, I don't know if we still have a band or not,' Don told me.

He showed me a handwritten list of every record company in Australia, with comments on why they didn't want to sign Cold Chisel. It was daunting, to say the least.

'Do you think Jim is really leaving?' I asked Don.

After a long silence, he explained that Jim had left numerous times before, but had always returned. But Don was apprehensive this time, especially with the lack of record company interest and no manager. Don suggested I talk with Feather's manager, Ray Arnold, a man who I knew had connections in the industry and who was feared and respected. Arnold had been part of the first generation of roadies and tour managers; he was a tough and uncompromising character.

Soon after, I stood at the front door of a house in Bondi, wondering what I was about to say. I pushed a button and the doorbell rang loudly. I heard a voice from inside.

'Who the fuck is it?'

Not a good start, I thought. The door opened to reveal an angry, broad-chested guy. My sphincter tightened like a rubber band.

'What do you want?' Arnold snapped.

'I'm looking at managing Cold Chisel and want to talk to you about Jim.'

He gave me the once-over. I hoped he didn't notice my shaking knees.

'Do you want a beer?'

'Sure,' I squeaked. It was midday, after all.

I sat on the edge of his leather couch and gave him my background—how I'd worked as a road dog in the UK and the US, but now with a pregnant wife I had decided to return to Australia and try my hand at management. A smile slowly crept across his craggy face.

'Mate, I love Chisel,' he said. 'They are a great band. As far as I am concerned, Jim should stay with them.'

I don't think I've ever felt so relieved.

★

Don assembled the guys in his tiny room at the Plaza Hotel in Kings Cross, opposite the notorious Bourbon & Beefsteak and a stone's throw from the El Alamein Fountain. Three members of the band were sprawled across the two beds, while Jim sat on the floor, looking uninterested, and Don commandeered the lone chair. The cheap room said a lot about their current predicament: a wire coathanger acted as a TV aerial, and empty beer cans and discarded orange peel were scattered about.

I launched into my spiel.

'You guys are world class,' I announced. 'I reckon I could make you the biggest band in Australia—maybe the world.'

Don sat and listened intently, Ian Moss fidgeted with a piece of paper, while Steve Prestwich and Jim stared blankly off into space. But Phil Small smiled; he seemed interested. However, I didn't feel confident that I'd won them over. Maybe they'd heard it all before. I left the Plaza sensing that my big pitch had somehow fallen well short.

The following day my phone rang.

'It's Don, mate. You've got the job.'

I was now managing Cold Chisel.

*

Cold Chisel had branched out from Adelaide in early 1976 and had been crisscrossing the country since. While they could find gigs, the money was lousy—maybe, if they were lucky, $150 a show—and they were living hand to mouth, gig to gig. Bands like Chisel were expected to play three 40-minute sets a night. Chisel's live repertoire was a mix of Deep Purple, Free, Jimi Hendrix and Led Zeppelin covers, interspersed with originals like 'Teenage Love Affair', 'Goodbye' and 'Daskarzine'.

It would be fair to say that Cold Chisel had never been fashion conscious. Even describing them as a 'ragtag bunch' in 1977 was a stretch. There was always a sense of style about the bands I'd worked with overseas, but in Chisel's case I think that the roadies were better dressed.

Don Walker was the most level-headed of the band, and I mainly dealt with him in the beginning. At least I could find Don; I don't even think Interpol could have tracked down the others most of the time. Don was the responsible adult in the room, a role I imagined he accepted reluctantly, but that he understood was necessary; otherwise, the band would probably die a slow and inconsequential death. He sculpted their music from day one and every night conscientiously constructed their live set list. Don's slow country drawl belied a deep intelligence—he held a degree in quantum physics and his mother was a university lecturer—and the security and comfort brought about by a daily chat with Don would endure for my 32 years with the band.

Steve was a Pom from Liverpool. I knew very well what Scousers were like from my time in the UK and dealing with the quirks of John and Pete from Savoy Brown. Yes, Steve could be rude, arrogant and opinionated, but he was also one of nicest guys you could ever meet. In these early days, he was a nuisance; if you said black, he'd say white, if you said go, he'd say stop, and the rest of it. Steve loved chip butties and wore oversized shoes, which while comfortable couldn't have been more unfashionable. He was also a great drummer, an integral part of the Cold Chisel sound.

Ian came from the Red Centre of Alice Springs. He was an enigma, all hair and no shoes. More than once he described himself as being from another planet, and at times I agreed. He had two pre-gig rituals: he'd shave, and then he'd tune his guitars. Ian always had a problem with time; one day he'll surely be chasing his own hearse.

Phil was such a friendly guy it's unlikely he ever had an enemy. He was the last to join the band, in 1975. His predecessor, co-founder Les Kaczmarek, had had trouble adapting to the new material and the band's change of direction when they'd started writing their own songs. Phil had been playing in an Adelaide covers band named Planet when approached to audition for Chisel. He had a great smile, the kind that could disguise a serial killer.

As for Jim, when we met at the Plaza, what stuck in my mind were his dirty jeans and filthy sneakers, and the wary way he scoped me out from behind his mop of hair. As we became more acquainted, I could sense him working me over; he tried to get away with murder and, more often than not, he did. But when I caught him out, he'd slip into his default mode—laughter—which made it almost impossible to get mad at the guy.

Gigging was the life source of bands like Chisel and I needed to get my head around how the game worked. Booking agents tightly controlled live work and the top dog in Sydney town was Solo Premier. They had a joint venture with Premier Artists in Melbourne, which was partly owned by heavy-hitter Michael Gudinski, whose Mushroom Records roster included the hugely successful Skyhooks. This gave them serious leverage.

Solo Premier was fronted by the brash young Chris Murphy, whose parents ran a successful booking agency out of Shellharbour, servicing the many licensed clubs of New South Wales. A week into my life with Chisel, I sat down with Chris in his North Sydney office. Chris was bright and super confident, bordering on arrogant, but he had the power—and the venues—that I needed to get Chisel moving. Like me, he was a surfer.

Chris liked my enthusiasm for Chisel, and took the band on, but a remark he made has always stuck with me. 'Chisel,' he told me, 'will never be bigger than Kevin Borich.'

★

Barbara was to be induced on 21 July 1977 and there was no way I was going to miss the birth of my first child. My train left Central station on a cold winter's morning, my destination Mudgee, 265 kilometres away. I figured I would arrive with plenty of time but, for some inexplicable reason, at every stop—even though most platforms were empty except for a few gum leaves pirouetting—the driver and the conductor would disappear into the ticket office for ages. While my journey dragged, my wristwatch didn't and my early-arrival plan was soon in tatters.

When I finally reached Mudgee Hospital, I was greeted by a nurse whose expression basically read 'So glad you could make it'. Then she gave me some news: 'Congratulations, you're now the father of a baby girl named Shannon Lorraine.'

So much had changed in twelve months. I was now married, with a baby daughter, and was actually managing bands, albeit small ones. Barbara stayed at the farm with my mother for a couple of months while I searched for a place in Sydney for the three of us. Every Monday I was back in Sydney trying to make a living in the music biz.

According to the list Don had showed me when we met at the Hilton, no record label was interested in Cold Chisel. One had described them as having 'no commercial potential'. This was the era of Sherbet, John Paul Young and Dragon, and while there were a few breakout rock acts like AC/DC, Skyhooks and Richard Clapton, if your music wasn't deemed fit for AM radio, most record companies weren't interested.

However, an astute music publisher by the name of John Bromell had been following the band's development since they'd arrived in Sydney. He was impressed with Don's songwriting and offered him a publishing deal. While this was great, what we really needed was a record contract.

David Sinclair was A&R manager at Warners and a close confidant of John Bromell. (A&R stands for 'artists and repertoire', which is basically the talent scout for a label.) He too had been keeping a watchful eye on Cold Chisel. David was also receiving encouragement from Warner's Victorian promotion guy Steve Hands. In Melbourne Steve and his mate John Hoffman acted like cheerleaders at Chisel gigs, shouting encouragement and telling anyone in earshot how great the band was. Collectively, they all sensed that Cold Chisel could be at the vanguard of a groundswell of young bands making their mark in the suburban pubs and clubs.

I would frequently run into David and John at gigs. What I didn't know was that while David was keen to sign the band, Warner's hierarchy expressed reservations about me, an unproven manager. So John Bromell, in cahoots with David (and without me knowing), cooked up a ruse. David told the Warner hierarchy that Peter Rix, manager of major acts Marcia Hines, Hush and Jon English, was interested in Cold Chisel—but it was conditional on a record deal. The idea was that Rix would be the main guy, with me handling things day-to-day. Warner's top brass bought the story and, in September 1977, they signed Cold Chisel. Peter Rix was totally unaware of the subterfuge, and I became the manager of a band with a three-record deal.

9

COLD CHISEL

Upon Chisel's signing, the main players I was dealing with at Warners were Paul 'The Dog' Turner, his second-in-charge Peter Ikin, A&R manager David Sinclair, and Phil Mortlock and Roger Langford who handled promotion. Chisel were unquestionably low priority; the label's main priorities were mega-selling internationals like Rod Stewart and Fleetwood Mac, plus local signings Ray Burton and Jeff St John.

Sinclair, Mortlock and Langford, as well as Steve Hands and John Hoffman in Melbourne, were all true believers, permanent fixtures at most Chisel shows. I'm sure, though, that there are many other ex-Warners staffers that have since falsely dined out on being at the Be, Bop & Loo Bar or the Southside Six in 1977. Funny that.

I wasn't at all fazed; I knew that the band was building a solid base from the ground up. But the reality of daily life was tough. For a week of six shows in Melbourne, Cold Chisel would gross between $1500 and $1800. After deductions for petrol, food, road crew, accommodation, and agent and management commissions, often the band survived on the generosity of others. I managed to scrape by on my meagre commission.

I could usually find Don at the Plaza Hotel—if the front desk was staffed. The Plaza Hotel was populated by hollow-eyed denizens of a nocturnal world. I guess this environment was stimulating fodder for Don's songwriting, but it held little fascination for me. The rest of the band lived like vagabonds. Where they were when not at a gig or rehearsals remains a mystery to me. Communication was either via a landline or hammering on a front door somewhere. All I could do was hope that at some time during the daylight hours the gypsies would surface, enabling me to provide a schedule for the next few days.

In order to survive, Chisel were almost always on the road, crisscrossing state lines, from the Elizabeth Rugby Club in Adelaide to the Orana Hotel in Swansea, just south of the blue-collar town of Newcastle. Outside of the band's hometown of Adelaide, Newcastle was one of their first solid markets. It was a rock-and-roll town. The band's loyal followers were led by Eck the Wreck, who I once described to the *Newcastle Herald* as an 'infamous character with a big mouth, an incredible reputation and a heart of gold', and the Ward brothers. A strong fanbase grew, ensuring that local venues the Redhead Surf Club, Mawson Hotel and Swansea Workers couldn't get enough of Chisel.

Slowly, a vibe grew out of their live shows. Prominent music journalists Andrew McMillan and Anthony O'Grady from *RAM* and *Juke*'s Christie Eliezer began to actively support Chisel, heightening their profile and in turn attracting more gigs.

Sometime around October 1977, during one of my many chats with Chris Murphy, I expressed concern that the agency specifically didn't seem to identify and nurture a pathway for the next generation of acts. I'd noticed that there were numerous promising young bands who risked falling between the cracks. I believed there must be a way to fast-track them to a point where they could make a living and build a career.

We tossed around the concept of setting up a sub-agency, but then Chris asked me, 'If you're so passionate about this, then why don't you run it?' Fair enough. This new role supplemented my earnings and allowed me to work within the confines of Solo Premier. We called the sub-agency Pyramid. Its roster included such young aspirants as Flowers (Icehouse), Big Swifty (Radiators), Teenage Radio Stars (featuring future Models James Freud and Sean Kelly), The Boys Next Door (fronted by a young Nick Cave) and a band called Midnight Oil. Chris also handed me the task of booking a new Sydney venue called the Stage Door Tavern, which helped launch many of these acts.

Seated behind my desk at Solo Premier, I was in a perfect position to further advance Cold Chisel's case. While I was a pest to people like Chris, always asking questions, the agency gave me a crash course in how the live industry functioned. This would raise as many questions as it provided answers, and would play a big part in upcoming events.

★

Trafalgar Studios was located at Annandale in Sydney's Inner West. I'd heard that the building was once a shoe and button factory during World War II. It was owned by producer Charles Fisher, who'd had great success with Air Supply and would go on to work with the Hoodoo Gurus, Radio Birdman and Savage Garden.

In early January 1978, Cold Chisel entered Trafalgar to record their debut album. I was a studio novice—my experience to date amounted to loading gear into the room, then sitting around waiting for food and drink orders. I'd done some live sound mixing in my Savoy/UFO days but had no idea how to do that in a studio.

Peter Walker, who'd been the guitarist with prog-rockers Bakery, was chosen to produce their debut. I had no real knowledge of Peter's credentials—or of Bakery, for that matter, who'd broken up a couple of years before I returned to Australia, after recording two albums. The band's—and Warner's—take on Peter was that he was an excellent musician who understood studio technology. I wasn't sure if these were the optimum qualifications for a great producer, although in fairness most good producers have been down a similar road. This was Peter's production debut, but David Sinclair was confident that he understood what everyone was looking for in feel, sound and style.

Without any other viable option, and with the band and record company keen, I concurred and the band got to work.

To his credit, David Sinclair negotiated a flat studio rate instead of the standard hourly fee. This turned out to be a wise move; sometimes the band would play a gig then party into the morning, which left them exhausted and not in the best shape to deal with the rigours of recording during daylight hours. The band were used to playing live and dictating how they sounded, and they found it hard to deal with Peter's direction. Being used to the spontaneity of live performance, they felt frustrated by the endless repetition required in the studio. They wanted to recreate their live sound—intense, passionate and dynamic—but Peter's approach was methodical, clinical and conservative.

★

While the band struggled inside Trafalgar, I received a call in February 1978 from Peter Ikin at Warners.

'Do you think the band would be interested in supporting Foreigner?'

The US band was touring Australia in April, and Peter was confident that he could get the four-city run for Cold Chisel. While I could see what an ideal opportunity it was to promote their album, I had to sell it to the band. Easier said than done.

In Adelaide, Cold Chisel had been the go-to band for touring acts. But those spots could be frustrating; the audience was rarely interested in the support act. I appreciated that now, with a record deal, they felt they didn't need to put themselves in that position anymore—and Foreigner definitely wasn't high on their favourites list.

I met with the band in the studio to talk it through and they gave me their rating of Foreigner.

'Fookin' wankers,' said Steve. '"Cold as Ice"—piece of crap.' Jim also expressed strong doubts that the two bands would be compatible.

Ian and Phil opted to sit back and watch the internal debate unfold. Four pair of eyes then turned in the direction of Don, who'd been silently chewing over the pros and cons.

'Well,' he finally said, 'I agree with Jim, but this is a good opportunity.'

He went on to say that they really needed to be onside with the record company and that this was one way to achieve that. It looked like we had a breakthrough; the only real dissenter was Steve, who continued arguing his point of view as we exited the studio and walked out into the night. With the decision made, the heat was now on the band to complete the album in time for the tour.

There was a consensus at the time that the sound quality of Australian recordings was compromised when locally mastered. From the outset it had been agreed that the Chisel album was to be mastered in the US. As the recording sessions dragged on, the reality of getting that done started to fade. It was decided that in order to have albums ready for the tour, we'd organise a locally mastered version, to be replaced later by the US master.

David Sinclair, however, was told that the local mastering would be delayed by ten days. For reasons best known to David, he left the tapes in the boot of his car. Ten days of heat exposure in a metal coffin meant that when the mastering finally did happen, the sound had been audibly undermined. The band was furious. I pleaded with Warners to do a remix from the multi-tracks, but they refused. Chisel, clearly, was a low priority. As a consequence of all of this the album wouldn't be ready for the Foreigner shows.

The Foreigner tour kicked off at Brisbane's Festival Hall, a venue better equipped acoustically for its original use as a boxing arena. This didn't seem to matter, because the next day *The Courier-Mail* described Chisel's performance as 'burnt red hot'. The Sydney show was equally good, but problems arose in Melbourne when the production truck arrived late and the promoter scaled Chisel's set down from 30 minutes to a miserly fifteen.

When I told the band, their faces basically said, 'I told you this tour was a bad idea.'

But totally unexpectedly Foreigner's main man, Mick Jones, caught wind of it and presented the promoter with a blunt ultimatum: 'Cold Chisel get 30 minutes, or we don't play.'

We got our 30 minutes.

★

Exactly one week after the completion of the Foreigner tour in April 1978, Cold Chisel's self-titled debut was released. The album launch, at Melbourne's Bombay Rock, was a sell-out, further indication that the hard slog on the road was paying off. Even though the band was somewhat disappointed with the studio results, music journalists and long-time supporters Anthony O'Grady, Andrew McMillan and Christie Eliezer finally had something tangible to crow about in the press—and crow they did.

Many of the songs on the album had been road-tested for a few years and were familiar to the faithful punters who now filled venues whenever the band played. The cover artwork, conceptualised by Don and Abby Beaumont, featured Micki Braithwaite, Daryl Braithwaite's first wife, superimposed over an Asian street scene.

Despite the support of the music press, mainstream radio was still immersed in the pop of Sherbet, John Paul Young, Marcia Hines, Ted Mulry Gang and Dragon. That old Chisel curse—'No commercial potential here!'—remained intact.

The band had no concrete plans about singles, but Warners pressed their case. They thought 'Khe Sanh' fit the bill. The problem was Don's lyrics, with lines like 'their legs were often open' and references to speed and hitting 'some Hong Kong mattress all night long'. The mention of drugs or sex was a big problem, especially as many of the largest radio stations were owned by church organisations.

'If Warners are so keen for it as a single, why don't they tell radio just to bleep it out?' suggested one band member.

'Maybe if you're The Beatles,' I shot back.

Don wrote alternative lyrics that were recorded but just as quickly erased. Everyone realised that the integrity of the song was far more important. Trouble was clearly on the horizon, but Warners felt strongly enough to let 'Khe Sanh' fly in early May—and fly it did, straight into controversy. Commercial radio refused to play it, apart from Adelaide's 5KA, which, ironically enough, was owned by the Methodist Church. Due to the unwavering support of David 'Daisy' Day and his fellow 5KA DJs, the song reached number 4 in Adelaide. In Sydney, the Catholic Church–owned 2SM banned the song. The only support came from 2JJ (Double J).

Warners believed that a number of radio stations were thinking about adding the song, but they needed convincing. Melbourne's promo man Steve Hands felt that if they could get *Countdown* behind the song, it might help break the impasse at radio. Steve was good mates with Molly Meldrum, the host of *Countdown* and the most influential figure in Australian music. *Countdown* had a huge national reach of more than three million homes every Sunday night.

When we talked it through, the band felt that *Countdown* wasn't their thing and they were fundamentally right. But while living in the UK I'd seen the effect *Top of the Pops* had had on the careers of everyone from the Sex Pistols to Pink Floyd and Jimi Hendrix who didn't fit the teenpop mould: in a word, huge. *Countdown* could reach areas that were starved of the motherlode: rock and roll. I explained this to the guys and then looked around the room.

'Okay. Agreed?'

Five heads nodded in unison.

The band had been at the studio in Ripponlea for barely ten minutes when Michael Shrimpton, head of ABC's light entertainment department, marched into the dressing room.

'Sorry, guys,' he said, 'but you'll have to modify the lyrics.'

Shocked, we were left to ponder our dilemma.

'I told you, Rod,' said Jim, clearly disgruntled. 'It was a bad idea.'

We shut the dressing-room door and had a show of hands. The decision was unanimous: Cold Chisel did not compromise. Meldrum and Shrimpton were taken aback by our decision; it was unheard of for a band to take Chisel's position, particularly given the impact and reach of *Countdown*. But the band's integrity was crucial. I was confident that the momentum from street level would keep growing and *Countdown* could wait.

Yet it wouldn't be until August that 'Khe Sanh' officially received an A-classification, which meant 'not suitable for airplay'. The record label may have fretted but I rubbed my hands together—a bit of controversy never went astray. The song would peak nationally at number 41, while the album reached number 38 and would remain on the national charts for almost six months, earning it a gold album in sales.

★

In early August, while at Solo Premier, Chris Murphy introduced me to John Woodruff, or 'Woody' as he was known.

'You two will get on well,' Chris assured me.

This would be an understatement—and an introduction that Chris would surely later rue. John Woodruff was managing The Angels, another young Adelaide band making waves. Woody had learned the trade working in Adelaide with agent/manager Bob Lott at the Sphere Organisation. A champion rower and uni rugby player, Woody had once been renowned for never wearing shoes, although he'd kicked that habit by the time we met. Woody and I hit it off from the get-go: we both had young bands on the rise and we shared a burning desire to break them in Australia and internationally.

The Angels—originally the Moonshine Jug and String Band, then The Keystone Angels—had developed into a powerful rock beast through constant touring and a shift in image. After moving to Sydney in the mid-seventies, their music developed fast, heavy riffing and an overt punk sensibility. The charismatic Doc Neeson was out front, and the band was supercharged by the two-guitar attack of the Brewster brothers, John and Rick, and anchored by the rhythm section of Chris Bailey and Buzz Bidstrup. Their first album, self-titled like Chisel's and released in August 1977, was produced by former Easybeats George Young and Harry Vanda. The band was signed to Albert Productions, the legendary 'house of hits'.

Although Solo Premier was doing a good job, with crowds and money on the rise, John and I shared concerns about how the business was being run. The live music circuit was primarily centred around the capital cities—the 'tyranny of distance' made it difficult to regularly visit Perth, although there were smaller centres like the Gold Coast, Newcastle, Wollongong, Ballarat, Bendigo, Mount Gambier, Whyalla and Port Pirie that provided profitable stops along the way.

The inner-city pubs and clubs were the main venues in the large cities, but as a new generation of young bands emerged in the late 1970s and demand for live music grew, the RSL and leagues clubs, especially in New South Wales, realised they could tap into a younger crowd. Once the sole domain of variety acts like Ricky May, Johnny O'Keefe and Julie Anthony, these clubs were able to capitalise on their lucrative poker machine revenue and large entertainment rooms. Not to be left behind, many suburban pubs that had never hosted live music saw its potential and by mid-1978 there were so many venues that acts could find work most nights of the week.

But the duopoly of Premier in Melbourne and Solo Premier in Sydney controlled most of the name acts and venues in their markets, and by way of proxy arrangements with companies in Brisbane and Adelaide they were able to exert immense power over much of the country. A second tier did exist—smaller agencies operating on a local level, and venue bookers acting exclusively for clubs—but they were all beholden to the major players if they wanted the big acts.

These new venues meant more work—and money—was available for acts, but it also gave agents unprecedented power. The venues needed the bands that the agents had on their books, so, in reality, agents dictated where bands played and for how much, greatly diminishing the control of acts and their managers. This power vacuum led to a number of areas of concern for people like me, Woody and many others.

Acts were paid 'flat' fees, a fee agreed between the agent and the venue promoter, which was unrelated to the amount of money coming through the door. Hypothetically, a band could generate $5000 in door sales but only receive a flat fee of $500 to $750, which meant that someone other than the band was doing very nicely. An additional concern was agency commissions. In simple terms, an act should receive a gross fee from a performance, less 10 per cent agent's fee, but this was often not the case. Often, a web of agents, sub-agents and venue bookers, all expecting their cut, lay between bands and their final pay packet.

Most acts and their managers had no idea that this arrangement even existed. The only documentation they saw was a simple worksheet from the agency that contained venue information, performance times and their fee. Double dipping and possibly more were commonplace, and the agents—the gatekeepers who were paid to look after the best interests of their clients (the bands)—were often complicit in this unfair arrangement. There was very little an act could do; they were usually told that this was the price of doing business. Their livelihood depended on the agent, who had the upper hand—and the agent knew it.

Bands were afforded no legal protection and there were no contracts with venues, which left the system wide open for abuse. Performances could be unfairly terminated and often without compensation or redress. Agents were reluctant to do anything about it for fear of losing the venue. Bands were also required to print posters and were often pressured to distribute them at their own expense.

Another concern was what seemed to me like a lack of interest from agents in the marketing and direction of acts. It appeared that they had little incentive to try to break into new areas or restrict overexposure in others. My read was that their overriding motive was based on a simple formula: the bigger the fee, the larger their commission.

This was the climate that Chisel, The Angels and many others operated in the spring of 1978.

*

Working within Solo Premier with Chris presented a bit of a moral dilemma for me. While I enjoyed the security of employment, I also had to wrestle with the concerns I had as a manager now wearing two hats. But when I looked in the mirror, it was a white manager's hat that sat squarely on my head.

Woody provided welcome respite from the world of the agency. Over a beer or two, I felt comfortable venting my frustrations with the status quo of the industry and it came as a great relief to learn he felt the same.

One September evening, while we sat in the pub reconfiguring the music industry on a soggy coaster, he suggested I come over to his place and meet his flatmate, Ray Hearn. Ray had at one time managed Cold Chisel in Adelaide but now was looking after Flowers, a young band from Sydney, who I happened to book through Pyramid. Beginning life as a punk/Bowie jukebox, Flowers had begun making solid progress with original material in the inner-city scene. They of course would change their name in 1981 to Icehouse.

Ray and Woody lived in a flat opposite the Waverley Bowling Club. From their lounge room, over copious amounts of alcohol and other substances, the three of us dissected the local music business. Initially, we considered joining forces as a management company, but that didn't solve the issue of control and direction of our acts' live work—that power would still remain in the hands (and pockets) of the agents. The longer we spoke, the more apparent it became that if we wanted overall control of our bands' destinies, we'd also need to incorporate the role of agent into our plans.

And that plan? An umbrella management/agency entity that would deal with all aspects of a band's career. We called it Dirty Pool.

10

JUMPING IN THE DEEP END

What we needed to find first were staff and premises. We had
a good working relationship with Solo Premier's head booker
Richard McDonald and office manager Jenny Elliott. We saw
them socially and they were avid supporters of our acts, so they
were a perfect fit for our new venture. And we felt confident we
could trust them without divulging our plans.

We arranged a meeting with Richard and Jenny at Waverley,
getting straight to the point—we knew the concept was an
immense gamble but felt it was worth the risk. Ray laid out our
strategy, which was to represent, market, promote and oversee
all aspects of our artists' live and recording careers, making
major (and far more reasonable) changes to the way things were
currently done. I watched Richard, imagining that his brain
must have been racing. He had a secure position at Solo Premier
and was being asked to leap into the unknown. A nervous smile
gradually appeared on his face.

'It's a fantastic idea,' he said, leaning forward on the sofa.
Jenny looked around the room, aware that we were waiting on
her decision.

'Well, I am definitely in,' she said with a cheeky chuckle. 'This could be fun.'

With this sorted, I carried on as usual at Solo Premier. Behind the scenes we were setting up premises beside a chemist shop on Oxford Street, Bondi Junction, all done behind a veil of secrecy straight out of a John le Carré novel.

★

In the middle of 1978, Warners started to put pressure on Cold Chisel for another album, even though their debut had only been out for a matter of months. They were also pushing for a more experienced producer to take control. Richard Batchens had been the in-house producer and engineer for Festival Records and was suggested by A&R manager David Sinclair. Batchens' track record included five albums with pop kings Sherbet and four with Richard Clapton. But he was light on harder rock credentials. The problem was that there simply weren't that many good local rock producers. The Vanda and Young team—which included young-gun engineer Mark Opitz—had struck gold with AC/DC, Rose Tattoo and The Angels, but were loyal to Ted Albert and Albert Productions. And trying to lure an international producer was simply too expensive. So Batchens it was.

Warners supplied a larger budget than the first album but it was hardly a blank cheque. Fortunately, Don had the material— he was always writing songs, scribbling ideas on pieces of paper. At least that was the case until he bought a dictaphone, which led to some embarrassing moments when he was on public transport and his fellow passengers wondered who that weird guy talking to himself was. As Don once expressed to me, if an idea or lyric comes to mind, you need to capture it immediately, no matter where you happen to be.

Sessions with Batchens moved between Byron Bay and the Alberts studios in Sydney, and it was in Sydney that things began to rapidly go downhill. Studio 1 was where Vanda and Young had made great-sounding rock records. But for some reason, Warners had booked Studio 2. Unaware of this, I bounded into Alberts, feeling great, but could sense that something wasn't right. Richard Batchens was hunched over the console and the control room was silent except for the sound of a kick drum. Four dour faces looked up and Jim flicked his head in the direction of the door.

'This room is fucked,' he told me. 'We should be in Studio 1. Who booked it?'

'The record company booked it, mate,' I replied. 'Frankly, I had no idea that there were even two studios.' I was kicking myself. I should have known.

'Studio 1 is where AC/DC recorded. That is the room!' Jim snapped. 'And the other thing—this guy is a fucking worry.'

I immediately called David Sinclair and suggested, strongly, that he get his arse down to the studio. 'We've got some serious problems,' I told him, 'and I can see it heading in a bad direction.'

David had a long-term relationship with Batchens that stretched back to their days together at Festival. 'Give the guy a go,' he told me. 'He'll make a great record.'

Our problem was that the more recording the band did, the bigger the problem grew. But to pull the plug without a viable alternative was a huge call.

As usual, Cold Chisel was touring around the recording sessions and packing out venues. While the exposure and the income generated were positive, it wasn't exactly a recipe for creativity. Looking back, if we had block-booked a solid month of studio time, the problem would have arisen earlier and been properly dealt with. But hindsight, as we all know, is a wonderful thing.

I was under a lot of stress: I had Barbara and a one-year-old daughter to care for, I had Chisel struggling in the studio, and I was immersed in a clandestine operation that would emerge in October as Dirty Pool. Then I got a call from veteran promoter Pat Condon, offering Cold Chisel the second support spot behind Sherbet on Peter Frampton's November tour.

Frampton was still basking in the glory of his 1976 worldwide smash *Frampton Comes Alive!* and the venues were larger than the Foreigner tour. Three shows were to be staged outdoors, with guaranteed huge crowds. I could see the positives. The record company was gushing at the prospect, but the band, predictably, hesitated. The dramas they were experiencing in the studio didn't put them in the most receptive frame of mind—and Frampton, like Foreigner, didn't feature in their record collections.

But I felt the tour was worth a shot. At the very least it would keep their name out there in the broader market. Doing 30 minutes before Sherbet didn't overly concern me, because Chisel was match-fit and not intimidated by big shows. After the usual drawn-out process—and my hard sell—they finally agreed.

In a classic case of déjà vu, Warners again pushed for the album to be fast-tracked and ready for the tour, but I threw cold water on that. I wasn't sure how long this recording was going to take: it could implode any second, or drag on indefinitely.

★

Dirty Pool officially opened for business on 23 October 1978. Amongst Ray, John and myself, I was the closest with Chris Murphy, and he certainly wasn't happy when I broke the news. Not only did we work together, but we were friends, our families were close, our kids were of a similar age and we socialised a lot together. But I knew it was a necessary move. We'd already met with agents and promoters in Sydney and Melbourne, advising them what was about to happen and assuring them that our aim was to represent the best interests of our three acts: Cold Chisel, The Angels and Flowers.

We knew that we would be seen as a threat to the duopoly and they'd squeeze promoters, insisting they not deal with us. But good fortune was on our side: our acts were some of the hottest in the country, and promoters and venues knew their potential to put bums on seats—and that was the bottom line. And we weren't the only ones to feel some animosity towards the major players and the power that they wielded. Our massive shake-up to the status quo was quietly welcomed by the majority of promoters and venues.

We brokered a deal with Zev Eisak's Nucleus Agency in Melbourne, Graham Hutchison's agency in Brisbane and Brian Gleeson's Adelaide Rock Exchange to represent our interests in their markets and book gigs under our direction. In the other states we set up similar arrangements (although on a non-exclusive basis) with local agencies.

At the beginning, we faced our share of problems. Venues were threatened, phones were jammed and syringes were left on our front doorstep, but we weren't going away. And it worked: our acts drew full houses while the competition suffered.

★

Festival Hall, the old boxing arena in Brisbane, hosted the first Frampton show, then we went onto Perth, followed by large outdoor shows in Adelaide, Melbourne and Sydney. Although Chisel were not keen to do the tour, that reticence was firmly left in the dressing room when they hit the stage. They knew that they needed to capitalise on every second of their 30 minutes. And they did just that.

We still had no idea when the second album would be finished, but we needed to find a way of utilising the post-Frampton tour momentum. Just before the Frampton tour, in October, 2JJ had presented a Chisel and Midnight Oil show at the Regent Theatre in Sydney. Fearing damage to the heritage-listed theatre, the staff were on high alert. During the Oils' set, every time someone rose from their seat they were met by overzealous ushers frantically waving their torches and demanding they sit down. Chisel had watched the frustration grow in the crowd from the side of the stage during the Oils' set. But how to get 2000-plus frustrated punters out of their seats and not piss off these torch-wielding ushers?

Chisel strode onto the stage to a massive roar, as ushers frantically strafed the crowd with their torchlights. Turning slowly, Ian launched into a Hendrix-inspired version of the national anthem 'God Save the Queen', and all the patrons in the house rose as one. It was a masterstroke.

That show had been recorded by Keith Walker in the ABC's mobile recording studio, and it captured a raw energy that had so far eluded the band in the studio. A five-track EP taken from the gig would be the perfect between-albums release. In addition to four originals, the final track—and the gig's closer—was The Troggs' 'Wild Thing', which had become a live classic for the band.

Keith Walker mixed the EP and all that was missing was a title. One night in the studio, I threw it out there.

'Guys, we need a name for the EP.'

It was late, there'd been a few drinks consumed, and the suggestions ranged from the ludicrous to the unprintable. David Sinclair from Warners suggested *You're Thirteen, You're Beautiful, and You're Mine*, and the room went quiet. We all looked at each other. It rang a bell: both Johnny Burnette and Ringo Starr had cut a song called 'You're Sixteen (You're Beautiful and You're Mine)', and it *sounded* risky. People would definitely notice it. For a nanosecond someone joked about changing thirteen to twelve. Thank god that never flew.

The cover was shot by Greg Noakes in the toilet of the home of Jim's then girlfriend Jan during a wild party. Jan's flatmate Georgina was topless, and a pair of panties dangling from the neck of Ian's guitar were clenched between her teeth as a kohl-eyed Jim looked on. Released two days after the Frampton tour, the EP and its artwork raised more than a few eyebrows, but the raw power of the music underlined why punters had been packing venues across the country to see Chisel. The EP charted a couple of places higher than their debut album.

The recording sessions, meanwhile, dragged on. Richard's recording method entailed getting the band to play a song over and over (and over) in the belief that it was how you got the optimum result. This frustrated the hell out of the guys. Maybe Richard's method worked with pop acts like Sherbet, but Chisel thrived on energy and spontaneity, and this approach left the songs lifeless. It seemed to me that Richard had no real empathy or understanding of what the band was after. I don't even think he liked Chisel's songs.

As the producer–band relationship crumbled, the band, and Jim in particular, began to openly antagonise him. Whenever I dropped in, I'd find Richard hunched over the desk, seemingly intent on minimising eye contact with anyone. It was a toxic environment.

Yet somehow things got worse. Late in the mixing process it was discovered that Richard had been recycling multi-tracks from early demos for the final recordings. This might have saved money, but it drastically affected the sound of the recordings. For the second time, the band's music had been compromised by someone who should have known better.

*

With mixing well underway, Don came up with the idea of shooting the album cover in the Marble Bar at the Hilton Hotel, where we'd had our first meeting back in May 1977. Typically, a cover shoot is a fairly straightforward event, but not when Cold Chisel was involved. Greg Noakes flew up from Melbourne for the Monday-morning shoot. Slowly the band straggled in, looking not too shabby given that it was the morning after a weekend.

'Where's Steve?' someone asked. 'He did know about it, right?'

Assurances were given that our drummer would be here soon—no problem.

As lights were set up, and Noakes's camera loaded, there was still no sign of Steve. I phoned around the usual suspects and got the standard replies: 'Yeah, saw him yesterday, not here now.' 'No, sorry, haven't seen him.' We were forced to cancel the session and the only excuse Steve could offer was a simple

'I forgot.' A week later, this time with Steve present, the shoot was finally completed.

The album was called *Breakfast at Sweethearts*—named in honour of a favourite cafe of Don's in Kings Cross—and the artwork was overseen by Warner's Ken 'Kenny Colouring In' Smith, who came up with the idea of a key line around the COLD CHISEL logo. It would become one of the band's most distinctive visual symbols.

★

With *Breakfast at Sweethearts* ready for release, Warners were keen for Chisel to land the support spot on the upcoming Rod Stewart tour, scheduled for early 1979. I was also keen. There'd be large outdoor shows in both Australia and New Zealand that fitted perfectly with the album's release plans. Stewart was a major act for Warners and, conveniently, Peter Ikin was a close confidant of Stewart's manager Billy Gaff. I had been a huge fan of Stewart when I lived in the UK. I'd seen him with Shotgun Express in 1967 and followed him through his Jeff Beck and *Gasoline Alley* days, but his career with the Faces was my favourite phase. I had caught them whenever they played at the Marquee.

But while he may have been one of rock's great vocalists, Stewart's current image left me a little cold, as he pranced about in his glam clobber, playing music underscored by a blatant disco beat. Once again, I had to wrestle with the band's concerns, insisting that the end would justify the means. And once again they reluctantly agreed.

The Blondes 'Ave More Fun tour began with two sold-out shows at the Perth Entertainment Centre in late January 1979.

Chisel fronted at 5 p.m. for their soundcheck only to find the Stewart crew still setting up. And when they finally got a soundcheck, it was cut short because it was time to open the doors to the public.

The mood in the Chisel dressing room was tense and the usual questions were asked of me. 'What the fuck are we doing here, Rod?'

It wasn't the perfect start.

The Rod Stewart extravaganza was in every way the opposite of Cold Chisel's raw, pub-honed rock show. Stewart, in his finest peacock mode, swanned across the stage, undertaking numerous costume changes and working his adoring female fans into a lather.

While the overall texture of the show was very glam, Stewart's band comprised some very down-to-earth lads who enjoyed nothing better than women and alcohol. But Billy Gaff, his manager, and publicist Tony Toon were very proudly gay. As the tour rolled on, we learned that there were two distinct camps: Rod with his band and crew, and Billy Gaff and the 'luvvies'.

Chisel weren't impressed by the show's glam/camp overtones but kept their feelings to themselves. But one night after a few drinks, Steve, blunt as a brick wall, asked one of Stewart's band how it felt to play in a 'less-than-heterosexual' band. The response was lighthearted but very quickly Steve's comment reached the ears of Stewart and his management.

I awoke to an urgent call from Peter Ikin. 'Stewart wants Cold Chisel off the tour now!' he roared.

I wiped the sleep from my eyes and convened an emergency band meeting in my room.

'We either come up with a solution really quick,' I told the guys, 'or we are off the tour.'

There was a bit of staring at shoes and nervous shuffling before Steve piped up and offered to speak to Stewart personally. Ikin hastily organised for Steve to meet with Rod and his future wife Alana in their penthouse suite. While Steve could be abrasive, he could also be charming and funny. I don't know if it was Steve's UK roots or his undeniable Scouser charm, but whatever happened between them worked a treat and Chisel were quickly accepted by Stewart, and his band and crew too.

We headed to New Zealand for outdoor shows in Auckland, Wellington and Christchurch. After the Wellington show, the Chisel guys, Stewart, and Stewart's band and crew gathered around a grand piano in the hotel, singing everything from soul classics to football anthems. As more drinks were consumed, someone decided that it would be a big laugh if we inched the piano towards the large floor-to-ceiling window that overlooked the loading dock three floors below. Slowly, the piano started to move, and the singing continued until a side door was flung open and an ashen-faced night manager appeared, pleading like a man about to face a firing squad.

'No! No, please!' he begged. 'Don't do it!'

This didn't help a bit, and the poor sod desperately tried to wedge his body between the creeping piano and the window. It was only the timely entrance of two of Wellington's constabulary that stopped the revellers from dispatching the Steinway into the cold Wellington night.

During the Stewart tour we had to contend with raids from what were known as the tour's 'sex police'. It was a mystery exactly who they were, but their self-imposed task was to punish any and all indiscretions. These ranged from being late for soundcheck to failing to last the distance during an after-show celebration. Their raids, which could be the ransacking of your room, or having the furniture in your room nailed to the ceiling, were conducted during show times, so these weren't band members or key road crew. They came and went like ninjas—the only clue to their handiwork would be a victim's room number clearly displayed on the large video screens during the show.

All up, the Stewart extravaganza was successful for Cold Chisel. On most nights, Jim would join Stewart for the encore—and the exposure to more than 300,000 people in just a few weeks was a great result.

*

Breakfast at Sweethearts hit the stores in February 1979. Although the band was disappointed with the overall sound of the album, that didn't deter fans. The record was gold by March, and Top 4 nationally by May. AM radio, which had pretty much ignored Chisel's debut album, were clamouring to get on board and show support—and, more importantly, identify with the band. It seemed that the penny had finally dropped, and AM radio was now zeroing in on acts like Chisel, The Angels, Australian Crawl, and Jo Jo Zep and the Falcons.

Back at Dirty Pool, while our introduction of contracts was broadly accepted by most promoters, the 'door deal' got a mixed reception. We proposed a different formula to what had come before: acts would receive a guaranteed fee against a percentage of ticket sales. While most pub promoters were okay with it, the licensed clubs were resistant. For years they'd paid a flat fee, whether it was Johnny O'Keefe, Julie Anthony or The Angels. Eventually they came around when it became abundantly clear how much potential revenue they were missing out on. They realised that bands only shared in the ticket sales, not the hefty bar and pokies revenue that a thousand Cold Chisel or Angels punters could generate. That would still go straight into the club's coffers.

While a percentage of the ticket revenue was okay in theory, it required careful monitoring: ticket stubs or cash in a drawer could be easily manipulated. The answer was the tally counter or, as it was affectionally known, the 'clicker'. It was a cheap handheld counter that I imagine was invented for counting livestock. But now, in the trusty hands of a Dirty Pool employee positioned near the ticket desk, this little contraption kept an accurate track of every sale.

The Dirty Pool HQ in Bondi Junction was a hive of activity as bands, promoters, roadies and journos jostled for attention. At times I'd have to weave through a throng of bodies just to get to my office. Although the chaos was a measure of how successful we'd become, we needed someone to help sort the riff from the raff.

I thought Gay Neller would be perfect. Starting out at 4BC radio at the age of seventeen, she'd gone on to work with power-brokers Harvey Lister and Rod Pilbeam at Tour Promotions in Brisbane. There were some upcoming Cold Chisel dates in Queensland, so I flew up to have a chat with her. Gay picked me up in a green Hillman Hunter, her pride and joy, affectionately christened 'Henrietta'. Within weeks, with Henrietta docked in Brisbane, and for the princely sum of $100 per week as a wage, Gay became the sixth member of Dirty Pool. She learned about her many tasks early on when an aggressive female drug dealer, with 'muscle' in support, lobbed on the Dirty Pool doorstep one morning demanding that Jim's account be settled—or else. Gay was alone in the office and realised she had no alternative but to head to the nearest bank to pay off this nasty piece of work.

Gay and I would soon play even bigger roles in each other's lives.

*

Flicks was a venue that had opened in late 1978 in the Sydney suburb of Manly. Chisel was booked for a show there in March 1979, but I was apprehensive. The lucrative live music scene had started to attract its share of shonky operators. If some of these characters weren't happy with a band's performance or drawing power, they'd resort to intimidation, often resulting in non-payment. I heard a rumour that one pub owner in western Sydney had brandished a shotgun when a band's roadies had taken too long to load out of the venue. Unlike the acts at Dirty Pool, many of these young acts operated without the protection of signed contracts, making them prime candidates for exploitation.

In the weeks leading up to the show at Flicks, word had filtered through to me that the promoter, a guy named Larry Danielson, was dodgy: some bands hadn't been paid, and they'd also been physically intimidated. We had a signed contract, but I still harboured concerns. I didn't need any bullshit, so I was recommended a guy who—for a fee—would accompany me to ensure nothing untoward occurred.

Paul was a big man, about six foot five, and impeccably dressed in a suit. On arrival, I politely introduced Paul to the venue promoter. Paul sat at the corner of the bar, his suit jacket open just far enough to allow a peek at his shoulder-holstered pistol. Larry beckoned me into his office for a quiet word.

'There's no hassles here,' he said. 'No need to be tooled up. Everything is cool.'

'Paul's a friend,' I assured him. 'He's just here to see the band.'

Larry's expression suggested that he didn't buy that, but nonetheless the show went on, the house was full, and we got paid.

In 1980 the same promoter was arrested, charged and convicted after he tried to extort money by threatening to place bombs in supermarkets, three of which were successfully detonated. Larry and his accomplice Greg McHardie were the 'Woolworths Bombers'.

Another dodgy character ran a well-known suburban venue where The Angels were booked to play, and I was with them on the night. Their contract stipulated payment up-front before they played. The house was full, show time was upon us but the promoter had seemingly gone AWOL. The crowd began getting restless and the promoter suddenly appeared, demanding to know why the band wasn't on stage.

'The contract says money before they go on,' I advised him.

'Mate,' he replied, 'they're going to tear the place apart if the band don't start playing.'

I stared him down while the band laughed the guy all the way out of the dressing room. A little later, by which time the crowd was making a hell of a racket, the promoter reappeared, ashen-faced and clutching a plastic bag covered in dirt. Inside was the band's fee and the show finally went ahead.

I knew where the promoter lived and, for some time afterwards, I joked about grabbing a shovel and jumping his back fence. Who knows what he had buried there?

*

After five months of relentless touring to support *Breakfast*, the band headed to Pyree on the NSW south coast in July for three weeks of rehearsals and a well-deserved break. In order to get some material together for their next album, I felt it was necessary to get them away from the various distractions of Sydney. Even though the band had not been happy with producer Richard Batchens, the record company was pushing for him to still be involved, so he accompanied them to Pyree. It was a good call to go there; I was happy with the band's progress, they seemed more focused on their writing, and the songs were more cohesive and commercially accessible. Steve's 'Best Kept Lies' was one of the songs that emerged from these sessions. The Batchens issue, though, still loomed on the horizon.

I arranged a gig at a local rollerskating rink in Nowra, where live music happened every Friday night. The 200 young skaters gleefully whizzing around the rink to the Pointer Sisters 'Fire' were slack-jawed with surprise when Cold Chisel—billed as Jimmy and the Sweethearts—suddenly ambled on stage.

After Pyree we headed north for a free show in Brisbane presented by radio station 4IP. A large Royal Australian Navy barge, complete with crew, was anchored in the middle of the Brisbane River to be used as a floating stage. Jo Jo Zep and Air Supply were in support, and thousands of 'Brisburbians' turned up for the free show.

By the time Chisel took to the stage, the well-oiled crowd was deep in party mode, and the more enterprising punters entered the muddy waters and started swimming towards the barge. The navy personnel who had been enjoying their ringside view began to freak out, rushing towards the front of the barge in an attempt to repel the advancing armada. Jim, sensing that things could get completely out of control, called a halt to the show and demanded that the sailors back off. The onshore crowd roared, as a dozen or so punters continued treading water in the murky, brackish river. Thankfully, the show went on—the radio station was happy, the audience was ecstatic and nobody drowned.

Warners were keen to get the band into the studio to build on the momentum from their Pyree rehearsals. David Sinclair was still pushing for Richard Batchens to be involved, so we grudgingly agreed to let him have a crack at a single. The band entered Paradise Studios at the end of July, but it didn't take long for the old problems to resurface. I pulled the plug. We needed a new producer.

Mark Opitz had worked with Vanda and Young at Alberts on AC/DC's *Powerage* album, and produced The Angels' Top 20 album *Face to Face*, which stayed in the charts for more than a year. Mark was of a similar age to the guys in Cold Chisel and had experience with rock bands. He was really what Chisel needed. Mark had been contractually bound to Alberts, but that changed when he became head of A&R at Warners. He was now free to produce Chisel's third album, with sessions to begin in October.

Until then it was back on the road for a run of pubs, clubs and universities as part of the Set Fire to the Town tour, a line taken from their popular song 'Merry Go Round'. The tour kicked off in August but soon struck controversy. I had been dabbling in conceptualising poster art. My first effort had been a poster featuring an image of an Aussie digger stripped to the waist that I felt tied in with Jim's thing for wearing khaki army pants on stage. For this new tour I chose artwork that I knew would provoke controversy: the infamous image of a Vietnamese Buddhist monk setting himself on fire.

Regional newspapers went ballistic—and punters turned up in record numbers.

One of the biggest shows on the run was called A Day in the Sun, which drew over 15,000 people to the Fairfield Showground in August 1979. Chisel were to headline with support from Jo Jo Zep and the Falcons, The Sports, Mental As Anything and The Radiators. As Chisel's onstage time drew near, Ian was nowhere to be seen. This was pretty normal, as he operated in a different time zone to the rest of humankind. But the minutes ticked by, and Ian was still AWOL.

I peered out from behind the stage curtain, desperately scanning the crowd for any vision of 'Wonder Boy'. By my side was promoter Harry Della.

'You know there's a curfew?' he reminded me. 'And the local licensing cops will enforce it.'

With just 30 seconds left until show time, The Sports' guitarist Andrew Pendlebury bravely slung his guitar over his shoulder and offered to step in. Just then, through the foggy haze of a cold August night, the crowd slowly parted to reveal a curly-haired man carrying a guitar case and ambling towards the stage. Ian made his way backstage, seemingly oblivious to the drama.

'Where the fuck have you been?' I asked.

'I guess I was on another planet,' Ian shrugged, and the show went on.

★

Jim was developing a reputation for consuming large amounts of vodka on stage—the full bottle he had at the start of a Chisel set was guaranteed to be empty by the encore. As the band's manager, this presented me with two big problems: Jim's health, for one, and the impact on his performance. The more he drank, the more he slurred his vocals, to the point of being indecipherable. The punters embraced it as part of the show, but I felt I had a responsibility to look after him.

Jim would come off stage every night soaked in sweat, his eyes blank—I called them his 'dead-man eyes'. If I suggested that he cut back, he'd say, 'I'm okay, mate' and carry on. One night I decided that I'd try to slow him down—or, more the point, slow down the effect. Mark Keegan was part of our crew, responsible for the stage area, which included rehydration: water for Don, Phil and Ian, and Smirnoff for Jim.

'Mark, look, I need to try and slow Jim down a bit,' I told him. 'I want you to water down the vodka.'

A look of horror crossed his face.

'He'll notice, Rod.'

'Don't worry mate,' I replied, 'he'll be too busy to notice.'

Jim took his first gulp as the band kicked off with their usual opener, 'Juliet'. The ensuing spray was silhouetted in the spotlights as he drenched the packed front row. Jim's head swung 180 degrees towards the hapless Mark, who was quivering side of stage.

'What the fuck is this?' Jim mouthed.

Mark swore that Jim resembled a 'red-eyed demon'.

By the time Jim unleashed on me, most of his anger had been exhausted on poor Mark, who I swear will forever be emotionally scarred. We didn't water down his vodka again.

*

Whenever the band was in Melbourne, they'd stay at the seedy Diplomat Hotel in St Kilda, known for its 'ladies of the night' who plied their trade in the neighbourhood. Towards the end of the Set Fire to the Town tour, after an exhausting five-day Melbourne run, everyone piled back into our Toyota Land Cruiser for the long haul back up the Hume to Sydney. Tour manager Chris Bastic had just climbed in behind the wheel when the shrill tones of one of the hotel's housekeepers caught everyone's attention.

'Mr Bastic! Mr Bastic!' she shouted, frantically waving a crumpled brown-paper bag.

I'm not sure what flashed through Chris's brain at this moment—all he could say was 'Fuck'.

Inside the bag was $18,000 dollars of takings, which Chris had stashed under his mattress for safekeeping. It's fair to say that for the next 878.24 kilometres, there were frequent reminders of his oversight from the back seats of the car.

Chris later moved into local politics and became mayor of Randwick in 1993. He couldn't have asked for better preparation than a stretch as tour manager for Cold Chisel.

11

LOUNGING IN PARADISE

Paradise was the number-one recording studio in the country, designed by blues/jazz musician Billy Field, whose 'Bad Habits' would be a massive hit in 1981. Located in a narrow lane in Woolloomooloo, it had a recording desk that resembled the flight deck of the starship *Enterprise*, but just as importantly its jacuzzi could accommodate a footy team. Paradise's reputation as a den of iniquity was well known. An illegal gambling establishment like something straight out of a Robert G. Barrett novel was located nearby. You know the drill—if you knocked three times and said something like 'Arko sent me', you were in. Observing the constant comings and goings certainly helped us deal with the tedium of the recording process, which for me was right up there with watching paint dry.

By early October, with Mark Opitz at the helm, the band seemed to be finally finding their feet in the studio. There's no doubt in my mind that Don, frustrated with the lack of commercial radio support for *Breakfast at Sweethearts*, had written some songs that radio simply couldn't dismiss. And in Mark, Don found someone he felt comfortable with, who could craft a song that would work on radio without losing that intrinsic Chisel sound. Mark had learned from Vanda and Young, the masters of the hit song.

Phil and Steve were also starting to emerge as songwriters. I'm not sure if this was a coming of age or the realisation that they could earn extra money if they wrote songs. Whatever the motivation, they came up with some strong contenders for the album.

★

The three-album worldwide deal that Chisel had signed in 1977 proved to be fortunate for the band. With this third album, entitled *East*, well underway, Warners faced the distinct possibility that it could lose the band. The label's managing director, Paul Turner, was astute enough to realise that the album had the potential to explode and that the vultures would soon be circling.: Warners had done a fine job in Australia, but they had achieved very little anywhere else. Dirty Pool stablemates The Angels had broken their contract with Alberts and secured a lucrative US deal with CBS—and Chisel wanted something similar.

In September, over a lavish meal at the Fortuna Court Chinese restaurant—Paul's second home—in Crows Nest, the matter of the band's future was raised.

'The band really want to break into the US and Europe,' I told Paul. 'We've got our sights set on bigger markets.'

'If I can guarantee you a US release,' said Paul, 'would the band consider re-signing for Australia and New Zealand?'

I explained that we would consider all offers, but deals in any territories would not be conditional on deals in others. I felt it was fundamentally important that I kept the Warners team focused and committed to the next album, and I didn't want them losing the vibe by worrying about what might happen when the contract expired. It was a tricky juggling act.

But I knew after meeting with Paul that a degree of panic had set in at Warners. The word coming out of Paradise was that this record was the big one and the label's need to tie up Chisel's Australian recording future was paramount. Paul put forward a proposal that I fly to LA and meet with Warners International, and they'd cover all my (non-recoupable) costs.

'They're keen,' he assured me.

'Great,' I told Paul, 'as long as you understand this isn't a quid pro quo.'

With the trip in place, it was time for me to shore up my position with the band. For nigh on two and a half years, my deal as Cold Chisel's manager had been based on a handshake. I knew that to properly pursue the international market would require a considerable financial outlay on my behalf. I needed to safeguard my investment and formalise our relationship.

On 26 October 1979, I signed a three-year exclusive contract with the band. Everything was in place. The irony was that when this deal elapsed, I continued for a further 27 years on a second handshake deal.

*

Two days later, I boarded a plane for Los Angeles, travelling with David Sinclair from Warners. I hadn't been to LA since late 1976, and this time my role was a bit more substantial than that of a roadie for Savoy Brown.

My first meeting was in Burbank with Julie Sayers from Warners International, whose role was to coordinate international releases through the domestic US labels. It was immediately apparent to me that she was aware of the band's strength in its local market and that Warner Australia's priority was to retain the act.

'Australia's a completely different matter,' I explained to her. 'We want to sign directly to a US label.'

Julie told me that the Elektra Records label was in a rebuilding stage and was looking for rock acts. A meeting was duly set up. Elecktra had been predominantly a folk label in the early 1960s, moving into rock in 1964 with the Paul Butterfield Blues Band, Love in 1965, and their most significant signing in late 1966, The Doors. Closely followed in 1968 were MC5 and The Stooges, a formidable roster.

It was a surreal feeling walking into the iconic Spanish-style building that was Elektra Records' home, diagonally across from the Alta Cienega Motel where Jim Morrison of The Doors once lived. I was to meet with Joe Smith, the head of the company, who during his illustrious career had signed Van Morrison, Grateful Dead, The Doobie Brothers, Bonnie Raitt, Black Sabbath and many more. Smith was a music man through and through.

He was also a very charming man who certainly knew the art of schmooze. During our meeting, random staff, clearly well rehearsed, were wheeled in to rave about how hot Cold Chisel was. I left the meeting with mixed feelings: but at the very least a door seemed to be ajar.

Later that afternoon I had a meeting with Kenny Loggins' brother Dan, a high-flyer at Warners International. He also put forward a strong case for Elektra, explaining that Joe Smith had been brought in a few years back to revitalise the company. The label was having major success with The Cars, Dan told me, and was actively hunting for new and exciting projects. Dan felt that Chisel was a great fit.

During our meeting, we were interrupted by an urgent telephone call.

'I need to take this,' Dan mouthed at me, and I looked out the window onto Warner Boulevard and pretended not to listen. It was obvious that this was a very personal conversation; I got the sense that whoever he was talking with was in a severe state of despair.

'It's okay, Dave, everyone loves you here,' Dan said repeatedly. 'You just need to get it together; we are all behind you.'

When he ended the call, Dan could read the perplexed expression on my face.

'Sorry, my apologies,' he explained. 'That was David Crosby. He's in a pretty bad way.'

That was an understatement: Crosby's drug problems were so bad that he would end up in prison in 1983.

I flew back to Sydney with a lot to consider. Elektra certainly seemed interested in the band. But how genuine were they?

*

Released in early November 1979, 'Choirgirl' was the first offering from *East*. It was the band's most pop offering by a country mile, but to appease the hardcore fanbase devoted to frenetic tracks like 'Goodbye (Astrid Goodbye)' and 'I'm Gonna Roll Ya', we added a live version of 'Conversations' to the B-side.

AM radio in Perth, Adelaide, Melbourne, Sydney, Newcastle and Canberra jumped on board. Though dismissed by many as a cute pop song, a closer analysis of the lyrics of 'Choirgirl' told a different story. As the song made waves at pop radio, I got a call from Glenn A. Baker, a friend, journalist and noted rock historian, a man who knew that Willie Nelson had been the bass player for Ray Price in 1958, and that Neil Young was once a guitarist in Rick James' band The Mynah Birds.

Glenn posed a question: 'Is "Choirgirl" about abortion?'

I was startled—all I could manage was, 'Ahhh, not sure, Glenn. Maybe call Don.'

This got me thinking: many of the country's radio stations were owned by the Catholic Church, so I figured I should check this with Don. Now, any conversation with Don on a subject other than rugby league does not progress at a rapid pace, so I got to the point.

'Don, is "Choirgirl" about abortion?'

There was a long silence. Just when I thought the line had gone dead, I finally heard Don's voice.

'Yes.'

No one caught on and the song became a hit, peaking nationally at number 14.

★

Pooled Resources was a five-date tour we put together at the agency, featuring our acts Cold Chisel, The Angels and Flowers. The costs of mounting such a tour were high; concert production, transport and promotion didn't come cheap. So we set the ticket price at $10, which was double what we charged in the pubs. Supports were some of the best acts currently doing the rounds: Paul Kelly, Mental As Anything, Hitmen, Rose Tattoo, Dave Warner and The Boys Next Door. US band The Motels were touring Australia at the time, and they were added to the Newcastle bill.

We kicked off in late November 1979 at Adelaide's Apollo Stadium, a 4000-capacity venue better suited to basketball than rock music. Thankfully it was a sell-out, and we were off and running. The rest of the shows continued in that vein, at Melbourne's Festival Hall, Canberra Showground—where Jim met his future wife, Jane—and Sydney's Marconi Stadium.

The final date was at the Newcastle International Motordrome, a dirt-track racing venue. Unfortunately the heavens opened up and we were forced to postpone the show by a few days, but then it went ahead without a hitch.

The tour was a success, making money, raising the profile of our acts even further, and demonstrating how much Dirty Pool had grown in its first year.

*

The year 1980 would be a defining one for Cold Chisel and for me. It couldn't have started in a better fashion when, as the band juggled live shows with studio sessions for *East*, they received their first gold album—for *Cold Chisel*—and a platinum award for *Breakfast at Sweethearts*. They'd go on to receive plenty more, but that very first gold album remains my most treasured.

After a Saturday-night show at the Manly Vale Hotel in April, everyone headed to the Bondi Lifesaver for a few well-earned beverages. The show had been a sell-out, and band and crew were in great spirits. But that was all brought to a sobering halt when we got word that two former Chisel roadies, Billy Rowe and Alan Dallow, had been killed in an accident in rural New South Wales while working for Swanee, Jim's brother John Swan's band. Their truck had blown a tyre, veered off the road and hit a tree, bursting into flames.

John Affleck, another former Chisel roadie, had been asleep in the bunk behind the driver's seat and was the only survivor. Although trapped, Alan had managed to reach back to John and drag him free before flames totally engulfed the cab. Alan was also one of Jim's closest mates. His partner was Jim's sister, and they had a two-year-old son named James.

This tragedy had a major impact on the band and me. It underlined the precarious nature of a working band, and how unforgiving and dangerous the road could be. I reflected on my years behind the wheel, the thousands of miles I'd travelled and how, apart from my one crash while working with Jonathan Kelly, incredibly lucky I'd been.

Alan and Billy's lives would in time be immortalised in the Chisel song 'Letter to Alan' and, later on, in 'No Second Prize' from Jim's *Bodyswerve* album.

*

We were all still coming to grips with this tragedy when the second single from *East*, 'Cheap Wine', again written by Don, was released in May 1980. It promptly went Top 10 and would stay in the Top 40 for more than four months. The song provided a much-needed antidote for the hardcore fans who thought the band had suddenly gone soft with 'Choirgirl'.

East was released in June and featured a strikingly original cover image. Don had come up with the concept, inspired by *The Death of Marat*, a 1793 painting of murdered French revolutionary leader Jean-Paul Marat by artist Jacques-Louis David. The cover was photographed at the Elizabeth Bay apartment of Warner's Roger Langford, also the site of the 'Cheap Wine' film clip. Jim, wearing a Japanese headband that he'd bought in Japan in early May, posed reclining in a bathtub that Roger and I had lugged up a few flights of stairs. Strewn around Jim were various pieces of bric-a-brac sourced from antique stores, junk shops and second-hand bookshops. In the background was a bamboo blind that seemed to be blowing in the wind (with the help of a few hands and a piece of cotton). It worked a treat, and remains the band's most iconic and recognisable cover.

East didn't just break through—it smashed through, going gold in its first week. The album would spend more than a year on the album charts and turn the pub band into a household name. AM radio support for both 'Choirgirl' and 'Cheap Wine' was great—and long overdue—but looming large was FM radio, with the new commercial stations EON FM in Melbourne and Triple M in Sydney embracing Cold Chisel and a whole new generation of rock bands.

The album tour was named Youth in Asia, a reference to a line in the song 'Star Hotel', which had been inspired by a riot at the Newcastle hotel. The tour was a massive haul, 64 shows in all, which drew more than 120,000 punters and ran for four months. My philosophy from very early on was that I wanted to expand the band's live base to more than just the main cities and the stopover markets in between. As my old Sunday School teacher had taught me, citing Matthew 7:24, 'A wise man built his house on the rock', I believed that if we created a solid base across Australia, it would pay dividends well into the future. From one end of 'girt by sea' to the other, this tour would capitalise on all those years of groundwork, those poxy gigs playing to three drunks and a bartender. This time Cold Chisel would triumph, and they would build an audience that would stay with them for years to come.

The fifth show of the tour, which we filmed and recorded, was on 7 June at the Manly Vale Hotel on Sydney's Northern Beaches. At an absolute squeeze, perhaps 1000 punters could be sardined into the room, and before the gig the line of fans stretched through the massive car park and wound down Condamine Street for blocks. The room was so full that the last few payers had to crawl under the ticket desk to get in, and they happily obliged. It was wild: moisture dripped from the ceiling; crushed beer cans littered the floor. I went backstage after the gig and found an exhausted Jim slumped against a wall, with so much perspiration dripping off him onto the concrete floor it seemed as if someone had left a garden hose running nearby.

Business was booming, but trouble was brewing at home. Barbara, Shannon and I were living in Rose Bay, but my relationship with Barbara was unravelling. My career was keeping me away from home so much that I was almost a stranger— hardly a recipe for a stable relationship. Barbara was also spending a lot of time clubbing and partying, and infidelity was an issue for both of us. Shannon was just three, and her welfare was constantly on my mind when I was on the road.

By early July, our relationship had hit rock bottom. We agreed to split and I moved out to stay with some mates in a flat in Bellevue Hill. My marriage was fucked and, crucially, my daughter was living in a situation that was less than ideal. At times I felt like I was trying to juggle chainsaws.

From Sydney to Adelaide, Melbourne to Cairns, the Youth in Asia tour was a relentless haul. When we reached Brisbane at the end of July, the demand was so strong that more than 3000 fans packed the Cloudland Ballroom. The famous venue had a unique floor that sat on a huge coil and enabled dancers to feel the movement beneath their feet. Now this was okay for the Canadian Three-Step or the Pride of Erin but not for a rabid Brissy rock audience, and the ecstatic punters revelled in its wave-like motion. As if that wasn't enough, Jim decided to scale the three-metre-high PA stack, which started to sway as if there'd been an earthquake. Frantic roadies formed a scrum behind the towering stack as Jim screamed 'Wild Thing', while directly below, tightly pressed against the crash barrier, several hundred fans moshed frenetically, unaware of the potential disaster. Finally, Jim dismounted, much to the relief of the road crew, whose effort to stop the monolith from crashing had come close to being an exercise in futility.

★

With *East* killing it in Australia, I knew that if I was going to lock in a US deal the time was now. I headed for LA in late July. Glenn Wheatley, Little River Band's manager, had become a mentor of mine and introduced me to Owen Sloane, one of the top music lawyers in the States. Owen had handled Little River Band's legal affairs, as well as The Angels' CBS deal, and Glenn assured me he was a man with serious clout, able to help us break into the US market.

I stayed at the Sunset Marquis, which had replaced the Riot House as the home-away-from-home for every visiting rock star, manager and music-biz person. In the centre of the complex was the pool, so the optimum room was poolside, where all you required was an extra-long telephone cord to comfortably conduct business *and* observe the day's circus unfolding. I spent one sunny afternoon sitting with my Marquis neighbour Peter Allen as we mused over the procession of young lovelies coming and going from the room of Thin Lizzy's Phil Lynott.

I spent the next month in meetings with most of the major labels. Having a heavy-hitter like Owen on board, who enthusiastically talked up the band, helped open plenty of doors, but I still had to win over the head of a label's A&R department. The A&R guys are the rock stars of the music business, tuned into what's happening on the ground, and their careers are built on their success rate.

But to sign Chisel, an act from Australia, required a lot more consideration than signing a group from, say, Dallas or Chicago. There was the big issue of distance and all the extra costs that would entail. And while Elektra had already shown interest, I had the nagging feeling that they might be simply doing Paul Turner a favour, so I needed to explore all alternatives before making any final decision. I met with the A&R managers at PolyGram, Chrysalis, Geffen, Arista, Scotti Brothers, Epic, Warner, MCA, EMI America and Capitol. Some gave me a simple 'Sorry our roster is full', while others had heard good things about the band and wanted to talk further. In the end it came down to two: Capitol and Elektra. Both were good options.

I met with Owen and we decided there was little more I could do in LA. Elektra was poised to make an offer and Capitol's decision lay with its vice president of A&R, Rupert Perry. I'd been away for six weeks and needed to get back to Oz. Chisel had a new single and more big shows coming up.

*

Bassist Phil Small wrote 'My Baby', the third single from *East*, which was released in September. It was Phil's first solo composition. He told me that the idea came to him while he was in the studio's toilet; he then picked out the melody on the bass, and the song grew from there. Apparently, it only took a couple of hours from toilet break to a fully written song—and it's now a Chisel classic. I believe that Phil has since spent many hours in the toilet searching for similar inspiration. Just kidding, Phil.

Around this time I got the news that Capitol had passed on the band, leaving only Elektra in the game. Owen's advice was this: they were keen, they had money, and he was sure that a very favourable deal could be achieved. I talked it through with the band and gave Owen the go-ahead to close the three-album deal, which also guaranteed healthy tour support. While this was playing out, *East* finally hit the number 1 spot nationally in Australia in mid-September; album sales were now well over 120,000 units, selling at a rate of about 6000 a week.

On 5 October the tour reached the Darwin Amphitheatre, where we drew more than 6000 fans and broke the house record. Not a lot of bands got to the Top End, and the rock-starved crowd went nuts. At one point we had to stop the show when punters bombarded the stage with flowers and fernery ripped from the surrounding Botanic Gardens in a strange parochial custom of adulation. It summed up the wild spirit of the tour.

By early November, Owen had the draft contract. The band's holy grail, an American deal, was in sight. Elektra had tentatively scheduled *East* for US release in early 1981, with a couple of track changes—'Ita' and 'Four Walls' would be replaced by a remixed version of 'Khe Sanh'. I now turned my attention to finalising a deal for Australia and New Zealand. While there was huge interest from local companies, it made good financial sense to stick with Warners, which owned the copyright on the first three albums. A new deal enabled Chisel to enter a distribution arrangement with Warners, and the band would own the copyright in all their future music.

And the Chisel live juggernaut rolled on. Youth in Asia had now morphed into the Summer Offensive tour, and the poster image—army tanks on the march—described it to a T. The demand was unprecedented.

Chisel hadn't played New Zealand since the Rod Stewart tour in early 1979. On 26 January 1981 they re-entered the Land of the Long White Cloud, third on the bill to Split Enz and Roxy Music at Sweetwaters '81, a massive two-day festival run by promoter Daniel Keighley on a farm near Hamilton on New Zealand's North Island. TVNZ, the national broadcaster, was covering the event and the band delivered a blistering performance. Jim clambered to the top of the hefty sound system, eliciting a huge response from the 65,000-strong crowd. Kiwi media unanimously proclaimed that Chisel had 'stolen' the show. It was the catalyst for breaking open the New Zealand market.

*

Back home in Sydney, I was growing increasingly concerned for Shannon's welfare. I believed that I had one clear option, so I contacted a lawyer, seeking full custody. Our case progressed through the Family Court and after the financial affairs were sorted out it resulted in me receiving full custody of Shannon.

Barbara and I would divorce in 1981. (Barbara would later remarry; she and Dallas Royall, the original drummer for Rose Tattoo, would have four sons. She sadly passed away from cancer in 2014.)

During all this turmoil I had come to depend on Gay from the office for support. I was concerned that because of our working relationship the lines might get blurred, but the stars were aligned and we began a romance. Eventually Gay, Shannon and I would move into a little house in Bondi Junction—it would be the first time for a long while that I felt some stability at home. Several decades, three daughters and six grandchildren later, Gay and I are still happily married, living on Sydney's Northern Beaches.

12

COUNTDOWN TO AMERICA

The *TV Week*/Countdown Music Awards were viewed by the general public and the mainstream music industry as the pinnacle of success. In 1980, Chisel had won awards for Best Australian Album and Best Cover Artwork for *Breakfast at Sweethearts*; this year it was set to be Chisel—and then daylight. The band had been invited to perform at the awards finale, which would be staged on 16 March 1981 at Sydney's Regent Theatre. Warners were frothing at the mouth over the prospect of an avalanche of gold statues and even bigger sales of *East*.

After our walkout from *Countdown* in 1978, I'd managed to convince the band to make four appearances on the show, miming songs from *Breakfast* and *East*. (Jim sported his famous headband during a performance of 'Cheap Wine'.) There was no question that those appearances broadened the band's reach and increased record sales. I figured that when it came to *Countdown*, we were in control and happy to play the game, but on our terms.

Of course, if you dabbled with the devil—in this case, the world of mainstream pop—there were consequences.

The reality was that I wanted the band out of the *Countdown* loop, but there was no clear way of doing that apart from a very messy public divorce. Cold Chisel was a rock band, not a pop act, and their success was underwritten by years of hard slog in the pubs and clubs of Australia. The fear of being anointed 'pop gods' by *Countdown* placed them in a tricky position. If they refused to perform at the awards, they'd be seen to be thumbing their nose at their fans; if they did go on, they'd be seen as the latest player in the old pop game.

I called the band together for a meeting and discussed the invitation to appear at the awards. The immediate reaction from some quarters was predictable.

'Fuck them. Not interested.'

I understood that. To the band, *Countdown* was just one factor in their success. What did they owe *Countdown*? The band also expressed some concerns about the role of *TV Week* in the awards. What did they have to do with Australian music? None of the big American awards—the Grammys, the American Music Awards, the Oscars—had a major sponsor. I also believed that we really didn't need *Countdown* anymore: the band had the momentum, it had the live market pulsing, and radio was totally on board. So the question was: how could we extricate ourselves from this association? What we needed was a positive solution, not a reactive one.

After a fair amount of discussion, we reached a decision: 'We have to perform live. No miming. And if they say no, we're not playing.'

With that agreed, I approached the ABC and managed to persuade them to let the band play live. 'They won't be collecting their awards on the night,' I advised them, 'because they're saving themselves for the grand finale. It'll bring the house down.'

If only the people at *Countdown* knew how true that would be.

It was then that the five band members and I hatched a plan that no one else (apart from our road crew) would know about until the night of the performance. At the dress rehearsal, the band ran through 'My Turn to Cry,' the closing track on the *East* album. It went really well and, to their credit, the ABC sound technicians, overseen by Mark Opitz, managed to get a very good live sound.

On the night of the show, the Regent was packed with the who's who of the Australian music industry, all decked out in their finest threads. True to prediction, the awards started to flow Chisel's way; over the night they would win seven, including Best Album, Most Outstanding Achievement and Most Popular Group, while Don was crowned Best Songwriter and Mark Opitz Best Producer. Warners staffers and I wore down the theatre's carpet as we collected their many awards. Then came the finale.

The lights dimmed and the stage curtain slowly rose as voiceover man Gavin Wood introduced the band to massive applause. Knowing what was about to happen, I'd sunk down deeper in my seat. Jim was in his favourite footy jumper, sculling from a bottle of vodka, a guitar slung around his neck; Phil, an avid collector, was resplendent in a German World War II uniform. Ian wore a black shirt and jeans, Steve a navy Jackie Howe singlet, while Don was in shirt and collar, his sleeves rolled up, ready to get down to rebellious business.

As they launched into 'My Turn to Cry', I hung on every word, waiting for what only a select few knew was about to happen. The crowd by now was on their feet, going crazy. Halfway through the song, the band suddenly went off script, by which point if I'd hunched down in my seat any further, I would have been on the floor. Gay tightened her grip on my hand as Jim exploded into a carefully constructed diatribe firmly directed at *TV Week* and the industry in general.

Jim sang:

I never saw you at the Astra Hotel
I never saw you at the Largs Hotel
I never saw you at the Fitzroy Street
Now you use my face to sell *TV Week*
I never saw you . . .
I've got four minutes ten
For just one shot
At this media wank
I think you want it hot
So eat this
EAT THIS!

I glanced around and saw that much of the audience was in shock, their jaws had collectively dropped. But the band wasn't quite done yet. Jim threw his guitar to the floor, followed closely by his microphone stand, as Ian, feedback roaring from his amplifier, smashed his guitar. Steve kicked the drums from the riser as the stage curtain slowly crept towards the floor. As a final statement, Ian's guitar slid out from under the curtain and skidded to a halt at the front of the stage. All this madness was beamed live across the nation to more than three million homes.

Ian's guitar was still wailing feedback when stunned *Countdown* compere, Molly Meldrum, who was watching from the wings, walked to centrestage. I didn't take in a word he

Mum and Dad at their wedding, 1946. Photo: Author's collection

Mum and us kids on Long Reef beach, summertime, mid-1950s. Photo: Author's collection

Me with my new Scott Dillon surfboard, 1960. **Photo: Author's collection**

Rod the mod, 1965. **Photo: Kim Hamilton**

Top Left: My first trip to Belgium with Little Free Rock in 1968.
Photo: Laurence Bernard

Top Right: Me at the famous Star Club in Hamburg with Little Free Rock, 1969.
Photo: Author's collection

Left: In Paris with Little Free Rock, 1969. **Photo: Author's collection**

Wild times with UFO
in the UK, 1972.
Photo: Rod Willis

West Palm Beach
Auditorium, US, with
Savoy Brown, 1975.
Photo: Rod Willis

Savoy Brown
performing at
the University of
Indianapolis, 1975.
Photo: Rod Willis

Southern rocker in the USA, 1976. **Photo: Author's collection**

Cold Chisel sign to Warners, September 1977. **Photo: Phil Mortlock**

Jim takes over my desk at the Dirty Pool Office, Bondi Junction,
November 1978. **Photo: Phil Mortlock**

Cold Chisel on the Peter Frampton tour, at Sydney Showgrounds, November 1978.
Photo: Rod Willis

Me, Steve, Ian and Phil Mortlock, at the Alberts Studio's recording of *Breakfast at Sweethearts*, 1978.
Photo: Phil Mortlock

Roger Langford (far left) and David Sinclair (far right) from Warners, with Ian, Steve, Don and me, at the *Breakfast at Sweethearts* cover photo shoot, Hilton Hotel, Sydney, January 1979.
Photo: Phil Mortlock

POOLED RESOURCES

THE ANGELS
COLD CHISEL
FLOWERS
LEMMY CAUTION

FRIDAY, NOVEMBER, 23rd
APOLLO STADIUM
Bookings at MITCHELLS BASS
DOORS OPEN 6.00p.m.

Pooled Resources tour poster, November 1979. **Photo: Author's collection**

A crowd lining up outside Manly Vale Hotel to see Cold Chisel perform, Sydney, June 1980.
Photo: Guy Finlay

Cold Chisel with Warners boss Paul Turner (centre) and me. At the bottom right is Richard Batchens, producer of *Breakfast at Sweethearts*, for the platinum award presentation, 1980.
Photo: Phil Mortlock

East album display outside Tower Records, Los Angeles, July 1981.
Photo: Rod Willis

Cold Chisel at the River stage,
Chicago Fest, Chicago, August
1981. **Photo: Rod Willis**

Above: Jim and our sound guy,
Gerry G., in Compton Terrace,
Phoenix, July 1981.
Photo: Rod Willis

Joe Ely, Jim and Ian, at Manor
Downs, Texas, July 1981.
Photo: Rod Willis

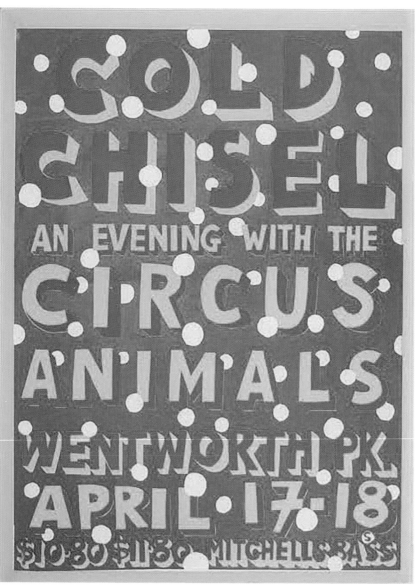

Circus Animals poster by Martin Sharp, April 1982. **Photo: Author's collection**

Elektra's Marty Schwartz and Vic Faraci, Ian and me, at the Country Club, Los Angeles, August 1981.
Photo: Author's collection

Steve and tour manager Mark Pope in my office, Crows Nest, 1982. **Photo: Rod Willis**

Jim on board the ferry to Denmark, December 1982.
Photo: Rod Willis

Cold Chisel at the Marquee Club, London, November 1982. **Photo: Rod Willis**

Me, Jim, Steve and Phil on the ferry to Denmark, December 1982. **Photo: Author's collection**

Paying irreverent homage at the *Radio Song*s cover photoshoot, Bilpin, NSW, 1985. **Photo: Phil Mortlock**

Dirty Pool staff, 1988. **Photo: Author's collection**

Financial guru Gino Principe, EMI Publisher John Anderson, Iva Davies and me, 1989. **Photo: John Anderson**

My 50th birthday party at Avalon RSL, November 1997. Jim and me, with Phil in the rear. This was the first time the band had played live together since 1984. **Photo: Roy Leggo**

Tour manager Michael Long with Don, Michael Gudinski and Don's wife Firoozeh at my 50th birthday party, Avalon RSL, 1997. **Photo: Roy Leggo**

'Under the sails.'
Cold Chisel in
rehearsals at the
Sydney Opera
House, 1998.
**Photo: Robert
Hambling**

Mixing at The
Chapel studio
in Encino Los
Angeles: studio
engineer, mix
engineer John
X, Ian, me, Don
and Jim, Los
Angeles, July
1998.
**Photo: Author's
collection**

Jim, me and Eric
Robinson of Jands,
at the Moonlight
Festival in
Claremont
Showgrounds,
Perth, February
2004.
**Photo: Robert
Hambling**

The Willis girls: Leigh, my wife Gay, Kelly and Shannon.
Photo: Rod Willis

Me surfing at Palm Beach,
Sydney. Photo: Adam Parsell

Cold Chisel with
John Watson (far
left), Gay and
me, Parramatta
stadium, 2020.
Photo: Robert
Hambling

said; my mind was racing as I tried to work out what would happen next. The band by now had made a quick exit and were no doubt having a drink somewhere else and laughing at the chaos they had left behind.

I'm sure they felt this was a joke masquerading as a political statement, but I was left to deal with the wreckage. I could feel eyes burning a hole in the back of my balding head. My good friend Eric Robinson, owner of Jands Australia, leaned forward and murmured in my ear, 'Oh well.' I guess he was unsure if I was part of the ruse or an innocent bystander.

As my brain fog slowly cleared, I was suddenly aware that Molly was announcing another award, the last of the night, for Best Record Cover Design.

'Please,' I whispered to myself, 'let someone else win it.' I had no desire to go anywhere near the stage.

'The winner is *East* by Cold Chisel,' announced Molly.

I looked around at the record company personnel, who sat like stunned mullets. It would have taken an incendiary to move them. No, the walk of shame was all mine.

I tried to focus on the stairs to the stage, ever-conscious of the many people watching my every step, who probably thought that a stumble would have been well deserved. An ashen-faced Molly, his hands noticeably shaking, handed me the award. I looked out at the crowd, and all I could manage was an inane 'Rock and roll!'

*

The reaction was huge—we copped everything from 'you have killed the band's career' to 'that was the greatest rock-and-roll event ever seen on Australian television'. Molly Meldrum attacked the band ferociously, and understandably so. It was his show, his baby. As for the record company, while they were initially shell-shocked, soon enough they were smiling as the band's record sales soared.

I had no qualms about what the band did. They got five minutes of prime TV real estate to put up their billboard for free. However, I did feel really sorry for Molly, who was a good guy, a friend, and someone who devoted his life to music. But I think that when the dust settled, even Molly would acknowledge it was a significant moment in local music history.

As for *TV Week*, many award ceremonies have sponsors but few had the magazine's overbearing presence, especially considering their minimal involvement in the music industry. They were really just a TV magazine. They never sponsored the event again.

The day after the awards, quite strategically, we released the double live album *Swingshift*, which had been recorded during the Youth in Asia tour in August 1980, at the Palais Theatre in Melbourne and the Capitol Theatre in Sydney. It featured sax player Billy Rogers and long-time Chisel sidekick Dave Blight on harmonica. It shipped gold and debuted at number 1. Many critics and fans said it was the greatest live album ever released in Australia.

*

As the dust from the *Countdown* carnage startled to settle, on the other side of the Pacific, Elektra released *East*. I was aboard an Air New Zealand flight to Los Angeles to oversee the release and discuss plans for a tour. Glenn Wheatley had put me in touch with John Marx at ICM, one of the most powerful booking agencies in the States, who agreed to represent the band. Everything seemed to be falling into place.

My daily schedule was flat-out hectic: not only was I dealing with the US market, but I was endeavouring to handle what was going on 12,000 kilometres away in Australia. Time zones played havoc when I was coordinating US radio and media interviews with the guys back in Australia. Invariably these would happen in the early morning Australian time, never ideal for a band that had played the previous night and probably partied into the early morning. Jim, who had married Jane in May—the first member of the band to wed—was the poor sucker usually tasked with having to be bright and chirpy when chatting with 'Bobby K' or 'Raindog' at such stations as WRKK Birmingham, Alabama, or WQDR Raleigh, North Carolina. This was usually at 9 a.m. Sydney time, sometimes earlier.

The Elektra brains trust had singled out 'My Baby' as their preferred first US single. Their view was that it had the best chance at radio—and it had already been a hit in Australia. This immediately set off warning bells for me. It was more of a pop song and I sensed there was confusion within the company about Cold Chisel. They didn't seem to understand the band. I explained their history in Australia, how their success was built on constant touring, and how loud rock was Chisel's raison d'être. I stressed that their first two albums were inherently rock and how it was only after success and the establishment of a solid fan base that *East*, a more pop-orientated album, was released. To me, Chisel's path in America should be via the AOR (Album Orientated Rock) route, not pop radio, a move that had worked wonders for Little River Band, who sold millions of records in America.

To underline my concern, I pointed out that reviews in the major trade magazines *Billboard* and *Cashbox* highlighted rock tracks 'Cheap Wine' and 'Tomorrow' as potential AOR tracks, while only *Record World*, the least powerful of the three trade mags, mentioned 'Choirgirl'. None had spotlighted 'My Baby'. Surely this was a sign.

I was confused. Elektra seemed to be sending out the wrong signal before we'd even started. Whenever I questioned their judgement, I'd be told: 'We are getting great feedback from our guys around the country.'

I was in a difficult position: if I pushed too hard, I might kill their enthusiasm, which was hardly an ideal start for a manager of a band with no history in the marketplace. Then I was presented with the draft marketing plan for the delivery of 'My Baby' to radio: the record was to be enclosed in a nappy. The proposed slogan was 'Hey, wrap it in a diaper and run with it.'

I had to stand my ground. 'Sorry, I think not,' I told them. Heaven knows what the guys in the band would have said about it.

Elektra was receiving reasonable radio reaction to the band in some markets but no major 'breakout'. Breakout markets, historically, were crucial factors in establishing a band—they were like the building blocks. American music radio was divided into so many different genres that it resembled a supermarket, and for it to work everything had to be in its correct aisle. And, as I had predicted, people were having trouble pigeonholing the band—were they pop, rock, heavy rock, or even country? *East* displayed all these elements.

There were two distinct approaches in breaking an act in the States. Either radio would go rabid over a single, or you hit the road. (MTV, which would become a game changer, hadn't yet launched.) Without a record going gangbusters on radio, Elektra agreed to bring the band over to tour. In early May, *East* debuted at number 193 on the US Top 200 album chart in *Cashbox*. Not a great start.

Live touring was time consuming and, in the case of Chisel and America, expensive. Without the power of a hit single or album, it would be a case of hoping to break into different areas, building local support and winning over fans, media and radio. It wasn't that dissimilar to Chisel's approach to the Oz market, just on a much larger scale. John Marx at ICM, who'd flown to Sydney to see the band in action, started putting together Chisel dates for late June 1981.

★

The band stepped off Air New Zealand flight TE6 at Honolulu airport on 28 June 1981, on route to LAX. They entered the terminal to the strains of a Hawaiian steel guitar and, somewhat predictably, their arrival was not without drama. The complimentary beverages had flowed on board and Steve had taken full advantage. In a vain attempt to turn Steve's volume down just a little, someone had slipped him a tranquilliser, but this did nothing except extend his session.

A little worse for wear, Steve gathered with the rest of our party in the customs area, a ghetto blaster poised on his shoulder spitting out reggae beats at earth-shattering volume. By now the eyes of the burly customs officers were clearly trained on our party, making everyone other than Steve, immersed in his inebriated fog, very uncomfortable. Our sound guy, Gerry G., leaned forward and whispered in Steve's ear.

'Maybe you should turn it down a little.'

Rocking slowly back and forth on his heels, with Yellowman's 'Nobody Move, Nobody Get Hurt' reverberating through the customs hall, Steve seemed oblivious not just to Gerry G. but pretty much everyone. The explosive sound the ghetto blaster made when Steve dropped it on the floor ricocheted throughout the packed hall and, like mice escaping a cat, its D-batteries skimmed the concrete floor in all directions. For a split second time stood still as everyone froze in anticipation of an armed response.

Yet, strangely, nothing happened. The men in blue kept their firepower holstered and their demeanour seemed to indicate it was an everyday occurrence. Welcome to America.

The strategy was simple: we had arrived in LA early to do press and radio, and—more than anything else—to get in the face of the record company. More than 150 radio stations across the US were playing tracks from *East* but sales were not responding. The album was at number 173 on *Billboard* and 180 on *Cashbox*.

The hope was that, now the band was actually on US soil and about to undertake a tour, sales would pick up. On Sunset Boulevard, a large billboard of the album cover took pride of place outside Tower Records, the most famous record store in the world, for a couple of weeks. Our agent John Marx planned to get the band on as support on big arena shows, and also headline clubs. But as complete unknowns in the US, Cold Chisel was a hard sell. Headliners were on the lookout for supports that could put extra bums on seats; they weren't going to hand out a favour for some band from the Antipodes. Various groups passed when offered Cold Chisel as a support.

Elektra currently had two acts out touring: heavy metal band Riot and ex–James Gang and Eagles guitarist Joe Walsh. I leaned on Joe Smith and four arena shows with Walsh became available. But Chisel's first US date would be as a part of the Rock & Roll Weekend, featuring Heart, Jimmy Buffett, Pat Travers and Loverboy, at the 50,000-seat Jack Murphy Stadium in San Diego on 5 July. As the opener, Chisel wasn't mentioned on the posters and had no soundcheck—and, as it turned out, even their twenty-minute set was cut short.

It was sweltering hot, Simpson Desert hot, and the majority of the audience seemed more intent on drinking beer and chatting than watching this unknown act from Australia. The band were not impressed, and agent John Marx copped some major grief in the dressing room after their set.

We were staying in the Sun-something Motel and the next morning the tranquillity was shattered by the loud hiss of air brakes when a bright orange Flxible Clipper bus—our new ride—came to a sharp halt outside. Once owned by Elvis Presley, its chrome and paintwork were so bright that you needed sunglasses simply to look at it. It looked more expensive than the entire motel. It was fully fitted out with seventeen luxury seats, a TV, a kitchen, bunks in the rear and, to top it off, a toilet. Smithy, our driver, was from Memphis. When the King had died in August 1977, he had bequeathed the bus to Smithy, who now made a living hiring it out to touring bands. Proudly emblazoned on the side of the bus was Elvis's signature TCB logo—Taking Care of Business.

Next stop was Tucson, Arizona, 100 kilometres north of the Mexican border. Night Train was the city's premier rock club and while it took some time for the audience to warm to the band, things improved as the show progressed. As the

Tucson Citizen newspaper reported the following day, 'By three-quarters of the way through the band's set they had filled the dance floor.'

From Tucson it was east on Highway 10 into Texas and the 17,000-seat Summit Arena in Houston, for the first of four shows with Joe Walsh, whose album *There Goes the Neighborhood* sat comfortably in the Top 20. This crowd was no more sympathetic than the show in San Diego, but it seemed to inspire the band. Jim stood tall on stage, essentially saying, 'We're here and we're not going anywhere.' The band understood that they were starting at the bottom again, but they'd won over those tough Australian audiences, so what would stop them doing the same in America?

The following show was four hours north, at Dallas's 18,000-seat Reunion Arena, the home of the Dallas Mavericks. Then on 11 July it was Joe Ely's 2nd Annual Tornado Jam, which would be the highlight of Chisel's US tour. Roadhouse rocker Ely was a singer-songwriter-guitarist whose music was a heady brew of rock and roll, honky-tonk, Tex-Mex and country.

Staged at Manor Downs, a raceway about twenty kilometres east of Austin, the Tornado Jam bill featured Ely, The Fabulous Thunderbirds, Stevie Ray Vaughan, Delbert McClinton and Al Kooper (who'd played organ on Dylan's 'Like a Rolling Stone' and was a founding member of Blood, Sweat & Tears). Chisel had third billing, a curious quirk of fate that we had no issue with whatsoever.

Al Kooper kicked off the day, followed by Delbert McClinton, then Stevie Ray Vaughan, who was soon to become a superstar. Then came the stage announcement, courtesy of our tour manager, Mark Pope: 'Ladies and gentlemen, from Sydney, Australia, COLD CHISEL!'

Some 30,000 Texans cheered as the band hit the stage and ripped into 'Conversations'. And Chisel pulled out all the stops during their ten-song set—Jim clambered on top of the PA stack only to discover he'd inhaled a 'lone star' moth, which he coughed up onto poor Mark who was standing behind the speaker stack. But that didn't stop Jim, who did his best to work the crowd into a frenzy. Ian was at his most dynamic, Steve and Phil locked in perfectly and Don channelled 'the Killer' Jerry Lee. The rowdy audience and the luminaries standing side of stage lapped it up. The band was called back for an encore and tore up 'Wild Thing'.

The Fabulous Thunderbirds followed Chisel; Don would later credit their influence on the recording of the *Circus Animals* album. Joe Ely closed the show and, for the encore, he welcomed on stage members of the Thunderbirds, plus Jim and Ian. Ian seemed in a transcendental place as he swapped licks with two of the best, Thunderbird Jimmie Vaughan and Ely's guitarist Jesse Taylor. (How I wished that Stevie Ray had stuck around.) Also on stage was a thirteen-year-old guitarist in full rockabilly attire and pomaded quiff, trading solos with his older peers. It was Charlie Sexton, who'd go on to a successful solo career and a long stretch in Bob Dylan's touring band.

Denver, Colorado, was one market where *East* was gaining traction on radio. This was helped along by our new fans Barry Fey and Chuck Morris, major promoters who ran a company called Feyline and had been the first promoters of Led Zeppelin in the US. They loved Cold Chisel and went out of their way to push the record to Colorado radio stations KBCO, KBPI and KIIQ. They also happened to be the promoters of Joe Walsh's next show in Denver, at Red Rocks, an outdoor amphitheatre that was literally carved into the side of the Rocky Mountains.

It was without doubt the most beautiful venue I had ever seen. U2 thought likewise and would shoot their legendary *Live at Red Rocks: Under a Blood Red Sky* concert film there in 1983.

Unfortunately for Chisel, the skies opened as soon as they hit the stage. It was torrential rain, much like a Queensland monsoon, although this didn't seem to faze the band or the audience. Side of stage was a different story; I stood there, fingers crossed, praying to the rock gods that no one went up in a shower of sparks. It was really dangerous. Ironically, the second Jim's waterlogged sneakers hit the dressing room carpet, the rain ceased, leaving Joe Walsh to serenade the faithful with 'Rocky Mountain Way' on a balmy July night.

The journey south to Phoenix through the desert scenery of New Mexico and Arizona was spectacular. For a reason only known to himself, Phil had decided that no shoes was the order of the day. Bare feet were fine for a jog on Bondi Beach but the desert blacktop of Highway 40, on the famous Route 66, was very different terrain. Joe, our driver, pulled our bus to the side of the highway so we could capture the amazing scenery. Phil meticulously adjusted his camera's aperture for that perfect shot. All of a sudden, the silence and serenity of the desert were disrupted by his bloodcurdling scream. Phil was now performing a dance not seen since the Navajo Nation had roamed the land. His sprint to the sanctuary of the bus would have left Usain Bolt languishing in the starting blocks.

With Phil's feet a mass of blisters, we reached Compton Terrace, an outdoor amphitheatre in Phoenix that was owned by Jess Nicks, father of Stevie from Fleetwood Mac. This was to be the last Joe Walsh show.

The Big Apple was next. The plan was to play some shows, do press and hopefully get in a little sightseeing, but the shows didn't eventuate and the guys were left to cool their heels in the Gramercy Park Hotel for six days. The Gramercy came with loads of history—its guests over the years had included Humphrey Bogart, The Beatles and John F. Kennedy. When we arrived, Debbie Harry, actor Matt Dillon and playwright David Mamet were residents.

Cold Chisel's US dream wasn't living up to our expectations. The live shows were often frustrating, radio support was weak and there were underlining concerns with the record company. Jim, in particular, took a strong dislike to Marty Schwartz, the label's promotions guy, who was the full cliché with his satin jacket and perfectly coiffed hair. Jim, who was always treated well back home, felt very slighted when Schwartz chose to attend another function in preference to a Chisel gig.

So there we were in a New York hotel, stuck for six days with no work. It was a sure-fire recipe for frustration and tension. One night the Gramercy exploded as Jim and Jane, who had just arrived in the country, went at each other and anyone else in earshot. I wasn't sure what started their blow-up, but they made it clear they'd had enough.

'We're hitching to LA,' they announced. 'Then we're going home.'

Tour manager Mark Pope tried desperately to mediate but it only added fuel to the fire. As for the rest of the band, they just shrugged, as if to say, 'Nothing to see here.' Jim had blown up like this before. Don was convinced it was the end result of indulgence in some illicit substance that had gone wrong. I was worried, naturally, and wasn't so sure we'd be able to laugh about it the next day. I also had my own problems to deal with. I was constantly on the phone to the west coast, either to the label or our agent. I needed to know if we had any other shows in the pipeline but could get no clear answers. By this late point in the tour, the feeling within the band was that Elektra didn't see them as a priority and everyone involved was just going through the motions.

Then I got a call from John Marx.

'I've got you some shows in Canada and the Midwest,' he informed me.

'Who with?' I asked.

'The Motor City Madman himself,' John told me. 'Ted Nugent.'

Ideal—well, tell me, what *was* ideal? I knew that even AC/DC had had to play second fiddle to the likes of REO Speedwagon, Charlie Daniels and Moxy on their first US tour. It was naive for an unknown support band to believe they could select who they played with. But Ted Nugent was right out there—he took the stage in nothing but a loincloth, guitar and cowboy boots, and pranced around like one of those deer he so loved to shoot. Still, the Chisel guys agreed—Jim hadn't split for LA after all—and tailored a more hard-edged set, which, as the shows proved, generally went down well with the Nugent crowd. And gun-mad Ted turned out to be a nice guy.

We travelled from Thunder Bay in Ontario to Michigan. Mark had booked us into a motel in Pontiac, just north of downtown Detroit, a leisurely half-hour drive to our next show at Pine Knob. Unbeknown to Mark, Pontiac was a predominately Black city with one of the highest crime rates in the US. When we arrived, we were a bit shocked by the motel's reception area, which was completely encased in steel mesh and bullet-proof glass. It was more like a bank than a motel lobby. There was a look of sheer bewilderment on the faces of the receptionists as a dozen white dudes entered. I think they checked to see if our spaceship had just landed outside.

That night at the bar, Steve was at a table talking with a local guy. From the bar we could hear Steve tell him, 'You're not Black, you're purple.' We all froze for a second before Steve's new buddy doubled up with laughter. We were the only white folks in the bar and I think the locals were fascinated by us, a group of Aussies speaking a strange form of English.

Just when we thought Ted Nugent had been a mismatch, we got to share a bill with The Marshall Tucker Band. Hailing from Spartanburg, South Carolina, the Tuckers were more country than rock, all cowboy boots and big hats—band and fans alike. It reminded me of being back in Texas in the 1970s with Savoy Brown. Pine Knob was a 15,000-capacity amphitheatre in the town of Clarkson, its sprawling lawn descending to a concrete-encased soundshell at the bottom of the hill. Tucker's laidback fans, and I mean *laidback*, reclined on the soft grass, the pungent aroma of weed permeating the night air. It may as well have been a Grateful Dead concert. Chisel went through their standard set to a reasonable reception—and the inclusion of the Hoagy Carmichael classic 'Georgia on My Mind' generated a respectful cheer from the big hats on the hill.

Then it was on to Chicago to play the major summer music event ChicagoFest, staged at the Navy Pier on Lake Michigan. Chisel was the main support to Illinois headliners Cheap Trick. The 'Windy City' lived up to its name—and delivered accompanying showers—but that didn't dampen the enthusiasm of the big crowd for a great Chisel set delivered in the afternoon's fading light before an impressive Chicago cityscape.

WOUR, the top radio station in the Syracuse/Utica area, had *East* on high rotation so we anticipated a warm reception for the band's next show, at Casa Boogie in Utica, New York State, which the station would broadcast. This was a killer gig; the full house went off, and it seemed that everyone in the room knew the band's music. At the end of their set the crowd chanted and stomped for more, which the band was more than happy to provide. It felt a lot like the gigs in small clubs back home. WOUR would rebroadcast their set on air several times.

Our seven-week run wound up in Los Angeles at the Country Club in Reseda. The club, 30 kilometres north-west of LA, had only just opened but over the years would present everyone from Metallica to U2.

Being the final date of the tour, I knew that the record company would be present in numbers. The backstage vibe was strained and awkward—all I wanted was for the band to get on stage before someone said something regrettable. The audience, which included a sprinkling of Aussies, was well supplied with record-label freebies (free tickets).

The band, fully aware that this was their last US show and feeling justifiably disappointed, took to the stage in a volatile mood. Jim immediately berated the crowd for sitting down; the company suits watching from the sanctuary of the mixing desk must have sensed his aggression was at least partly directed at them. Chisel's performance was menacing, angry and one of the best of the whole tour, but was unlikely to endear them to the Elektra hierarchy.

Ten days after that final date, Elektra released the second single, the remixed 'Khe Sanh' included on the US version of *East*. Again, there seemed to be no logical reason to choose the track—it was absent from any US critics' list of faves, and its live performance didn't stand out above any of the other album tracks in their set. It was a frustrating end to a disappointing tour.

13

CIRCUS ANIMALS

On my journey back to Australia my mind was occupied with differing emotions. The US experience had been difficult and frustrating at times, but it had also had its share of highlights and positives. In my mind, if Chisel was serious about breaking into the US market then there would be no shortcuts. They had to start at the bottom and work their way up, as AC/DC had done. But I wondered whether the guys still had the drive and the passion for it, and if they were willing to make the necessary sacrifices. Considering their massive success in Oz, I had the sense that the comfort factor might set in. It was easier back home. Perhaps it was all too late.

Even though we had a US deal, a foot in the door, a big budget for recording, and tour support etched in stone, I was still unsure if Elektra viewed Cold Chisel as a serious long-term proposition. Warner Australia had not been that crazy about the band initially, and it had taken various factors for them to really get on board: Chisel's live work and great records, me in their face all the time, and the true believers at Warners—people like Steve Hands, Phil Mortlock and Roger Langford.

So why didn't *East* work in the US market? We all had our theories: financial woes within Elektra; the company having no personal involvement in making the record; no one pushing their cause within the company and marketplace confusion on where the band fitted; I tend to believe that Cold Chisel weren't an Elektra priority. I think they went for the pop market with 'My Baby', thinking that would be the easiest way to get a good result, overlooking the simple fact that Chisel's history was underpinned by years as a live rock act.

As an adjunct to all this, I was surprised and bemused when I read Tom Zutaut's comments in the 2001 Mötley Crüe book *The Dirt*. In 1980, he had been a junior sales kid in Elektra who, with determination and unbridled belief, managed to convince Joe Smith to sign Mötley Crüe. He spoke about his frustration at getting Crüe taken seriously, as he said that Elektra's priority at the time was 'the Australian band Cold Chisel'. Crüe's debut *Too Fast for Love* would end up selling more than a million albums. I wished that we had had our own Tom Zutaut inside Elektra.

*

Soon after returning from the US, Chisel was back in Paradise Studios for three months, making a new album with Mark Opitz, which they'd title *Circus Animals*. I was very interested to see what effect the tour and exposure to America would have on their new songs.

From the outset, there seemed to be a concerted effort to ensure that it wouldn't be a pop album like *East*. Don and the band had been particularly impressed by The Fabulous Thunderbirds, the manner in which they could 'sit back in the groove' but still rock. Don's songs for the new album, especially tracks like 'Houndog', 'Wild Colonial Boy', 'Numbers Fall' and 'Taipan', were much heavier. Similarly, Jim delivered 'You Got Nothing I Want', inspired by his personal disdain for Elektra's Marty Schwartz. Not to be outdone, Ian came up with two great songs: 'Bow River', plus 'No Good for You', a song that in my mind could easily have fitted the criteria for a US single.

East had been a commercial success, but the new songs that Opitz had to work with didn't include an obvious single. Steve came to the rescue with two pop gems: 'Forever Now' and 'When the War is Over'.

*

Album cover shoots could either be simple and fun or a potential logistical nightmare. For *Circus Animals*, Don had come up with a concept, something totally Australian—a flat, wide-open space, the band in front of an old caravan, with infinity stretching out behind them. In my mind the concept was brilliant, a great idea, despite presenting a major production headache.

Mascot Airport was suggested as a location and then rejected, so I told the guys, 'If we are going to do it, let's go and do it properly.'

We opted for Lake Eyre, a vast salt pan about 700 kilometres north of Adelaide, and fifteen metres below sea level, which would provide the vastness that Don envisaged. On the rare occasions it actually fills with water, it is the largest lake in Australia. It was also the site of Donald Campbell's famous land speed record attempts in the early 1960s.

First up, we needed to source a caravan, but not your everyday Millard or Viscount. We needed a 1950s-style vintage van, small, rounded, with a two-tone colour scheme, not something found easily in the *Trading Post*. I called Chris Loft, an old friend in Adelaide, and gave him the onerous task.

'I've found one,' he said when he called a few days later.

'Sounds perfect,' I told him when he described it to me. 'Buy it, Chris. Oh, and by the way, I need you to tow it 700 ks to Lake Eyre.' There was a deathly silence at the other end before Chris finally said that yes, he could do it.

Now we needed to work out how to ensure band and caravan could rendezvous in this vast wilderness and find a base for the few days we needed for the shoot. By chance there was a remote sheep and cattle station about 60 kilometres from the coalmining town of Leigh Creek, a spot where small planes could land. Over a dodgy phone line, I explained our concept to the station owner.

'Yeah,' he replied in an outback drawl. 'That sounds like fun, mate!'

I then called Pam Scott, a film producer friend, and asked if she and her husband Peter Levy, a future Emmy-winning Hollywood cinematographer, would be willing to fly to Lake Eyre and shoot the cover. Of course they were. The band and photographer's party would take a commercial flight to Adelaide, then travel in two privately owned Cessnas to the remote outback station—where, hopefully, they'd meet up with Chris, who was already on route in his Land Cruiser, towing the caravan. This was beginning to resemble a military operation.

Just try to imagine the look on the station owner's face when these strange characters emptied out onto the makeshift airstrip in 35-degree heat. They were as out of place as a nudist on George

Street, in downtown Sydney. The accommodation was outback luxury—the shearing-shed quarters, which the team shared with its resident spiders, bugs, moths and *Musca vetustissima*, the ever-present Australian bush fly, which took up residency on everyone's faces, backs, ears and wherever else they fancied.

Come morning there was still no Chris, although he had called in a few times from truck stops along the way. With nothing else to do but swat flies, everyone settled back and tried to remain cool with numerous red-tinned West End Draught as the temperature gauge headed towards the 40-degree mark.

Then, finally, the rising dust on the horizon signalled Chris's arrival, and the band and camera crew headed for the lake. The glare was as fierce as the flies. To get the optimum shot, it was vitally important that the landscape was pristine, which meant that everyone had to be acutely conscious of not leaving footprints in the crusty salt surface. That was a tough call but somehow it worked. Finally, after three days of heat, salt, sand and flies, the intrepid party headed back to Sydney with the 'money shot' safely in the can.

The caravan's future wasn't so bright. Chris tried and failed to tow it back to the cattle station. Its wheels sank so deeply into the soft salt pan that it had to be abandoned—or so I was led to believe. For years I wondered whether the station owner had somehow retrieved it and used it to house his chooks. Or did it just float away or sink when the big rains came? Then I learned the truth: the band and Chris blew it up with explosives supplied by the station owner.

I can only imagine the conversation: 'Don't tell Rod we blew the fucking caravan up. Tell him it was bogged too deep.' *Snicker, snicker, snicker.*

★

We kicked off January 1982 with shows on the east coast, then undertook the band's first headlining tour of New Zealand. Nine sold-out shows across both islands culminated in headlining Sweetwaters '82, the same festival that had gone so well for the band the year before. Our support on tour was INXS, a band we all loved and could tell was destined for big things. They had great songs and smart management—Chris Murphy, my old boss at Solo Premier—while Michael Hutchence's X factor screamed 'superstars'.

One of the shows was at the seven-sided Mount Maunganui Sound Shell in Tauranga. Both bands were staying at the same motel, your classic rectangular box. The weather was chilly, as New Zealand can often be even in January. The meeting point before the gig was the bar. Don was a huge Clint Eastwood fan; you could safely say that Clint was his idol—his bandmates considered it a fixation. Given that Don was tall, slim and often had a cheroot placed strategically in the corner of his mouth, there was also a passing resemblance.

Both bands were huddled around the bar enjoying a few drinks when the door swung open and Michael Hutchence entered, draped in a woollen poncho, dressed like Clint in *A Fistful of Dollars*. Those present swore they witnessed Don's eyes squint like a man in bright light, as he stared down Michael, as if in a scene from one of Clint's films. At least that's the rumour that has circulated ever since. I am not a mythbuster, so I'll leave it to linger forever in the ether.

★

Soon after returning from New Zealand in February, Gay and I were married at our house on Sydney's Northern Beaches, on a magic summer's day, surrounded by close friends and relatives. My daughter Shannon was our bridesmaid, my best man was tour manager Mark Pope, and my groomsmen were close friends Phil Mortlock and Peter Ikin from Warners. Gay and I had now been together for over four years, and apart from being an amazing mum to Shannon, she had been at my side during all my ups and downs.

★

The first single from the *Circus Animals* album was 'You Got Nothing I Want', which reached number 12 nationally. *Circus Animals* was released on 8 March in Australia, shipping over 35,000 units in its first week. It soared to number 3 nationally the following week, by which time I was on a flight to Germany. Over the past year I'd been in negotiations with Polydor Records and had secured a deal for Europe and the UK. There was some awareness of the band in Germany via early releases on the indie label Line Records, which had been organised by Warners.

Armed with master tapes and artwork, I travelled to Polydor's head office in Hamburg to coordinate the release, and then onto London to meet with the team at Polydor UK. There was genuine excitement in Germany, but the response in London was a bit tepid. It was an interesting year in music; trends like new wave, electro-pop, Brit funk and rap were all fighting for prominence. But Cold Chisel had never been fashionable—the diversity within their music made it hard to pigeonhole them, and the emergence of these new trends made it even harder to find a place where Chisel fitted. I wasn't unduly concerned; in fact I was optimistic that if we could get the band to the UK for live shows, the mood would change.

My next stop was LA and a week of meetings with Elektra. They were setting up for an early May release for the new album and although *East* hadn't set the States alight, we still had a deal, and it was crucial for me to maintain a positive and upbeat stance when dealing with the company. And they said all the right things, affirming their ongoing commitment to breaking the band in America. It seemed that the last show at the Country Club hadn't left any scars—not noticeable ones, anyway—but I was extra careful not to mention the subtext of 'You Got Nothing I Want' in my discussions with Marty Schwartz.

★

Chisel concerts have always been wild and unpredictable events, right from the band's earliest days in the pubs and clubs, where punters were inches away from the band. Jim fed off this proximity; it was almost as if the band and its audience were connected at the hip. As time went on and the band got bigger, so did the venues, and that crucial distance between band and punter widened.

We'd found ways of addressing that problem in bigger rooms; Jim would often grab the microphone and venture into the unknown, trailed by a nervous road crew. The connection was electric and the crowds loved it. I do recall one mishap, though, when Jim had decided to stage-dive into what he assumed was an audience versed in the art of catching. Apparently, no one knew the rules because the audience parted and Jim did a header onto the venue's floor, leaving him with one hell of a shiner.

As a warm-up for some large-scale shows, we had booked four nights at the Embassy Ballroom in Perth. During one encore,

Jim unloaded his ice bucket over the front rows as he often did, cooling off the punters who'd endured stifling heat for the past two-and-a-bit hours. The ice usually did what ice did in extreme heat—it melted. But on this night, that didn't quite happen. Either the bucket had recently been replenished or one large iceberg had miraculously survived, and a chunk of ice felled an unlucky fan. He was quickly lifted back to his feet by those around him, blood flowing down his face. As the crowd filed out, Mark Pope managed to intercept the poor guy and brought him backstage, a dirty tea towel clasped to his forehead.

Jim was genuinely concerned for the guy and offered his sincerest apologies.

'Are you kidding?' the wounded warrior exclaimed. 'This is the best day of my life!'

★

As I've noted, sometimes a great idea emerges from a brain-storming session, be it a tour name, a poster design or even the idea of a show on a mountain top. Now, during another of these sessions, Mark Pope came up with an idea.

'Why don't we try and incorporate rock and the circus under a big top? A rock show in a circus tent.'

After all, the new album was named *Circus Animals*.

Most of these out-there ideas are met with rational argu-ments—'Logistically a nightmare' or 'It's going to cost a fortune'—but in this case the band loved the concept. We agreed on two shows under the big top, ideally in Sydney where all the band members resided.

There were a couple of provisos: the shows needed to be outdoors and preferably close to the CBD. Someone suggested

Wentworth Park, in the parkland adjacent to the greyhound track. To our surprise, the Sydney City Council granted us permission. We reached out to Bullen's, one of the oldest and most famous Australian circuses, about hiring their big top and some of their animals and acts, and they too jumped at it.

When the tickets went on sale for 'An Evening with the Circus Animals', to be staged on 17 and 18 April, I genuinely didn't know whether it would be a resounding success or a financial disaster. My relief was palpable when I learned that the 10,000 seats were sold out within hours.

The shows began as tradition dictates—with a Grand Parade. Elephants, camels, horses, clowns and other circus acts marched around the sawdust-covered ring, while trapeze artists flew like birds through the air, and the punters, who seemed to be reliving their childhoods, cheered loudly. A giant metal globe was then wheeled to the centre of the ring. Inside were two motorcyclists who roared away inside the sphere at incredible speed, somehow managing not to collide.

As soon as the two-stroke fumes cleared, Chisel took the stage for a solid two-hour show. During their encore, the Bill Haley classic 'Shake, Rattle and Roll', Jim was perched precariously on a swing 15 metres above the ground connected below a motorcyclist riding on the high wire. Mark Pope deserves full credit for the triumphant two-night stand; no rogue elephants stampeded the crowd, and our death-defying lead singer suffered no misfortunes. Everything ran perfectly.

*

When *Circus Animals* was released in the US, Germany and Japan during May, I moved into the Oakwood Apartments in LA's Studio City. I set up my desk and lived on the phone from dawn to dusk. I'd be calling radio stations across the US and Canada, and Elektra promo staff in the field, trying desperately to get some traction. At times I felt I was just wasting time and money, while visiting the Elektra office was equally frustrating. 'We're working on it, it's a priority,' I'd be told repeatedly, but I couldn't help but feel that I was being given the old run-around.

Just as they'd done with *East*, the label led off with a pop-edged single, 'Forever Now', once again creating confusion at radio: was Cold Chisel a rock or pop band? I wanted to repeat what we did in Australia and lead off with a rock song like 'You Got Nothing I Want', or maybe Moss's 'No Good for You'. But Elektra's promo and marketing team were adamant that 'Forever Now' had the better shot—as they had been with 'My Baby'. It duly sank like a stone, and I saw the writing on the wall. In a neat ironic twist, 'Forever Now' was at the time in the Oz Top 5 and the album had hit number 1.

On the flipside, initial reports from Germany and the Netherlands were looking extremely promising, while on the home front, Gay called to say that she was pregnant. Finally, some good news. And within the world of Dirty Pool, business was booming: The Angels, Icehouse and Cold Chisel were killing it domestically and all were now venturing into overseas markets. *Circus Animals* had sold 20,000 copies in Germany, while Icehouse's 'Hey Little Girl' had made the Top 10 in Switzerland and Germany, and the Top 20 in Sweden, the UK, the Netherlands and numerous other European countries.

In early August, frustrated with the US situation, I headed back to Australia. I could monitor things in America and Europe from my Sydney office. The dismal record sales for *East* and now *Circus* made it clear that things were not working with Elektra. I advised our lawyers to get us out of any future album commitments, which they finalised in October. We decided to put the US on ice and look to Europe as a more viable option.

★

The fights between Jim and Steve were legendary, ranging from a simple push-and-shove to the occasion when Jim tried to dangle Steve out of my first-floor office window. It'd be reasonable to speculate that their volatility was partially due to their backgrounds: Jim born in Glasgow, Steve in Liverpool, two uncompromising cities with a culture and attitude to match.

During a second New Zealand tour in July 1982, while staying in a quiet countryside motel, the pair went at it again. I don't recall the spark; most of the time it was something trivial, but up and down the hallway they went—one would get in a good shot, usually followed by, 'Had enough, have you?' 'No way,' would be the response, and they would go at it again like two bucks in the rutting season. Usually, the roadies would intervene and guide the protagonists back to their rooms, only for hostilities to resume minutes later.

Don had the enviable capacity to ignore these frequent altercations. He'd lived with it for so long that I guess he just saw it as a part of everyday life. But on this night, as Don quietly reclined in bed sipping a glass of Irish, he looked up to find the two combatants bursting through his door.

He uttered one word—'Guys!'—and with that Steve and Jim picked themselves up off the floor like naughty schoolboys, muttered, 'Sorry, Don' and resumed their battle elsewhere. The next day, the motel owner was compensated for two broken doors, and Jim and Steve went about their day as if nothing had happened. Situation normal.

By the time we reached Hamilton for the final New Zealand show, *Circus Animals* was at number 1.

14

THE LAST STAND

Germany might not have the rich musical history of the USA, but it's less fashion obsessed, less market driven, more eclectic in its taste—and it's the third-largest record-buying country in the world. Polydor were completely different to Elektra: they were effusive, buoyed by positive results in sales and radio in Germany and the Netherlands, and keen to get the band touring Europe as soon as possible.

On an unusually sunny winter's day in early November 1982, the band arrived in Hamburg for a couple of days' press before heading to London to kick off their tour. The Hamburg welcome was in striking contrast to that of Elektra almost eighteen months earlier—there was a tangible excitement within Polydor, from the executive level to the front desk. After a night of frivolity, schnapps and tenpin bowling, we headed out the following day, very hungover, on a boat tour of the port of Hamburg—not comparable to Sydney Harbour, but the gesture was appreciated.

The UK tour began with two nights at one of my old stomping grounds, London's famous Marquee Club. 'So this is what happened to you!' the venue's manager, Jack Barrie, said to me, a smile on his face, when I walked in. 'I hope they are good.' Much to Jack's delight, the shows were packed out—albeit with the predictable Oz and Kiwi expats, but also, thankfully, a healthy smattering of curious Brits and music media.

Mark Pope and I had decided that instead of flying we would let 'the train take the strain', figuring it was an ideal way to see the countryside on both sides of the Channel. We planned to take a 30-minute hovercraft ride from Dover to Calais, and then a leisurely train ride into Paris. This was all great apart from one small detail. The night before, after the final Marquee show, we'd met up with producer Steve Smith and his girlfriend Debbie, the daughter of Paul Raymond, 'the king of Soho'—club owner, girly-magazine publisher and property developer. It degenerated into a powder-fuelled non-stop party stretching well into the early hours.

Most of the band, including myself, were well aware of the travel day ahead and retired to our hotel to catch some sleep, a challenge with all the residual cocaine in our systems. Just before I bade farewell to our hosts, I asked Jim if he was coming.

'No,' he said through grinding teeth. 'I'll see you back at the hotel.'

As we settled into our seats at Victoria train station the following morning, Jim was immersed in a white puffy jacket; he resembled a hibernating polar bear. The look on his face clearly said, 'Don't talk to me, don't look at me, just leave me alone.' When we reached Dover, its famous white cliffs were shrouded in thick fog, while the howling wind and stormy white caps on the English Channel suggested this was going to be a very bumpy ride to the land of croissants.

No sooner had we taken our seats aboard the hovercraft than Jim upped and bolted for the toilet. As the engines fired up, the attendant checking seatbelts immediately noticed the empty space between Ian and me.

'Where's this passenger?' she asked.

Steve, who was in the seat behind, smirked and pointed, and the attendant headed off towards the toilet.

'Sir,' she said from the other side of the door, 'you need to resume your seat.'

No reply. She knocked again.

'Sir, we are ready for take-off, you need to resume your seat.'

'Fuck off,' was all Jim could muster.

After a few more attempts she shrugged her shoulders, looked at me and said, 'Well, you're in charge of him now.'

The crossing was like a scene from a disaster movie—we were tossed around mercilessly, and the windows were so fogged that the only time they cleared was when hit by a wave. I wondered if we were still on top of the water, or underneath it.

When we finally docked in Calais, to the strains of muzak playing from a speaker somewhere, it was time to retrieve Jim. I went over and knocked on the toilet door.

'Jim, we're here.'

No response.

Eventually, the door creaked ajar and our ashen-faced singer literally crawled out. Jim was sick, really sick; his pleading eyes seemed to suggest, 'Shoot me. Please shoot me.' Ian took one of Jim's arms, I took the other, and we basically dragged him through French customs.

After 'Jim's Excellent Adventure', it was little wonder that the Paris show at Le Rose Bonbon—which sounded more like a box of chocolates—is best forgotten. While the subsequent club shows in the Netherlands, Germany and Denmark went well, the first serious indication that Germany was somewhere worth investing in was at Hamburg's Markthalle. A crowd of more than 800 enthusiastic punters turned up. The gig was filmed for the influential music television show *Rockpalast*, which not only had national reach across Germany but was beamed into bordering countries. We drew another large crowd at Berlin's Quartier Latin, before heading south to Munich's premier venue, the Alabamahalle.

This being the time of the Cold War, Germany remained divided and that was nowhere more evident than in Berlin, where the wall separated east and west. A small group of us decided to have a closer look at life on the other side; I hadn't been since 1976, in the Savoy Brown days. This was reasonably straightforward as long as you followed strict protocol. First, you went through the mandatory passport control on the western side, known as Checkpoint Charlie, then traversed a 100-metre stretch of ground commonly referred to as 'no-man's-land' before entering East German passport control.

A large sign in English stated very clearly: 'NO PHOTOS'. But Steve operated by different rules. Approximately 50 metres into no-man's-land, he decided to whip out his camera and start taking holiday snaps as if he was enjoying a day at the seaside. Within seconds, the loudspeakers from the east and the west were competing in a medley of English and German, which we read as meaning he'd be shot dead any minute. The rest of our party stopped, looked at each other and took a couple of large steps backwards into West Berlin passport control. Steve was left standing alone in no-man's-land, his camera poised. We waited nervously to see if he would be mowed down in the crossfire. Thankfully, common sense prevailed, Steve put the camera away and, with a trademark shrug and a bounce of his heels, he continued eastwards unscathed.

Our last headline show was in London at The Venue, where almost 1300 punters squeezed into the room, an encouraging indication that word had got around about the band. I'd received a call from our agent about playing eight UK shows with the glam-rock band Slade, who'd staged a major comeback at the 1980 Reading Festival in front of 65,000 fans. Once the guys in Chisel recovered from their usual apprehension—'Slade? Really?'—they accepted that this was an opportunity to play outside of London, and to audiences that weren't necessarily awash with expats.

The first date was at Nottingham University; after their set, Chisel congregated side of stage, displaying more than a fair degree of curiosity about the headliner. Slade's flamboyant lead guitarist Dave Hill suddenly burst on stage bedecked in his finest glam gear, silver angel wings and all, as the eyes of the Chisel guys all rolled in unison. As they had done in the States with Ted Nugent, Chisel had opted for a harder set of songs, which, after some initial apprehension, went down well. The Slade run climaxed with two full houses at London's Hammersmith Odeon.

It was noticeable, especially in the wake of the Marquee show, that interest in Cold Chisel was growing. Members of Motörhead and Girlschool, and ex–Thin Lizzy guitarist Gary Moore were heard to talk them up, while the local music press began to show genuine enthusiasm. Major mags like *Melody Maker* and *Record Mirror* were keen to talk to the band, while *Kerrang!* had the final word, stating that Cold Chisel were 'the best thing to come out of Oz since AC/DC'. High praise.

★

After this first foray into the European market, I felt optimistic. It was a great result and Germany in particular looked very promising. Our agent told me he'd received strong signals from German promoters, who were super keen to get the band back for the northern summer. Polydor was also excited, and genuinely believed they could help break the band throughout Europe. As for America, that stayed on hold until I could find a label that really wanted the band and would commit for the long term.

Our broad plan for 1983 was a run of regional shows and a couple of major events in Australia, back to Europe, then commencing work on a new album. One of those major local events was the Narara Music Festival. We at Dirty Pool, along with Michael Coppel and Peter Rix, had for some time been planning a four-day all-Australian music festival to run over the Australia Day long weekend. The location we chose was near Old Sydney Town on the NSW Central Coast, about an hour's drive north of Sydney.

Named for a small town nearby, the Narara festival had an impressive line-up, featuring Cold Chisel, The Angels, INXS, Men at Work, Goanna, Mi-Sex, Choirboys, Dragon, Australian Crawl, Rose Tattoo and Richard Clapton. There were about 30 acts in all. Chisel headlined the Sunday night, putting in a marathon three-and-a-half-hour set, playing more than 40 songs—including covers of 'Twist and Shout', 'Georgia on My Mind', 'Don't Let Go' and Little Richard's 'Rip It Up'—in front of 35,000 punters.

For us at Dirty Pool, the festival was a big step up from 1979's Pooled Resources, and thankfully the gamble to feature an all-Aussie bill paid off handsomely.

Another big event was Bathurst's Australian Motorcycle Grand Prix, which was staged at Mount Panorama over the

Easter holiday weekend and drew crowds of around 30,000. It seemed like the perfect vehicle for a Cold Chisel concert—or so I thought. The logical spot for a stage was an old quarry near the track that provided a natural amphitheatre, which could be easily set up. The perimeter could be secured by a chain-link fence covered in hessian strung along the rim of the quarry. Our plan was for the band to go on at dusk, just after the final race. It was a great idea in theory, but we hadn't considered that after three days of serious partying, the punters would be either too exhausted or would simply have no money left for the entrance fee.

The gates opened late in the afternoon, but ticket sales were slow—snail's-pace slow. Then we noticed something happening with the chain-link perimeter—small tears began to appear in the hessian as inquisitive racegoers peered through to have a look at the stage area below. As the opening strains of 'Wild Colonial Boy' echoed around the quarry, the fence began to sway. After three songs, that gentle sway grew to a vigorous push-and-pull; the fence resembled a willow branch blowing in the wind. When it finally buckled, a human avalanche began thundering towards the band and the terrified punters already inside.

The Grand Prix officials who had been standing by panicked; anticipating the worst, they called for the cops. At the time we were totally unaware that Mount Panorama had turned into a battlefield, with fights erupting between racegoers and police, resulting in 150 arrests. By now, the concerns we had about making money from the show were replaced by fears for the safety of the band, stage equipment and those who had paid to get in. Minutes later, a lone paddy wagon arrived at the front gate; three young constables got out, took one look at the chaos and immediately called for the riot squad. Shortly after we could hear the sirens of the approaching cavalry, the NSW Police Tactical Response Group.

Even though the gatecrashers meant no harm and just wanted to party, it was a very tense scene, especially with the arrival of the riot squad. I wondered whether the band would finish their show before Armageddon was upon us. Serious mayhem was now a real possibility. Thankfully, a full-scale blow-up was avoided—even though some newspapers later reported 'a riot between police and bikies'. Peace was restored and everyone went away happy. The only real damage was the fence—oh, and the band's bank balance, which was about $20,000 lighter.

*

As expected, an offer soon arrived for a run of 25 dates in Germany during the northern summer. The band were to be special guests of Roger 'Chappo' Chapman. Chappo had been the lead singer of the British band Family, one of the premier acts on the psychedelic/prog scene of the late 1960s and early '70s, and had since forged a solid solo career in Europe, predominantly in Germany. I knew two of Chappo's players from my days in London: bass player Boz Burrell, formerly of Bad Company and an old drinking buddy; and Tim Hinkley from Jody Grind, a trio that had been on the Transatlantic label with Little Free Rock. I had a fair idea what the Chisel guys were going to say about the proposal, something along the lines of 'Not another has-been', but they grew more enthusiastic when I told them about the size of the venues and Polydor's enthusiasm for the band to tour.

The first show, in early May, was in Hof, a town tucked away in the east of the country, close to the borders of East Germany and what was then Communist Czechoslovakia. The band's stage equipment would be freighted in Chapman's truck, while the band and entourage, which included Jim's wife Jane and baby Mahalia, would travel in Chappo's tour bus. The band played really well over the first few shows and received a positive reaction each night. But at the Hall Polyvalent in Luxembourg, things suddenly went south; their performance didn't seem to gel. Heated words were exchanged and for the first time Steve's playing was called into question.

The following night in Karlsruhe was much better; the band seemed happy and the reaction from the 1800-strong crowd bore that out. Yet in Rosenheim, in front of 800 people in the echo-ridden Stadthalle, problems resurfaced. Steve's playing was again singled out—either he was playing too slow, or Jim wanted him to play faster—and I could sense a growing frustration within the group. I wrote about their performance in my diary, describing it as 'slack'.

Unbeknown to me, another issue was building. Jim's decision to include Jane and Mahalia in our entourage had become a concern for some members of Chappo's party. I was only alerted to this when I was pulled aside by Chappo's tour manager. I knew from past experience that touring was predominantly seen as a boys' club, and that the presence of Jim's wife and baby might have had an effect on that.

As much as I hated to, I had to discuss this with Jim before it became a real problem. To his credit, he was calm and accepting.

'We'll arrange our own travel for the rest of the tour,' he told me.

But allowing this to happen drove a further wedge within the band at a time when solidarity was crucial. I now realise it wouldn't have been difficult for me to arrange alternative transport for our entire party; we did have the resources.

For the remainder of the run, the crowd reaction was excellent, but this didn't calm the frustration that was simmering within the band. I could see them imploding before my eyes. They'd given far worse performances in the past and had always found a way to regenerate themselves, but now it felt that the oxygen was being sucked out of the group. Steve, rightly or wrongly, was considered the major culprit, and the situation hit rock bottom when Jim impulsively phoned ex–Daddy Cool drummer Gary Young to see if he would fly out and take over the drum stool. Gary, wisely, declined the offer. His presence would have only made a bad situation worse.

As the tour rolled on, Jim and the rest of the guys became more convinced that Steve's playing was the root cause of their poor performances. When confronted, Steve would simply shrug his shoulders and brush off their criticism. I was convinced that the problem was more than Steve's playing. I think it was a couple of factors: frustration with the situation in the US, and the simple fact that these five guys had been living in each other's pockets since 1974. There was clearly something very wrong.

We returned to Sydney on a Sunday, a meeting was set for the Wednesday and by Friday, 17 June, the news had broken. The headline read: 'Steve Prestwich leaves Cold Chisel'. Ray Arnott, who had covered for Steve when he had been injured in a car accident, was quickly drafted into the band. Six days of rehearsals later and Cold Chisel was back on the road for a run of shows in Victoria and South Australia.

Although the gigs with Ray went well enough, I could feel that Cold Chisel's energy, their fire, was fading. It was as if they were going through the motions. Steve was an integral element in the band, a key part of the Chisel DNA, and it was hard to accept that he was gone. Ray tried his hardest to fit in, but the feeling that something was missing permeated every gig. Steve's absence on stage was subconsciously affecting the band's performance, and the fans could sense that too.

To exorcise all this negativity, it was agreed the band would record a new album, hoping that new songs, new sounds and new energy would get them back on track. Don was a big fan of Tony Cohen, an engineer/producer from Melbourne who had worked with Nick Cave's post-punk band The Birthday Party. Although most outside of the band—and maybe a few within—felt that this was a very left-field idea, arrangements were made to lay down some tracks with Tony at Richmond Recorders in Melbourne.

Tony was full of raw enthusiasm and he threw himself into the sessions. Yet even his zeal did little to stem the feeling in the band that things were spiralling downward. The studio didn't prove to be the magic bullet; it simply wasn't a great environment for Cold Chisel at that point. The guys returned to Sydney to consider their next move.

*

Cold Chisel was a business, a partnership that generated income from touring and record sales. Out of this came business costs, touring expenses, recording costs, management and agency commissions. Once that was done, the remaining money was split equally between the band members. Now, these dividends were paid subject to there being enough funds in reserve to cover ongoing and future costs. If one partner required an additional amount to the others—an advance— then an equalisation had to take place. If that equalisation put a strain on the band finances, the only way to resolve that was either to sell more records or go back on tour.

On 17 August I received a call from Mark Pope. His role as tour manager often resulted in him being the meat in the sandwich between band and management. There had recently been a tour reconciliation, and each member had received a sizeable dividend. But due to previous advances he'd received, Jim's share was reduced. It wasn't unusual for Jim to be in this position; it'd been a battle from day one.

Mark informed me that he had a request from Jim for an additional advance. Unfortunately, the amount wasn't the issue; we were really talking about a larger problem, because all the guys would have to be paid the same amount, putting an untenable strain on Chisel's finances. Being very aware of the fragile nature of things within the band, I felt that this could be the tipping point. I called Don and Mark to an urgent meeting.

During our meeting, the phone rang. It was Jim.

'I want to speak to Mark,' he said down the line.

But Don took the phone. 'Sorry Jim,' he said, 'but we can't do the advance.'

Jim said very little before hanging up. Don then phoned Ian and Phil to further discuss the situation. The following morning Don called me and said that both the guys were of the same opinion regarding further advances, and asked me to organise a band meeting.

Around 2 p.m. the next day, at Don's place, the band and I sat down to talk. The tone of the meeting was cordial, there were no raised voices, but the decision was made for Cold Chisel to call it a day. This outcome came as no real surprise considering the current environment. I'd known the final whistle would blow sometime; I just hadn't known when.

Interestingly, once we agreed on the split, a calm descended on the room. I guess everyone was expecting this outcome and felt relieved.

'So what do we do now?' I asked the guys.

Jim, Don, Phil and Ian looked at me for an answer.

'How about we go out with a bang?' I suggested. 'Let's finish the album and do a final tour.'

The unanimous response—hell yes—was the most positive reaction I'd heard from the guys in ages.

'Now, before we go,' I said, 'what about a drummer?'

The answer was obvious. Just eight weeks after leaving the band, Steve Prestwich was back in the saddle.

★

Over the following days, Mark and I met up with Richard McDonald, Dirty Pool's booking agent, to work out the tour run. Our strategy was to play the biggest indoor venues in Australia and New Zealand, which meant the production would need to be on the scale of an international touring act. The only company that could provide that sort of grunt was Jands, run by my old mate Eric Robinson. Of course this came with a hefty price tag, and without being able to accurately predict ticket sales we were flying blind, especially when we factored in promotion, advertising and fixed costs. It was a big risk; the band could conceivably finish in the red, the last thing anyone needed.

I dreaded my next meeting—with Paul Turner and Peter Ikin at Warners. They'd believed in and supported the band since Warners had signed them six years earlier, and they had been integral to the band's success in Australia. The news completely blindsided them; they were gutted, visibly shaken. I tried to put a positive spin on it—big tour, new album—but disappointment was etched on their faces. Record companies plan and depend on future financial predictions, so I could only imagine the budget recalculations going on in their heads.

The tough calls continued—I now had to break the news to Ray Arnott. For almost two months he'd been the drummer with Australia's biggest band; it had been his 'Jimmie Nicol moment'. (Nicol was the drummer who replaced Ringo in The Beatles for two weeks when they toured Australia in 1964.) But there was an upside for Ray, because he'd get to work on the upcoming farewell album.

We released a press statement on 22 August, which stated simply:

Cold Chisel has today announced that on their 10th anniversary in October 1983, they will be disbanding following a final tour. The band's final album is being prepared. The tour will take in the major cities of Australia and New Zealand.

By 6 a.m. on Monday, my phone was ringing off the hook with people from all over the industry. So much for an unlisted home number. 'Who did what?' I was asked repeatedly. 'Why, how, what's the real story?' Rumours began to buzz about what went down, but all I could do was to try to remain calm and focused, and to concentrate on getting the tour and album sorted.

Box offices across the country were going to open at 9 a.m. on Monday, 5 September. By Sunday evening, news began filtering through that diehard fans across the country were camping outside venues to buy tickets. We'd predicted playing a couple of shows in each city, but we were genuinely unprepared for the avalanche of demand. On opening day, four Sydney shows were sold out and another 20,000 seats were sold in Melbourne. A similar pattern emerged across the country. The tour was on fire.

There was still a month before the tour launched in New Zealand, time we'd utilise for the final album. Although the end was sudden, the attitude within the band in the studio was civil. I guess everyone figured, well, the explosion happened, the world didn't end, and tour sales were extraordinary, so it was a case of, 'Okay, then—let's get on and make an album.'

For that final album, which would be called *Twentieth Century*, Don was particularly keen to capture the kind of energy, sound and performance that were the essence of Chisel live. The band had been really impressed by the acoustics of the Capitol Theatre in Sydney's Chinatown when they had performed there with Mentals and INXS on the Youth in Asia tour in 1980, so we stationed the Jands mobile recording studio out the front of the theatre for six days and got to work. Tony Cohen flew up from Melbourne to engineer. In theory it was a great idea but unfortunately it didn't work in practice. Tony was a bit out of his depth with the multi-tracking equipment, so we rushed in Peter Walker, who had engineered and produced the first Cold Chisel album, to oversee things.

With so much now happening so quickly, I had little time to think about the future or what the others might have planned. I'm sure the band was still a bit stunned by all that had happened and was about to happen, but I was sure that Jim, for one, wasn't going to let the grass grow under his feet. Rumours were rife about their split and their future, but rumours were always rife. My task was to get the job done. Everything else, I figured, would be revealed in due course.

*

With Steve back behind the drums, the Last Stand tour kicked off in New Zealand on 20 September. Two capacity nights in Auckland were followed by sell-outs in Wellington, Christchurch and Dunedin, where the house record at the Town Hall set by The Beatles in 1964 had been smashed by Chisel the previous year.

Merchandising was a fairly new phenomenon for us. Although we had printed promo T-shirts for album releases and achieved some sales at gigs since the Summer Offensive tour of 1981, the size of this run, about 30 gigs in all, was a whole new paradigm. Trying to assess the actual sales potential was difficult; if we printed too many T-shirts we'd be out of pocket, but if we produced too few, sales would go begging. In the end, we just took a punt and hoped we'd got it right.

As for the design, we knew the iconic COLD CHISEL block logo would work, but we needed a great visual graphic. In the end, we settled on the four black-and-white images of Jim and Ian from the inside sleeve of the *East* album. These abstract images had been created by Phil Mortlock on the Warner office photocopier, the same machine that staff were known to use creatively at Christmas parties. We employed Neil Wright's fledgling merchandising company Floggitt to oversee the logistics of dealing with venues and sellers.

A couple of days before the tour began, Jim dropped by my office and asked Denise, my trusty PA, if he could have a peek at the finished product. Denise opened up one of the boxes and proudly displayed the T-shirt.

'Fantastic, hey, Jim?' she said.

The expression on Jim's face said it all—he was horrified and began stabbing his forefinger accusingly at graphic number three.

'Fuck, look at my nose, I look like fucking Pinocchio!' he gasped. 'They cannot be sold. Dump them!'

Then Jim headed out the door. When I reached the office, I found Denise sitting cross-legged on the floor in a state of shock and panic.

'Oh shit,' I said when she explained how Jim had reacted.

'I think I can fix it,' Denise reassured me.

She spent the next couple of days reshaping Jim's nose with a black texta on thousands of T-shirts, which was well and truly beyond the call of duty. I can't recall if I told Jim, or just assured him we'd done a reprint.

A dark shadow was cast over the first of three nights at the Newcastle Workers Club in late September when we learned that Scott Howlett, a long-time friend and ex–Chisel employee, had been involved in a car accident en route to Sydney that had claimed the life of his fiancée.

Then it was on to full houses at Canberra, Brisbane and Surfers Paradise before we arrived in Melbourne for four nights. By then, the first taste of the new album had been released: a double A-side single, 'Hold Me Tight'/'No Sense', which would go on to peak at number 14.

At the end of October, the Last Stand juggernaut rolled into Sydney for the first of five shows at the 11,000-seat

Entertainment Centre. Unfortunately this came off the back of four emotional nights in hometown Adelaide, and Jim's voice was shot. He could hardly speak, let alone sing. He managed to get through the first night but it was obvious that the hectic schedule, plus the hometown festivities in Adelaide, had taken their toll. I cancelled the remaining Sydney shows and rescheduled them for early December.

★

Seven weeks later, on 12 December, with Frank Sinatra blaring from the sound system, Chisel took to the stage for the first of their four remaining Sydney shows. Assuming that these were the last concerts the band would ever play, we had decided to record the four nights and film two of them. The Jands mobile recording studio, with Mark Opitz in the chair and Jon Lemon assisting, was parked at the rear of the Entertainment Centre, while an eight-camera shoot directed by John Whitteron and Tony Stevens was overseen by John McLean's Captured Live.

This Sydney swansong was all a blur to me, a whirl of conflicting emotions. I was caught between a sense of relief that it was finally over and a feeling of not wanting it to end. After the final show, I sat staring at the dressing-room floor, trying to put all the craziness into some kind of perspective. The band that I had nurtured for the last five-and-a-bit years had left the stage, leaving me wondering where life would now take me. In my heart and my guts I knew that we could have achieved so much more; I fervently believed the band was destined for international success. But in the end, I accepted that it was down to the five guys in the band to determine and agree on their future.

Everyone else had left for the afterparty, but I was struggling. I didn't want to go but felt compelled to. I had to remind myself that this was really the end of Cold Chisel.

Or was it?

★

If anything was going to clear my head and cleanse my soul, it was surfing—and that's exactly what I did when the Chisel carnival was over. Mother ocean was calling.

I'd thought things might be quieter in 1984, but I was wrong. Early in the new year I was approached by my good friends Martin Fabinyi and Cameron Allan, who ran the indie label Regular Records. They formed Regular in 1978 and signed some of the best young acts around: Mental As Anything; I'm Talking, featuring Kate Ceberano; The Cockroaches, who became the nucleus of The Wiggles; comic Austen Tayshus; and Dirty Pool's very own Icehouse. Regular had some structural issues that required sorting out, and they asked if I could help them out for a couple of months as a consultant. They'd recently moved their distribution to Warners, and given my strong relationship with the label, they could see the merit of having me onboard. I really enjoyed my stint at Regular and to this day remain friends with Martin and many of the acts on the label.

Dirty Pool, meanwhile, continued to grow—our agency division was expanding with new bands on the roster, and we were seriously looking at setting up a touring arm for international acts. But during the winter of 1984, the landscape of Dirty Pool changed significantly. Richard McDonald had been running the agency side of the company since its inception in

1978, but unfortunately a conflict of interest arose so he left. We needed a top-line replacement. Initially we considered a shortlist of bookers, but no one stood out. We were left with only one alternative—to sleep with the enemy. We needed to meet with the people from Premier.

The Cheshire cat grins on the faces of Michael Gudinski, Frank Stivala and Sam Riggi when we walked into their office in Melbourne were impossible to miss. But I had to put my personal feelings aside; our acts' security had to take precedence. We put in place a deal with them, but one that still allowed us the final say on gigs and was in keeping with all our Dirty Pool standards.

*

A fair amount of acrimony existed between former Chisel band members for quite some time after the split. I guess this was understandable as old wounds were exposed. Financial meetings were not pleasant; Jim turned up at one wearing a T-shirt that read 'My lawyer can beat up your lawyer'. It was funny but hardly helpful. The liquidation of their assets, which included a property in Glebe, proved to be difficult. The property had been bought as a long-term asset but was sold prematurely due to the split, and as a consequence of the real-estate market declining up to 17.4 per cent over an eleven-month period it lost money.

I took some heat, much of it inaccurate and disputable; some issues still persist today. Slanderous remarks credited to a band member appeared in a popular publication, requiring me to hire well-known lawyer Chris Murphy to defend my name—a situation that brought me more sadness than satisfaction. Yet our business relationship managed to remain intact for a further 25 years, and on a personal level has survived to this day. As I have said before: 'Chisel forever, forever Chisel.'

After The Last Stand, most of the Chisel guys headed off in their own directions, leaving Don and me to oversee the completion of *Twentieth Century*. There were still a few minor overdubs to do and cover artwork to create, and Mark Opitz had to do the final mix.

Eduardo Guelfenbein was a Chilean friend of Don's, an artist, painter and photographer who'd produced two quirky film clips and artwork for the 'Hold Me Tight'/'No Sense' single. We hoped he'd do the cover artwork. His apartment was above a shop on Bondi Road, reached by rickety wooden stairs. Don and I were met at the door by Eduardo's stunningly beautiful wife, a baby at her breast. The apartment walls were a mass gallery of Eduardo's unique, evocative art. Eduardo agreed to do the cover art. Even now I'm still perplexed as to why it didn't raise more eyebrows.

Richard Lowenstein was Australia's most sought-after video director, his reputation forged via cutting-edge clips for Hunters & Collectors and The Church. He produced the clip for the next single, 'Saturday Night', captured over two nights in Kings Cross. Richard's camera shadowed Jim and Ian as they mingled with the denizens of that seedy, red-light world. Don captured ambient street sounds on his mini recorder and they were woven into the soundtrack. The song was a hit, reaching number 6 nationally at the end of March, while the clip is still lauded as Chisel's most iconic and enduring. *Twentieth Century* was released the following month, shipping gold and reaching number 1 in its second week. (By Christmas 1984 it would sell 100,000 units.) Then, in July, *The Last Stand* movie gave cinemagoers across the country a taste of the experience of those final shows in Sydney. The 1000-watt stereo system left their ears ringing for days.

With the success of *Twentieth Century* I knew I needed a solid future strategy for the sake of Cold Chisel's legacy. I'd devoted nearly six years to getting Chisel to the top and I wasn't going to let it all disappear into obscurity. By then, FM radio was the key driver in the marketplace, and while Chisel was no longer active, radio needed reminding that they were still relevant. The release of Jim's debut solo album *Bodyswerve* in September achieved that by default, but I needed to find a way to surf the Jimmy Barnes wave for the sake of the band.

Considering the positive reaction to the *Last Stand* movie at the box office, I approached Don with the idea of releasing some of those live tracks on an album. Don thought that another release on top of the tour, the *Twentieth Century* album and the movie might be overkill. Yet my gut told me that Jim's album would be big, and I didn't want Cold Chisel to be lost in its slipstream.

We came up with a compromise: what if we released something so humble that it would look like a bootleg? The band, including Jim, agreed, and the end result was an album in a plain dirty-green cardboard cover, rubber-stamped with *The Barking Spiders Live 1983*. Simple. Capitalising on the lucrative Christmas market and the success of *Bodyswerve*, by the end of January 1985 sales of *Spiders* had exceeded 60,000, which wasn't too shabby for such a low-key release.

*

It had been twenty years since I'd watched The Beatles arrive in Sydney and I was still a huge fan. In November 1984 I was thrilled to be invited to a function at the Sydney Opera House to launch *Fifty Years Adrift*, a book by Derek Taylor, the band's long-time press officer. Taylor, often referred to as the 'fifth Beatle', was accompanied by a very special guest, George Harrison.

I was at a table with members of INXS and Divinyls, and other assorted music-industry luminaries. During proceedings, George was escorted around and I'm sure his right hand was getting a bit tired from all the handshakes. When he reached us, the Divinyls' guitarist Mark McEntee rose to greet George, and his hand accidentally brushed a full glass of chardonnay, sending a spray of Burgundy's finest all over George's pristine white-linen suit. An audible gasp swept across the room, and a mortified Mark apologised profusely while George's minder tried to wipe away the darkening patch. George didn't look too impressed.

'Don't worry, mate,' I whispered in Mark's ear. 'Not many people can claim to have thrown a glass of wine over a Beatle.' Mark was not amused.

15

DIRTY POOL TOURING

In early February 1985, Gay and I welcomed a new baby girl to the family; we named her Leigh. I now had three daughters, which as I have joked, was God's retribution for my evil ways. Life was good on the Northern Beaches, even if it was a long daily drive to Dirty Pool's offices in Kings Cross.

And things were changing at Dirty Pool. It was inevitable that we'd eventually get into tour promotion and I now was at the helm of Dirty Pool Promotions. We'd already dabbled— with XTC in 1979 and Simple Minds two years later. Both had come to Australia in support of Icehouse on a run of clubs and pubs; in return, Icehouse would support those bands in the UK. Our relationship with their booking agents now opened doors for our acts in the UK and Europe, and also gave us access to acts keen to break into the Australian market.

Although we were experienced and successful on a pub/club level, we needed an alliance with a more experienced partner. Australia seemed to have more promoters than kangaroos; the major players at the time were Michael Coppel, Michael

Gudinski, Michael Chugg, Garry Van Egmond and Paul Dainty. Behind them was a long list of promoters skilled in touring everyone from punk acts to juggling monkeys. We had teamed up with Michael Coppel at the Narara Music Festival, so he was our pick. Chris Cole had toured some of our acts in New Zealand and seemed a perfect fit to represent us across the ditch.

Our first joint venture with Michael and Chris was a tour by UK punk pioneers The Stranglers. Being our first foray, we took a cautious approach, booking mid-range venues in Sydney, Canberra, Brisbane, Newcastle, Melbourne, Adelaide and Perth, with a solid support in Hunters & Collectors. The tour was a financial success, apart from the cost of a backstage door at Melbourne's Palais, which was ripped off its hinges by a sideways kick from Jean-Jacques Burnel, their sometimes-aggressive bass player.

Feeling more confident and adventurous, we took on the larger Entertainment Centre–sized venues in June with English blue-eyed soul singer Paul Young, who was enjoying worldwide success with his cover of Hall & Oates' 'Every Time You Go Away'. His fanbase was mainly young girls, so 'screamsville' was go.

Tears For Fears was next, arriving on the back of their monster hit singles 'Shout' and 'Everybody Wants to Rule the World'. The tour was a runaway success. For reasons that still escape me today, I also had UK synth-popster Howard Jones touring at the same time. Talk about jumping in headfirst.

*

In the wake of these successful tours, my partners Ray Hearn, John 'Woody' Woodruff and I, and our financial guru Gino

Principe, booked some R&R in Ray's destination of choice, Japan.

Our first stop was Hakone, a beautiful resort town in the mountains west of Tokyo, famous for its hot springs and stunning views of Mount Fuji. On our arrival at the hotel lobby we were confronted with the sight of Japanese businessmen quietly shuffling around in their yukatas, the male equivalent of the kimono, and thongs. We stood out like the proverbial.

Central to the complex was a large bathing facility known as an onsen, fed from the famous local hot springs. It was full of naked Asian men. We quickly learned that the protocol of modesty was very important in Japan. On our entry, we were each supplied with a small washcloth; its purpose was to cover our most intimate region. Through the rising steam, the serene demeanour of those already in the pool changed to sheer horror as we four, sans washcloths, made our entrance. As we settled back against the tiled wall, enjoying the soothing water, our fellow bathers glared at us, waiting to see what new atrocity we were going to perpetrate.

Woody didn't want to disappoint them, and he decided that it would be fun to see who could swim the most laps under water. The water temperature in an onsen normally sits between 40 and 44 degrees, so undue physical exertion was ill advised. Regardless, Aquaman submerged and, like a torpedo, headed for his target on the other side of the pool. As if in a synchronised motion, the bath guests clutched at their genitalia, fearing the worst. It was a safe bet that at 40-odd degrees Woody's subaqueous passage would be short-lived and, like an overcooked whale, he breached from the steamy depths as an audible gasp echoed around the onsen. Our departure the following day was, I can safely assume, gladly welcomed by both staff and house guests.

But Ray was by no means finished with the Land of the Rising Sun. In September 1985, after seven years of Dirty Pool business, he packed up and moved to Tokyo, his favourite place in the world. Our team had achieved amazing success and I was sad to see the original combination split up. Ray had played such a huge role in our accomplishments. He was wild and funny, with a great mind and an amazing memory for detail. Ray was a visionary, and his departure left a huge hole in the company.

★

I continued spruiking Dirty Pool Touring with a trip to LA and New York in late September 1985, soon after Ray's departure. While in New York I caught up with an old mate named John Stainze; he was the man who had discovered and signed Dire Straits, and in 1979 he'd signed Kurtis Blow as the first rap artist on a major label. John and I had met when he ran A&R for Polydor in LA and had become great friends.

John was a music aficionado, with an amazing knowledge of early blues, rock, R&B, soul and rockabilly. He had turned me on to blues shouters like Wynonie Harris and Big Joe Turner, and rockabilly legends Charlie Feathers and Warren Smith, and he knew which Little Richard reissues contained the original performances, or which obscure R&B artist I just had to check out. John and I had a ritual whenever I was in LA: before I left for home, we'd go to Tower Records on Sunset to load up on essential vinyl.

While in New York with John, he invited me along to a gathering of British music expats known as the Curry Club. They got together once a month at Good Karma, a tiny Indian restaurant on 6th Street in Little India. This clique of mainly expat record-company personnel also included John Lydon, aka Sex Pistol Johnny Rotten, who lived in the Big Apple. Like most Poms, they had an almost religious addiction to curry; blazing hot was the default setting. After a long afternoon of fire eating, washed down by copious cold beers, we indulged in an evening of club hopping. Dressed in his baggy powder-blue suit, Lydon's legendary status was on full display as we swanned through the doors of one club after another, always with a free bar tab. I'd be left with a huge hangover and a 'ring of fire' to remind me of another great day.

*

I'd first floated the idea of a Cold Chisel greatest hits record in early 1985, as part of my strategy to not let their catalogue go cold. Some in the band felt it might be seen as milking it, but my counterargument, put simply, was that a best-of was the most viable way to maintain a presence in the marketplace without new product. And it would also generate income. We agreed to release what would be known as *Radio Songs: A Best of* in late 1985.

While out scouting for inspiration for an album cover with Phil Mortlock, we discovered a rusted van dumped on the side of the road near Bilpin, the apple-growing area just west of Sydney. We glued an old gig poster from Newcastle Workers to the side of the van, which Phil photographed with his box brownie camera. That photo became the cover for *Radio Songs*, which soared to number 3 on the national charts, and with Jim's monster hit 'Working Class Man' at number 1, made for another stellar Chisel/Barnes Christmas.

In January 1986, when *Radio Songs'* sales clicked over the double-platinum (140,000 units) mark, it helped achieve a huge milestone: Cold Chisel had now sold one million albums in Australia. I was incredibly proud of their massive achievement, but that was offset, to some degree, by the harsh reality that the band no longer existed.

★

A cruise on the magnificent Sydney Harbour was pretty much a given for any visiting international artist. Accompanying the artists onboard would be your usual posse of company players, all expertly coached in how to blow smoke up the act's arse. Some specially selected media would also be invited, a quid quo pro for positive column inches. It was all part of the game.

After the success of Paul Young's 1985 tour, we at Dirty Pool brought him back for six more shows in early 1987. While we were all out on the harbour with Paul, I did a double take when I spotted a very special guest, Tony 'I Left My Heart in San Francisco' Bennett, sitting quietly at the rear of the boat. Years ago, while in Chicago with Savoy Brown, I'd seen his signed portrait in a restaurant but here he was in the flesh, a living legend.

While the usual boozy rock-and-roll shenanigans continued around him, Tony sat quietly sketching on an 8-by-10-inch pad. My inner fan took over.

'May I sit down?' I cheekily asked.

'Sure, take a seat,' he replied in his distinctly Queens New York tone.

I couldn't believe my good fortune—and I'd had no idea that Tony's favourite pastime was painting, or that his work was highly sought after and displayed in major galleries. To this day I wonder whether his painting *Boy on Sailboat, Sydney Bay*, on display at the National Arts Club in New York, was inspired by that afternoon on the harbour, with me looking over his shoulder while he sketched.

★

In the early days of Dirty Pool I didn't really know Iva Davies very well; we'd mainly cross paths in the agency's corridors, or backstage at gigs. Other than the Pooled Resources tour, Icehouse (at that time still known as Flowers) and Chisel had never appeared on the same bill. Ray Hearn had looked after Icehouse since the Flowers era, guiding them through success in Europe with the breakout single 'Hey Little Girl' from the album *Primitive Man*. When Ray left for Japan, Woody took over as manager. At the time, Icehouse was in great commercial shape: *Measure for Measure*, their fourth album, was in the Top 10 in Australia, while their single 'No Promises' was in the Top 10 on the US dance music charts. They'd sold more than 150,000 albums in America, where they were signed to Chrysalis Records.

There was great optimism within Chrysalis that if the band got the next album right, with great songs and production, it had the potential to be massive. Singles were crucial, and the idea of a co-write surfaced. Among the names tossed around was John Oates of the mega-selling US duo Hall & Oates, and he agreed. John spent a couple of weeks with Iva in early 1987, working at Iva's home studio in Erskineville. The standout track was a song called 'Electric Blue'.

With the completion of the *Man of Colours* album in September 1987, it was all hands on deck at Dirty Pool. Woody would handle the international side from an apartment we leased in New York, while Gino Principe, Keith Welsh (original Icehouse bass player)—who managed Do-Ré-Mi and Boom Crash Opera, two other Dirty Pool acts on the rise—and I would cover the home front.

In Australia, the first single 'Crazy' peaked at number 3, and the album hit number 1 on 5 October and stayed on top for eleven straight weeks. By the end of October, Oz album sales in Australia were in excess of 100,000; it was a monster hit. 'Electric Blue' was the second single and hit number 1 in Australia during early November, soon reaching the US Top 10, peaking at number 7. By early 1988, *Man of Colours* had sold more than 325,000 units in Australia. Huge numbers.

Icehouse cleaned up at the ARIA Awards, winning Album of the Year and Highest Selling Album. With the US success of 'Electric Blue', their album sales soon reached 450,000 there, while in Australia LP sales tipped over the 500,000 mark. *Man of Colours* made Icehouse superstars in Australia and upped their profile considerably in the US, Canada and Europe.

★

The first album I ever owned was Jerry Lee Lewis's 1958 debut; I was eleven years old. It still sits proudly in my vinyl collection. Some 30 years later, in August 1988, I found myself standing a few metres from 'The Killer' as he pounded the keys at the 86 Street Music Hall in Vancouver. I was in heaven. Gay and I and our three daughters were there to attend a friend's wedding, but with all due respect, Jerry Lee was the highlight for me.

With the strains of 'Great Balls of Fire' still ringing in my ears, I flew to Memphis to catch up with Angels drummer

Brent Eccles and a new Dirty Pool band, Johnny Diesel and the Injectors. Brent had discovered them in Perth, convinced them to relocate to the east coast and now, under the watchful eye of Dirty Pool, was co-managing the band with Woody. With plenty of points on the board after the success of Icehouse, Woody landed them a deal with Chrysalis.

Chrysalis had booked the band into Ardent Studios to record their debut LP with producer Terry Manning. Manning had learned his craft at Stax Records, the home of Memphis soul, before going on to a highly successful relationship with ZZ Top. He'd also engineered the *Led Zeppelin III* album. They were in good hands.

Whenever I was in a hotel room, pretty much by instinct, the first thing I would do was turn on the TV. I guess it was a security thing. I'd usually end up with Bert and Ernie to keep me company but on my first morning in Memphis it was a tele-evangelist doing the whole fire and brimstone thing. He offered added redemption, for just a few dollars, courtesy of a PO box somewhere. I passed and headed for the studio.

My hotel was a leisurely four-block stroll to Ardent. Once on the street, I realised I'd forgotten how hot and clammy the South got in August; the air-conditioned studio was a welcome relief. Equally comforting was to be in a studio with a young band again: the Injectors' exuberance was like a breath of fresh air.

Although unplanned, my visit to Memphis coincided with the eleventh anniversary of Elvis Presley's death. A candlelight vigil was planned at Graceland that night, and Brent and I knew this was an event not to be missed. I had always imagined Graceland to be out in the countryside, but I was surprised to discover that it was on a main road, directly opposite a strip mall where cheesy tourist shops flogged everything from nodding Elvis car ornaments to 'I Love Elvis' T-shirts.

Brent and I joined the orderly queue that formed at the famous 'musical note' gates at Graceland and stretched down Elvis Presley Boulevard. Only days earlier I had seen Jerry Lee Lewis in Vancouver, and my mind flashed to an event in November 1976 when Jerry had turned up right here, at the Graceland gates, drunk and waving a .38 Derringer pistol, demanding to see Elvis. 'The Killer' was arrested and thrown in the slammer—and not for the first time.

The vigil, however, was a much more sombre (and sober) occasion. At 8.30 p.m. sharp the gates slowly opened and the hundreds who had gathered made their way up the winding driveway, all to the melancholy strains of an Elvis ballad. The Meditation Garden was just past the swimming pool; the gravesites of Elvis, his brother, mother and father were nearby. People passed quietly, paused to pay their respects, said a prayer, shed a tear. It was all done in silence, making for a surreal moment in the funky humidity of Memphis, Tennessee.

Returning from Memphis, I headed to Cairns for an important meeting to determine the future of Dirty Pool. A lot had changed since we'd set up shop in the spring of 1978. Of the founding five, three had left: Ray went to live in Japan in 1985, Richard had left the year before that, and Jenny Elliott had moved on to have a family. We'd been highly successful, but after almost ten years, at least to some involved with the company, it seemed like a prudent time to go our own ways and chase down other dreams. I had mixed feelings about this. I felt we had plenty of scope to further expand, and in hindsight I believe we made the wrong move, but not everyone shared my point of view. In September 1988, Dirty Pool officially shut its doors.

It was hard to say farewell to our wonderfully loyal staff. They weren't just staff—they were an important part of how we functioned at Dirty Pool. Their contributions had played a huge part in our success, and the bond between us would continue. After all: once a Dirty Pooler, always a Dirty Pooler.

★

We ex-Dirty Poolers had plenty to go on with. Woody continued with The Angels and the co-management of Johnny Diesel with Brent Eccles. Keith Welsh retained Boom Crash Opera and Do-Ré-Mi, while Gino Principe, our financial guru, would establish his own business management company. As for me, I took over the management of Icehouse from Woody, and continued to oversee the careers of Don Walker and the legacy of Cold Chisel.

Since the Chisel split in 1983, I'd kept in regular contact with Don. We'd have Cold Chisel business to discuss, or we'd blather on about anything from rugby league to politics. Don had adopted the gypsy lifestyle, travelling in the US, Europe and even the Soviet Union, all the while observing and writing, enjoying the freedom, and occasionally checking in with me from some exotic location.

During 1987, I'd commenced negotiations with Warners for a solo deal for Don. He had a collection of songs that had either been unsuitable for Cold Chisel or that he'd written with a future solo project in mind. Initially, Warners was a little apprehensive; even though Don was the major songwriter for Chisel, he'd not been a frontman. Still, a deal was done and under the intriguing pseudonym of Catfish, *Unlimited Address* was released in October, within weeks of the closure of Dirty

Pool. Don co-produced the record with Peter Walker, who'd worked on Cold Chisel's debut. It was a stunning set, full of amazing songs like 'The Early Hours', 'Subway', 'Pre-War Blues' and 'My Backyard', and a major departure from the signature Chisel sound. One critic described it as 'a weird amalgam of torch songs, Eastern European cabaret, and funk'.

Although chart results were disappointing, the album and the single 'When You Dance' were nominated for Best Breakthrough Album and Single respectively at the 1989 ARIAs.

★

Taking over full management of Icehouse after the massive success of *Man of Colours* brought its challenges. Woody had driven that album hard and now that he was gone there would certainly be questions about me within Chrysalis—namely, who was this new guy, could I replace Woody, and could I keep the momentum going? I thought it best to start with a consolidation of the live market in Australia and New Zealand. Under the banner Life in a Paintbox, the band undertook a fourteen-date Australian tour in early 1989. It was a mixture of indoor and outdoor shows in regional and capital centres, culminating in a major Sydney concert. Turn Back the Tide— or 'Turn Back the Turd', as it was jokingly referred to—was designed as a protest about the polluting of Sydney's beaches. Staged on Bondi Beach, and featuring Midnight Oil, INXS, Divinyls, Noiseworks, Rose Tattoo and Icehouse, it drew in excess of 250,000 people.

Clearly, everything was in good shape for Icehouse in Australia. But what about America?

In April 1989, I flew to New York for my first face-to-face with the people at Chrysalis. Changes were taking place with the label; EMI had acquired a 50 per cent stake in the company, and a new CEO had been appointed. He was Joe Kiener, a German who until recently had worked for shoe giant Adidas, and been brought in by Chrysalis chair and founder Chris Wright. But there was industry speculation that Wright was thinking about offloading the remaining 50 per cent to EMI. Chrysalis's president Mike Bone, meanwhile, had quite the reputation. Legend had it that Bone, while still a promotions guy, had promoted The Boomtown Rats by mailing packages containing live sewer rats to radio DJs.

To say I was a little unsure of what to expect at Chrysalis HQ was an understatement. Much to my surprise, I found Bone to be a quietly spoken guy in jeans and cowboy boots, which was a departure from the usual Armani-suited east coast record guys. I soon found we had a connection: Mike was from Georgia, where I'd spent a great deal of time while working with Savoy Brown. Mike told me that when he was sixteen he'd managed a young Ronnie Hammond, who'd go on to become the lead singer of the Atlanta Rhythm Section, who I knew from hanging around the bar at Alex Cooley's Electric Ballroom. And Mike was a big Icehouse supporter.

Late in Woody's tenure with Icehouse there'd been plans for a compilation album featuring tracks from early albums plus a couple of new songs. It would provide some interim product between *Man of Colours* and a new studio album. Proposed tracks included 'Hey Little Girl', which had been successful in Europe and Australia. Chrysalis liked the plan; this compilation would make it clear that Icehouse was far more than a one-hit wonder in America. It would also ease the pressure on

Iva Davies, giving him crucial breathing space before tackling a new studio album, an album Chrysalis hoped would break the band worldwide.

When in New York I shared an apartment on West 72nd Street with Woody and Laurie Dunn, MD of Virgin Records in Australia. This arrangement worked well; it was far cheaper than a hotel and was close to everything on the west side of Manhattan. Most weekdays I'd work out of the Chrysalis office on Madison Avenue. My daily commute would take me down 72nd Street and past the constant crowd of mourners outside the Dakota, where John Lennon had been murdered in 1980. Then I'd tackle the busy Central Park West, trying my best to avoid becoming the latest pedestrian statistic. I'd welcome the sight of Central Park, Manhattan's green oasis, as I strolled by the tranquil Strawberry Fields, then over the 'Sheep Meadow' and through to the Upper East Side and the Chrysalis office.

I'd dreaded New York when I first visited in the 1970s. I was troubled by its size, its pace, its seemingly unfriendly atmosphere. For me, Los Angeles was easier to take, more laidback and sunny—it reminded me a lot of Sydney. But I realised very early on that doing business on the west coast was way different to business in New York. In LA it could take days, sometimes weeks, to get a straightforward answer. 'Hey, let's do lunch' was great for the stomach but not good if you wanted a quick response. In New York it was different; people there cut to the chase, abrupt to the point of being rude. But I came to understand that in the Big Apple time was money.

My good friend George Sewitt lived next door to our building on 72nd. George had been KISS's tour manager and was married to an Aussie. George was the go-to guy for shows. I noticed in *The Village Voice* that Al Green was playing a couple of nights at the Beacon Theatre, just two blocks from our apartment. The Reverend was a must-see and I called George. The show was a sell-out and scalpers were on the block flogging tickets at absurdly inflated prices, but George told me not to worry, he had me covered. Security at the Beacon was mainly moonlighting NYPD cops, hard-drinking types, street-tough characters. George knew them well and, with a chair in hand, an off-duty detective from Brooklyn called Steve led me to the last row of the Beacon and set me up in the middle of the aisle. The 99 per cent Black audience must have wondered who the fuck this white dude was—and what was he doing with his own chair? I didn't mind; I was too mesmerised by Reverend Green to take much notice of anything else.

But soon there would be big changes in play at Chrysalis. In August, Mike Bone was fired and Joe Kiener, now president and CEO, assumed a hands-on approach. During our first meeting back in April, I'd found Kiener to be condescending, abrasive and aggressive. I knew he wasn't going to be an easy person to work with. Kiener was feared within the company but not overly respected. A lot of people there wondered what a former shoe salesman knew about selling records. I found the rest of the company relatively easy to get along with, supportive, but I could sense an air of uncertainty; it seemed that everyone was on edge.

The Icehouse compilation, named after their anthemic song 'Great Southern Land', was released in October 1989, peaked at number 2 in Australia but barely caused a ripple in the US. I was really concerned for the band's future there.

*

The set-up in Australia for a new album would be relatively easy considering how big *Man of Colours* had been; both that record and the *Great Southern Land* compilation had passed triple-platinum sales. Icehouse's Oz label was incredibly keen, as was radio in both Australia and New Zealand. But internationally it was a different scenario. Granted, *Man of Colours* and 'Electric Blue' had made waves for the band in the US and Europe, but Iva had a troubled relationship with Chrysalis. Fairly or unfairly, Iva had developed a reputation for being difficult, something I'd become acutely aware of from my earliest meetings with the label.

At Chrysalis's New York HQ, the shuffling of key staff continued. Ex-MTV vice-president John Sykes had taken over Mike Bone's role, while Kiener was putting his stamp on everything: choice of singles, album tracks, even cover artwork. I figured that he had me pegged as some hayseed from Kangaroo Land, so I had to stand my ground. If I didn't get his respect I might as well have packed up and gone home, which really wasn't an option. I believed that the personal issues with Iva were not that significant. I also needed to convince the label that the band and their new record were worth supporting.

David Lord was the producer of *Man of Colours* and he was booked to work on the follow-up. But I received a call from him advising that he was embroiled in a domestic issue and couldn't leave the UK. After some SOS calls, Nick Launay, whose impressive résumé included records with Public Image Ltd, Killing Joke, Gang of Four, INXS and Midnight Oil, was brought in to produce.

Given the commercial success of *Man of Colours*, there were expectations that Iva's next record would be more of the same. *Man of Colours* had made Iva a fully fledged star, with his flowing hair, rock-star looks and some big hit songs. At first Iva enjoyed the adulation but he quickly came to realise how shallow that world was. I think Iva saw himself as a serious musician who was being dismissed as a pop star. He wanted respect, he wanted to be taken seriously—as, like Bowie, someone who could explore the line between pop and innovation.

Accordingly, Iva took a different approach with *Code Blue*. Its subject matter was more parochial, darker and deeper: Iva wrote about notorious 1920s Sydney madam Tilly Devine and the persecution of Indigenous peoples; he even tackled the uncomfortable topic of domestic violence. If the industry and public were expecting *Man of Colours* Mark II, *Code Blue* wasn't going to be that record.

Armed with the tapes of the new album, I bounced between New York, London, Germany and Canada in May 1990 for meetings with the label. I quickly discovered that Chrysalis, too, was hoping for *Man of Colours: The Sequel*, and I was right up against it. The spectre of *Man of Colours* hovered over me like a dark cloud.

'Where is the "Electric Blue"?' I was asked repeatedly.

While I heard what I figured to be lip service—'It's great, can't wait to start working it'—I could sense the underlying negativity towards Iva, and this, combined with Chrysalis's mixed feelings about the new record, really had me concerned. Ensconced in our apartment on West 72nd, it felt a lot like my days at the Oakwood in LA in 1981 trying to work Cold Chisel. After watching the *Great Southern Land* compilation disappear into a sinkhole, I was hoping the new album wouldn't suffer the same fate. I divided my day between the apartment and the Chrysalis building. I'd place calls to the label's local branches across the US and Canada and I got the same responses over and over: 'We're working it hard' or 'They're looking for the "Electric Blue".' It was so frustrating.

Iva chose 'Big Fun' as the lead single in Australia, which to me was a strange option. I wasn't far off the mark, unfortunately, as it struggled to reach the Top 50 in Australia when it was released in July. The second single, 'Miss Divine', did better, peaking at number 16 and setting up the album release for the end of October. But reception from Oz media and radio was mixed; again, *Man of Colours* was constantly used as a yardstick, which became unfair and infuriating.

Predictably, the album never got off the ground in the US and Europe. Radio wasn't interested and the poor sales reflected that. With strong echoes of my troubled time with Cold Chisel and Elektra, it became clear that Chrysalis didn't believe in the album.

In 1991, EMI acquired the remaining 50 per cent of the company, which meant that Iva was now free to shop for a new label. The last couple of years with Chrysalis had been turbulent and had taken their toll. We agreed to step back and focus on the local market for the time being, until a positive suitor came along.

My occasional flatmate Laurie Dunn, who'd had a successful career in the UK before running Virgin Australia, had started his own indie imprint named Massive Records, and it seemed a good fit for Iva in Australia. *Masterfile* was a sixteen-track compilation comprising singles from the first four Flowers/Icehouse studio albums and, as a bonus, featured a new version of 'Love in Motion', recorded with Chrissy Amphlett from the Divinyls, and produced and mixed by American Bill Laswell. By Christmas 1992, the compilation had sold in excess of 50,000 units.

★

Two years after the release of *Unlimited Address*, Don Walker returned to the familiar surrounds of Trafalgar Studios, where Cold Chisel had recorded their debut LP. Don was still using the Catfish moniker and his studio line-up included Charlie Owen, Dave Blight, Paul Burton, Sunil De Silva, Buzz Bidstrup and Hinemihi Kingi, as well as Tony Cook and Ron Laster, two heavyweight funk guys from James Brown's band. Ian Moss added some familiarity and Peter Walker again co-produced.

This new record, which Don titled *Ruby*, was more Australian in subject matter than *Unlimited Address*, as he explored the noir-ish world of sex workers and bodgies, rape and murder; heavy themes that somehow sat comfortably alongside the twangy 'Charleville', which Slim Dusty would turn into a country classic. While *Ruby* was warmly received by music critics, Warners again found it difficult to get any real traction on mainstream FM radio. Alternative darlings Triple J showed little interest, likely a consequence of Don's history with Cold Chisel, who weren't considered a Triple J kind of band. Fortunately, this attitude wasn't shared by community radio stations like 3RRR and 4ZZZ, who supported the record.

In October 1991, we organised a brief run of shows in Sydney and Melbourne. Don decided that instead of sitting behind the piano, away from the spotlight, he'd take on the frontman's role. I disagreed with him. I felt that the absence of keyboards would compromise the performance, as piano was featured on every album track. And Don was known as a keyboard player, not a lead singer.

'Nobody wants to see a frontman sitting behind a piano,' Don countered.

I didn't dare mention Billy Joel or Elton John—or Nick Cave, for that matter, someone Don respected. I lost that argument, but my persistence paid off and Don agreed to give it a go, leading to a comfortable compromise between piano player and frontman.

In all the years I worked with Don, arguments were a rarity. I'd prefer to simply call them differences of opinion.

16

MOVING ON

By the late 1980s, the CD had become the preferred format for selling and buying music. For some time I'd been giving serious consideration to a CD revamp of Chisel's *Radio Songs* greatest hits package. A CD could potentially include up to twenty tracks, compared to a vinyl record's twelve, which gave us something to work with. This was one idea I didn't need to sell to the band—it was a no-brainer.

The criteria for track selection would be strictly the group's most popular tracks—such songs as 'Breakfast at Sweethearts', 'Forever Now', 'Choirgirl' and 'Cheap Wine'—and to avoid any internal ructions, the sole arbiter would be the record label. Simply titled *Chisel* (all the hits to give you the shits), it featured eighteen tracks, and because of its distinct gold-flake artwork it became known as 'the Gold album'.

Warners predicted that it would be a monster and they were on the money. It debuted on the charts at number 3 in August 1991 and by Christmas sales had exceeded 210,000. It was a runaway success, hogging the charts for almost a year.

★

In August 1991, I was in LA for meetings with various record labels, in my suitcase a bunch of demos and albums by Catfish, as well as Judge Mercy and The Hurricanes, two up-and-coming rock bands I'd been managing.

While in LA I had a meeting with Bryan Huttenhower, the head of A&R at A&M Records. Bryan had a prediction, which he shared with me. 'The days of big-budget albums and promo clips are over,' he told me, citing Nirvana, a young Seattle band that had been around for a few years playing the clubs and building a sizeable following along the way.

Nirvana's first album, which was recorded for peanuts compared to what the majors were currently spending, was released on an indie label and had sold more than 30,000 units without any major radio play. As I travelled to New York, the vibe on Nirvana seemed to precede me. Every company I visited told me the same story: change was definitely in the air.

It was a very frustrating trip; the labels liked my acts but no one was willing to commit. It seemed like every record company was waiting to see what was going to happen to the musical landscape. By the end of September, the predictions I'd been hearing became a reality with the emergence of Nirvana's *Nevermind*. Nothing would be the same again.

*

Things were changing for me on a personal level. Gay and I split up in early 1992 and I moved in with Gary Rabin, a good friend who managed Ross Wilson and The Poor Boys. While away from Gay and the kids, I became strongly aware that I had unresolved issues from my childhood that I felt played a role in my current situation. I knew I needed to deal with these issues but didn't have a clue where to start.

My guilt load was heavy: our kids were still young and, being the product of a broken marriage myself, I had an inkling of how they must be feeling. I made a concerted effort to see them every weekend, but I knew that this didn't make up for my absences. My eldest daughter, Shannon, was fourteen and she took the split badly. She'd already had to deal with my break-up with her birth mother, Barbara, who'd returned to Canada; Shannon had grown very close to Gay, who she accepted as her mother, but now her father was absent. It must have been incredibly painful, something I didn't fully understand at the time.

I knew I needed to confront these personal issues. I tried counsellors, group sessions and meditation, but nothing worked for me. A close friend recommended a psychologist who she'd heard good things about, so I made an appointment. Still, I was very apprehensive as I approached a tiny terrace house in Cleveland Street, Surry Hills. The tarnished brass nameplate read 'Acey Choy Psychologist'. A diminutive Anglo woman answered the door and invited me in. Mrs Choy to my surprise was not Asian.

I was aware that I had either ignored or repressed childhood traumas, figuring that they had little or no bearing on my adult life. I quickly discovered from speaking with Acey that this was not necessarily so. Acey had a straightforward approach, homing in on something I'd repressed from my past that she believed was still having an impact on my life. I was overwhelmed by a fear I hadn't experienced since I was an adolescent.

Around the age of eleven or twelve, I was molested by someone close to the family, something my parents never knew about. I guess the thought of not being believed, or the fallout from dropping that bombshell, made me hide it away. I just got on with my life, or I thought that I did. In 33 years I hadn't told anyone, shoving it deep down inside, pretending that it had never happened and would simply go away. Acey explained that it wasn't uncommon for adults who were sexually abused in childhood to have difficulties with relationships, particularly intimate relationships.

I visited Acey a number of times, and with her help I believe I was able to come to terms with what had occurred all those years ago. What happened had happened; it wasn't my fault and I couldn't do anything to change it. I realised I had a choice: let it continue to affect my life, or accept it and break on through. I chose the latter.

I moved into an apartment at Palm Beach, to be closer to Gay and the kids. The situation with some of my old friends grew frosty because of the split; the only ones who didn't seem to pass judgement—or straight-up ignore me—were my surfing buddies. That was a bond that nothing could ever break.

Finally, after two years of my aimless wandering, Gay and I got back together and I returned home to Avalon. I felt as though I'd just been let out of jail after strict confinement. I didn't want to be like my father, who had lived alone in a small apartment for the last 28 years of his life after splitting from my mother. I wanted to be with the woman and the children that I loved, and I wanted a home. I'd never lose sight of that again.

*

Cold Chisel's deal with Warners had expired and they were now free to pursue a new recording set-up. They could go to another label with the obvious guarantee of a substantial advance, but this would mean splitting the catalogue up, as Warners would retain ownership of the first three studio albums. It made much more sense to keep the catalogue together, so I proposed to Warners a pressing and distribution (P&D) arrangement, which, of course, would come with a hefty advance. In essence the band was now its own record company, with Warners handling the manufacture, marketing, promotion and distribution of their catalogue. It was a win–win for both Chisel and Warners, and continued a successful alliance that had started back in 1978.

It was a different situation for me, however, with Icehouse. During 1993, after a fifteen-year association, we agreed to part ways. There was no animosity between Iva and me. It was simply time for both of us to move on.

*

Carmel Noonan was a Warners staffer, someone I trusted within the walls of the company. She was a good friend, and a long-time supporter and fixture at Don Walker's gigs. Over a coffee in a Surry Hills cafe, she raised the idea of a collaboration between Don, Charlie Owen and Tex Perkins (of The Cruel Sea and Beasts of Bourbon). The impetus was a live radio session that Don had recently recorded for Triple J with Charlie, Tex, and James Cruickshank of The Cruel Sea. I could only imagine the puzzled looks on the Triple J hipsters' faces when Don wandered in. 'Alien, alien! Cold Chisel alert!'

'Sounds like a great idea,' I said to Carmel, 'but I'm not sure Don will go for it.'

Yet over the following days, the more I thought about it, the more I saw the merit in it. I took the idea to Don and, predictably, he was lukewarm. I think he had concerns that it could be seen as an attempt on his part to buy 'indie credibility' by working with Tex and Charlie. But I felt that musically it was an interesting concept that would challenge Don and get him out of his comfort zone, which had to be a good thing. Still, I didn't want to push him too hard, knowing that was a sure-fire way of killing the idea stone dead.

I phoned Carmel.

'Maybe you should approach Don?' I suggested. And that did the trick.

In early January 1993, Don and I sat down with Tex over a beer at the bar in the Crest Hotel in Kings Cross, a place known to locals as the Goldfish Bowl. Tex loved the idea of working with Don, but there was a caveat: he was signed exclusively to PolyGram.

In an ideal world, to get the best possible deal for a project like this, it would have been preferable for none of the parties to be signed. Don and Charlie were free agents (Don's contract with Warners had expired), but Tex's contract stymied any approach to other record labels. I knew that it wouldn't be long before the 'jungle telegraph' started sounding about a possible Tex/Don collaboration, so I needed to establish exactly where PolyGram stood.

I spoke with Tex's manager, Wendy Boyes-Hunter, who felt that with my experience in dealing with record labels, I should take the lead. I convened a meeting with Sue Cohen, head of business affairs at PolyGram. She was the lawyer who did the deals.

Sue's response was straight out of the record-company playbook: 'Tex is our artist, we have a long-term investment in him', and so on.

I knew that to try to extricate Tex would be too difficult, perhaps impossible. No one needed a legal stoush that would cost money and possibly kill the vibe. And Tex's contract was airtight. The upside was that PolyGram was a good company with a proven track record and they could do a great job. I proposed that Don and Charlie agree to record with Tex but on a non-exclusive basis. Of course that wasn't how record labels did business; their nature was to own everything, from artists to product. So negotiations began. It was all a bit of a poker game: we knew what we wanted, they knew what they wanted, we just had to play the game. It shouldn't have been a long negotiation, but Sue Cohen adopted a pitbull-like approach.

At times it was intense and frustrating but, in the end, we got what we wanted. Don and Charlie were each able to ensure their independence; Tex, Don and Charlie made the album *Sad But True*; and PolyGram got a very successful record.

'The songs bring to life a low-life world of late-night bars, transvestites, girls with tattoos and lives gone wrong,' noted Lynden Barber in *The Sydney Morning Herald*. *Sad But True* would go on to feature in the *100 Best Australian Albums* book and launch a great musical partnership.

17

TEENAGE LOVE: THE CATALYST TO HEALING

Ten years had passed since Cold Chisel had called time on their career. During that decade I'd managed to keep their legacy alive—and profitable—with careful marketing and strategic releases of their music. Cold Chisel had become a staple of FM radio, a big achievement for a band that was once seen as having no commercial potential. While FM radio kept the flame burning, the impact of Jim's solo career and Ian's 1989 number 1 album *Matchbook*—for which Don had written six tracks and co-written three more with Ian and one with Steve—couldn't be underestimated.

By the end of 1993, Cold Chisel had sold in excess of three million albums in Australia. Even though all the studio LPs were readily available and continued to sell, I needed something to give their catalogue another good kick along. The 'Gold' greatest-hits package was still very much the flagship, but after releasing *The Last Stand* concert in 1992, the archives seemed to be bare. Contrary to popular belief, the release of Chisel's back catalogue wasn't strictly about preaching to the converted. In order for the band's legacy to not just survive but grow, we needed new fans.

Now and then rumours swirled around that the band might re-form, but they were just rumours—nothing more. Jim was in the headlines in mid-1994 when, after financial problems, he decamped to France to get away from the noise and clear his head. His stocks were down: his two most recent releases hadn't done great business. Ian's follow-up to *Matchbook* hadn't met expectations, either. The one positive was Don, who was gaining real traction with the Tex, Don and Charlie project.

Michael Lawrence was a Chisel advocate and a good friend, who'd later write the definitive Cold Chisel and Midnight Oil chronologies. Michael had told me over the years about Chisel bootlegs that diehard fans had in their collections. He spoke in hushed tones, as if he was passing along the secrets for making an atomic bomb. There were live recordings and copies of studio demos that had been surreptitiously acquired. Michael claimed that among them were some unreleased songs. I was intrigued.

I had a sizeable collection of Chisel recording tapes, some pre-dating 1977, stored in a climate-controlled vault in Botany. I'd often spend time in the vault trying to catalogue the contents of several old, mostly unlabelled cardboard boxes. Sprinkled among the album masters and live recordings were tracks I didn't know or had forgotten about. Many were songs that hadn't made it onto a finished album. I'd ask Don if anything was releasable and he'd dismiss them as incomplete songs, sketches or tracks that just weren't good enough. I had learned from my years with Don that when he dismissed something, the last thing to do was try to change his mind. The man was an immovable object.

But fuelled by Michael Lawrence's enthusiasm and without

telling the band, I set out on a clandestine mission to track down these mystery bootlegs and explore if anything stored in the vault was worth releasing. Perhaps the appeal would be strictly for Chisel trainspotters, but I wondered if there might also be some important historic markers in the band's development. I felt like I was panning for gold.

A source of some of these early bootlegs was demo sessions at Pepper Studios in Adelaide during June 1976, before the band shifted to Sydney. After a bit of detective work, a quarter-inch reel-to-reel tape landed on my desk. It contained eight songs, seven of which were new to me, along with a very early version of 'Daskarzine', which was on the first Chisel album.

At the same time, I continued to rummage around in the storage vault in Botany. As Don had told me, much of the material there was incomplete; some songs were album cast-offs while others were fragments that would surface later in new songs. But when I listened to the recordings, what jumped out at me were the rawness and excitement that so often formed the pure essence of a great band in its infancy.

I compiled some tracks that I felt had promise and mailed five cassettes off to the guys. A week passed with no response. But the phone eventually rang—it was Jim, and he was enthusiastic. Over the next few days, Ian, Phil and Steve also called. They laughed about some songs, but they also said, in a few instances, 'I'd forgotten about that one.'

The clincher, however, would be Don and I awaited his call, fully expecting a response along the lines of, 'Mate, I thought I told you it was a waste of time.' But much to my surprise, when Don did call, he said he liked what he heard.

So where exactly would we go from here? There were plenty of suggestions: they'd make good B sides, or bonus tracks, but of course we didn't have any new material to add them to. After taking a very deep breath, I said: 'I think they could stand on their own as a legitimate release.' After a long pause, the guys' response was a unanimous yes.

We set out some guidelines: the material could not have been commercially released before, and it had to be put out as per the original recording—there'd be no overdubbing of vocals or instruments. Of the fourteen tracks selected, we fudged the rules on two songs: 'The Party's Over', which had appeared on a limited-edition single with the *East* album, and 'A Little Bit of Daylight', which Jim had included on his *Bodyswerve* album. The other twelve songs had never before seen the light of day.

Due to their vintage and the poor quality of the recordings, they required work and money to get them to a releasable standard. Over time, magnetic tape can deteriorate; when you run the tape through a playback machine, it can shred, leaving it ruined. The only safe method to preserve the performances was to bake the original tape in an oven—yes, you heard right—then run it through a playback machine onto a digital hard drive. Even then, you might only get one run-through before the tape made like a snake and started shedding its skin.

Don Bartley had mastered many of the Cold Chisel albums and was the guru given the onerous task of saving some of the bad tapes. He sat huddled in a tiny room in Studios 301, surrounded by banks of strange machines. We watched anxiously as the old tapes, oven baked, safely made it onto the computer hard drive. As each song finished its journey, we'd look at Don, who'd give us a reassuring nod.

I could sense that working together on this project helped heal some of the wounds that had existed since the band's split in 1983. The five guys were genuinely interested in the process and excited by the results. Perhaps this project gave them a chance to reflect on how good they were, and what could have been. We called the album *Teenage Love* and it reached number 6 on the charts in October 1994, eventually going gold. I even convinced the wonderful Ita Buttrose, the subject of the *East* song 'Ita', to feature in the TV commercial for the album, which was filmed at Vaucluse House in Sydney.

★

When Jim was preparing to leave for France in June 1994, all the members of Chisel and their partners attended a fare-well party. Band relations were pretty amicable—working on *Teenage Love* had definitely eased old tensions. Towards the end of a boozy evening, Jim pulled me aside.

'Are we ever going to get the band back together?' he asked.

I was a bit taken aback. 'Well,' I replied, 'I guess it's up to you, mate.'

'No,' Jim said, looking straight at me. 'It's really up to you.'

Hmm, I thought to myself, *maybe there's a real chance it might happen*. I figured what Jim meant was that I was the only person who could put the pieces of the band back together, which was true. Within the Chisel camp, however, it was no secret that Don had the casting vote—without his thumbs-up, it would never happen. And right now Don's stocks were looking good: he had plans for a new solo album and was about to go out on a national tour. My gut told me it wasn't the right time to raise the subject.

★

In early 1995, Don released his third album, the first under his own name, the morbidly titled *We're All Gunna Die*. Once again, he was exploring places off the map and their colourful characters, all set to a soundtrack of country/bluesy rock. Like his first two albums, *We're All Gunna Die* received glowing reviews and he drew good crowds to his live shows, although album sales weren't great. These solo projects helped to lift Don's profile, drawing attention away from his all-too-familiar Cold Chisel association.

For more than eighteen years I'd been in almost daily contact with Don, talking business or rugby league: Don supported Brisbane and I was a Manly fan, so our conversations could get very lively. We always talked freely, although I understood that the subject of a Cold Chisel reunion was a no-go zone. But the conversation I'd had with Jim stuck in my mind; I just had to work out how to approach Don. One thing I knew was that it wasn't a conversation to have on the phone.

Don was booked to appear at the 1995 Maleny Folk Festival, an annual event at Woodford on the Sunshine Coast, staged around Christmas time. I flew up with him. Don played on the Saturday night to a boisterous crowd of hippies, ferals, hipsters and folkies. On our return flight to Sydney the next morning, I decided that the time was right to pose the million-dollar question. I knew I had a captive audience—unless Don had somehow stowed a parachute in his carry-on. Looking back, I wish I hadn't raised the issue of a new Chisel record then, because for the duration of flight QF513 I was subjected to a complete revisiting of the band's history and the multitude of reasons why a reunion was not on Don's radar—and why oh why would I raise such a stupid question in the first place? We couldn't have reached Sydney quickly enough.

When I got home, I spoke about it with Gay.

'Don't worry,' she smiled, 'it's only Donald. He'll come around eventually.' I admired her positivity.

I returned to the office in the second week of January and the phone rang. It was Don. I braced myself for a rerun of his in-flight diatribe.

'Well,' Don said down the line. 'When are we going to talk about this Cold Chisel album?'

I was lost for words. Had I heard Don right? For a moment I thought he was taking the piss, but then he continued. 'If we're going to get this together, then we have to do it properly.' He invited me to his place to talk more.

Don lived in a Victorian terrace in Elizabeth Bay, a locale with an interesting history. The house next door was owned by former prime minister Paul Keating, while Don's place was once the site of an infamous illegal gambling club, The Roslyn Social Club, owned and operated in the 1950s and '60s by 'colourful Sydney identity' Perce Galea.

As we had done over the years, Don and I headed for the basement, his personal sanctuary. The room contained a grand piano and an elegant but comfortable leather lounge that rested against a wall. Cuban cigar boxes sat on a makeshift shelf, housing a variety of tapes, containing the songs and ideas that were his stock in trade. As we settled in, we were served tea in pure-white china by Firoozeh, Don's Iranian-born wife. She was an amazing woman who'd escaped her country by fleeing over the mountains during the revolution in the late 1970s.

Don made it clear that he had several conditions if this reunion was to happen.

'Mate,' he said in his deep drawl, 'this has to be done for the right reasons. It's not a cash grab.' He went on to say that there needed to be a new studio album and he didn't want to be the sole songwriter; everyone had to contribute. Finally, he told me, everyone had to come to this contractually unencumbered. The reunion needed to be complication free.

On a warm Sunday morning in mid-February, Gay and I headed over to Kensington, to the home of Jane's sister Jep and her husband Mark 'Diesel' Lizotte. Jim and Jane had arrived from France for a quick visit and were staying there. During a large breakfast—every meal with the Barneses was big—we discussed the possibility of a reunion and what that would entail. I made sure that I laid out Don's conditions fully so that there were no misunderstandings.

'In particular,' I stressed, 'everyone has to be contractually free to make a record and perform it.'

Jim smiled and nodded his head in agreement. He understood. He also seemed very keen.

By the end of March, Steve, Phil, Ian and Don had been getting together regularly, jamming and going over song ideas. Steve and Don had quite a selection of songs, Phil had a couple, but Ian had nothing at that stage. During one of these get-togethers they put a call through to Jim in France to see if he had any songs.

Apparently he did, because ten days later a six-song cassette landed on my office desk. I wasted no time and headed over to Don's. The cassette contained, among other things, an early version of 'Never Stop Loving You'. As the tape played, Don seemed to be gazing at a spot on the floor, his head nodding gently. Don was not the kind of guy to get overly excited, but when the tape ended, he looked across at me.

'Mate,' he said, 'there are some good ideas here.'

Jim and Jane were back in Sydney at the end of April 1996

and all of the band, apart from Phil, got together for dinner at the Bayswater Brasserie in Kings Cross. The atmosphere was very positive, everyone was in high spirits, and I went home thinking that there was a real chance of this actually getting off the ground.

Our business manager Gino and I carefully put together a business plan, which we took to Don in early June. We sat on the couch in Don's basement and watched him carefully study the pages. At times he would pause to clarify a detail. Finally, he laid the plan down and looked up.

'The numbers are great,' he said. 'They make sense. We just have to make sure that we're totally free of any impositions.' Gino and I both knew what he was referring to: Ian and Jim currently had record deals. They weren't yet free agents.

★

Hernandez was Don's 'go-to' place where he wrote and pondered new songs in quiet anonymity. It was just up the hill from the site of the old Sydney Stadium. Its walls were covered in old bullfighting posters, while hessian bags of coffee beans were stacked behind a tiny counter, and the aroma of freshly ground coffee permeated the air.

In early July, I met with Don and Ian, and Ian's manager Mick Mazzone, at Hernandez for coffee. I was reminded that I was only a short stroll from Kings Cross when I looked up to see a well-known Sydney identity stroll past the cafe.

I got straight to the point: a Cold Chisel reunion was very much on the cards, and the only stumbling blocks were Ian and Jim's current deals. Ian had signed to Mushroom Records in 1988; after the success of *Matchbook*, his follow-up *Worlds*

Away hadn't done the business the label had hoped for. Since recording his third album, *Petrolhead*, Ian had run into problems with Mushroom, who expressed concerns over the LP's commercial viability. Mazzone had advised them bluntly that if they didn't like the album, they should drop Ian. In a move that Mushroom would regret, they agreed. *Petrolhead* was released by the independent distribution label TWA. But it was a one-off deal, which meant that Ian was now contractually free.

One down, one to go.

The day after the Hernandez meeting I received a call from Jim in France, checking on the current situation. I explained that the only impediment remaining was his deal with Mushroom.

'Jim,' I told him, 'you need to sort it out or nothing will happen.'

'Okay,' he replied. 'I'll talk to Gudinski and get back to you.'

Six days after speaking with Jim, my phone rang. It was Ian Smith, who was in France acting as Jim's personal manager. He asked how things were going with the Cold Chisel reunion.

I gave him the rundown. 'It's down to Jim to sort out the Mushroom side of things,' I told him. 'If that's not resolved, then frankly it's not going to happen. Has he spoken to Michael?'

'Yes, they've been talking,' was Smithy's not-so-convincing reply.

A week later, on a chilly winter's morning, I got a call from Michael Gudinski. The tone of his call was so predictable I should have placed a bet at Ladbrokes. 'Jim is a major Mushroom artist,' he made clear. 'We have invested heavily in his career and there is no way we will give him a release.' He was basically telling me that Jim was Mushroom's property.

Gino and I had anticipated that this would be Michael's reaction, and there was nothing to gain by arguing with him. The long game was our only option.

I called Don with an update.

'Well,' he said after a long silence, 'I'm just going to get on with my own career. If it's sorted out, great. Otherwise we get on with our lives. Good luck.'

I knew that Jim wanted to come home from France and work with Chisel, so I had to sit back and see what his next move would be. Meanwhile, Gudinski called to tell me he'd be in Sydney the following week and that we should meet. I had known Gudinski reasonably well for many years. During most of the Dirty Pool era we'd been in direct competition with his agency, Premier. And Mushroom was one of the labels that had passed on Cold Chisel before my involvement, which I'm sure they regretted.

I'd once been in LA on Chisel business when I ran into Gudinski and Michael Chugg. They were going to see The Allman Brothers Band in Santa Barbara and asked me to come along. They'd rented a brand-new red Mustang that had some serious grunt. Gudinski took the wheel and during the entire trip up the coast, he and Chugg argued about anything and everything like old friends sometimes do, Gudinski's foot flat to the floor the whole time. As the Mustang weaved in and out of traffic and the two Michaels continued bickering, I sat in the back, gripping the seatbelt and praying the journey would soon be over. As much as I loved the Allmans, it was the car ride that stuck with me.

Soon after his call, Gudinski and I sat down at the Ritz-Carlton in Double Bay. Michael wore his game face. If we wanted a Chisel re-formation with Jim involved, he told me, then he wanted the reunion album for Mushroom—oh, and in addition, he wanted the distribution rights to the four Cold Chisel albums owned by the band.

I looked at Michael with a wry smile and shook my head. 'No way!'

I wondered how he knew that the current pressing and distribution deal with Warners was up for renegotiation. Then it hit me. Thanks, Jim.

★

The Barneses arrived back in town in early August, and Jim phoned me for a progress report.

'It doesn't look promising,' I told him. 'We've hit an impasse with Michael.'

Jim was clearly frustrated but laid out a defence of Mushroom's position.

'They have invested serious money in my career,' he said, 'so their stance is understandable.'

I told him that I appreciated what he was saying but Gudinski's proposal was totally out of the question. 'This is your problem, not Cold Chisel's,' I told him. 'Don is free, Ian's free; in fact, everyone's free except you. If you really want to do this, then you have to sort it out with Mushroom.'

A week later, Gudinski, Jim, Smithy, Don, Gino and I had a sit-down, again at the Ritz-Carlton. I knew where it was going to go, but at least Don was along to express his point of view. Michael led off, enthusiastically prosecuting the case for Mushroom.

'Unless Jim gets a full release to record with Chisel, then there will be no reunion,' Don told him. When Michael replied

'In your dreams', I knew we had a Mexican stand-off on our hands.

By September, the wall of secrecy had started to crumble. With Jim back in town for good and in the wake of the Gudinski meetings, people were talking. I received lots of calls: 'I heard on the street that Chisel are getting back together—is it true?'

'No, there's no substance in that' became my standard reply.

Then an old nemesis from days gone by re-emerged: *TV Week* ran a story suggesting that both Cold Chisel and Australian Crawl were re-forming and may be going out on tour together. How the journalist had come up with that ridiculous scenario was a mystery to me. Chinese whispers, perhaps.

★

Another month passed and I got on with other Chisel business. I was in serious discussions with Brian Harris, the chair of Warners, as the current distribution deal that covered the four Cold Chisel–owned albums—*Circus Animals, The Barking Spiders Live, Twentieth Century* and *The Last Stand*—was set to expire.

Gudinski called me again. He reiterated that there was no way he was willing to release Jim, but he had a compromise: he was willing to let Jim record with Chisel for another company, but only with an override (that is, Mushroom would get a percentage of sales, even if the band signed with another label). He again made it clear that his overall desire was for Mushroom to release the Cold Chisel record—and he believed that he could match any other offer.

I hung up the phone with mixed feelings. I discussed this with the band; some could see it was potentially a way around the impasse, others were adamant, 'no way'. At least we now had a potential release for Jim, albeit with a Mushroom imposition hanging over it like a big black cloud. I sat down with Gino and tried to work out what to do next.

We came up with a strategy to test the market, to see what offers might be made. Then at least we'd be able to see what effect Mushroom's override would have on the bottom line.

I began confidential discussions with the major labels, and by mid-December I'd had offers from all of them, including Mushroom. As we'd predicted, all were highly lucrative and extremely attractive, but Mushroom offered the best net-revenue return.

Gino and I headed over to Don's with the breakdown. Don pondered the spreadsheet for a while; his reaction was that all the other companies had tailored their offers subject to a Jim/Mushroom override.

'Why on earth would they under-pitch deliberately?' I countered. It made no sense. In all my discussions with other labels, I'd never raised the subject of an override—my position had been that Jim was free to record with Cold Chisel.

Don wasn't convinced; he felt that the band was being forced into a Mushroom deal. I shared his frustration and was also reluctant to jump into bed, so to speak, with Gudinski, having spent most of my time in Australia in direct competition with him. But all I could do was play the cards in front of me.

I'd never felt so disheartened dealing with Chisel matters before. Furthermore, for the first time in my relationship with Don, I sensed an element of mistrust. I think he felt that Gino and I were pushing him into making a decision motivated by our own financial self-interest. All I knew was that if I gave up on the reunion now, it would never happen. The band would probably never play together again.

*

Don phoned me in early January. 'I'm pulling out of the project,' he told me.

I knew there was no point in arguing with him—he had a set of parameters and they hadn't been met, so he was out. But I had invested too much of my life in this band over the past twenty years; I wasn't going to let it die. I was convinced that there was light at the end of the tunnel—albeit a very long, dark tunnel—and I had to keep going.

Things went strangely quiet for a couple of weeks after Don's call; I figured everyone was in a state of shock over his decision. But in mid-January Steve called me—he'd only just spoken to Don and learned about his exit. Over the next couple of days the others called, expressing their disappointment and frustration. Some of the guys felt that if the price of getting the band back together was an override to Mushroom, then it was worth it; they also felt that Don was being unreasonable. At the same time, they agreed that there would be no reunion without Don.

I knew that if the impasse was going to be broken, Jim and Jane needed to be involved. Gino and I arranged a meeting with them. They clearly felt that Don was being unrealistic; their contention was that as Jim was under contract, it wasn't unreasonable to assume that Mushroom should be compensated if he recorded for someone else. It was just the price of doing business.

While they may have had a valid point, the fact remained that the other four guys were free to record unencumbered: why should they be penalised because of Jim's situation? Jim and Jane agreed to discuss it with their lawyer Peter Thompson, and with Gudinski.

I'd known Peter Thompson for a number of years and he was unquestionably one of the best negotiators in the Australian entertainment industry. I hoped that Peter might be able to take some of the heat out of what was a seemingly irreconcilable situation. Gudinski and I were getting nowhere; Don had dug in; Jim was stuck between a rock and a hard place; and the other three were standing on the dock looking on as the SS *Cold Chisel* slowly drifted towards an iceberg.

Jim and Don met with Peter at his office at Tress Cocks & Maddox, one of the country's biggest legal firms, and finally Mushroom agreed to drop their override demand if they had the option to match the best offer from another label. Don, while still cautious, agreed, conditional on receiving a letter from Gudinski verifying this. Finally, it seemed like we had some kind of solution.

18

OPERA HOUSE

The letter from Mushroom had a calming effect on the band, and in mid-April 1997, they entered Jim's home studio in a relaxed and positive state of mind. New ideas for songs were tossed around, while the laughs and irreverent banter that had always been a part of their chemistry returned.

Jim's home studio was okay for a few days, but to get down to serious work we needed a safe and discreet place for the band to rehearse and write songs. Hiring a rehearsal room was far too open to the general public; it'd be a matter of hours before the place was swarming with media and rubberneckers. I wanted a pressure-free situation for the band. After all, they hadn't played together for thirteen years and needed to ease themselves back into the process of writing and playing. They needed space to do what they did best.

Rehearsal Room 2 lay deep within the bowels of the Sydney Opera House. The space was big enough for an orchestra to rehearse, and it was secure, soundproof and air-conditioned. There was an unobtrusive place for the guys to park their cars, and the Opera House staff, more than likely, would have zero interest in Cold Chisel. It was the perfect spot.

On the day of my first visit, I left my car at Manly and caught the ferry across the harbour. I looked over to the Opera House and pinched myself; somewhere deep beneath those majestic sails was Cold Chisel, back together again. It was a very strange sensation, quite surreal. As I ambled along the Circular Quay forecourt past the hordes of tourists and workers, I wondered how they might have reacted if they knew Chisel were playing just a few hundred metres away. Perhaps most people wouldn't give a fuck, but it mattered to me. A lot.

I entered the Opera House and paused for a moment outside the rehearsal room. The only sign that it was occupied was a note on the door, scrawled in felt-tip: 'Keep Out'. I suddenly asked myself a question: what if they couldn't play anymore and had lost their old magic? *What if it was Spinal Tap?* I placed my ear against the door and heard some familiar sounds coming from inside. I smiled and walked in and within minutes realised that yes, they could still play. It sounded ever so sweet.

Jim was perched on a stool, a sheet of A4 paper in his hand. Amps, drums, keyboards, several guitars and a small PA system were spread out in front of a large whiteboard, upon which was written a list of song titles. The song they were working on stopped and started, and the guys laughed at any problems they encountered. Don and Jim seemed to be conducting proceedings, with the others falling in behind them as a song began to take shape. The mood in the room was great.

★

When the possibility of a Chisel reunion arose, I had an idea to document it on film. I knew that if it did come to fruition, the footage would be a very valuable asset. This wasn't the realm of a big production company; I needed someone who could blend in, fly-on-the-wall style. The person who came to mind was Robert Hambling. Before moving to Sydney from the UK, Robert had worked on *Pink Floyd—The Wall*. Robert's father Gerry was an award-winning film editor with such credits as *Midnight Express* and *The Commitments* to his name.

I'd known Robert since he'd produced a clip for the 1992 rerecording of Icehouse's 'Love in Motion', featuring Chrissy Amphlett. Our connection continued when he filmed some super-8 footage of a Don Walker show at the Metro in Sydney. Robert's wife, Adrienne Overall, had shot the cover of Ian's *Matchbook* album.

I phoned him well before the reunion was finalised and admitted up-front that it might not happen, but if it did it would be a fascinating ride. Robert said he was in. He first joined us when the band began meetings in early April 1997; initially the guys were aware of his camera but as time went on Robert blended in, becoming a sort of invisible presence.

I had known journalist Anthony O'Grady (known as AOG) since his days as editor and founder of *RAM*. He'd followed Chisel's career even before their move to Sydney and had forged a close personal friendship with the band. After the demise of *RAM*, AOG continued his career as a much-respected music writer for *The Bulletin*, *National Times*, *Sydney Morning Herald* and *Financial Review*. In early February 1998 I received a formal letter from him outlining an idea for a book built around the re-formation. It fell right into line with my desire to properly document the Chisel reunion.

It was now time to finalise a recording deal for the new record. Most offers had been textbook: long-term, big advance, big royalty. But I was looking for something entirely different—a joint venture deal. That was where the costs of recording, promotion and marketing were initially funded by the record company, but these costs were then deducted from the wholesale sales. The end profit would be split between the distributor (record company) and the owner (Cold Chisel).

The initial response was predictable: 'You must be kidding!' Occasionally I heard something a little stronger. While I didn't hear the actual words from *The Castle*—'Tell him he's dreamin''—I'm pretty sure a few people thought it. And when I advised the various label heads that the profit split was not a straight 50/50, a look of sheer horror crossed their faces. The paradigm had changed. The guys in the band were backing themselves to sell a lot of records, and therefore the distributor wouldn't be at risk, but at the same time the distributor wouldn't make as much as they would from a standard record deal. Yet as far as I was concerned, Cold Chisel was not your standard band.

By early June, all the record company offers were ready to be tabled to the band. Gino passed around five spreadsheets for final analysis, but my eyes didn't leave Don as he scrutinised every figure. It was clear that Mushroom's offer was the pick, but unless it received Don's imprimatur, it was a no-go. The rest of the guys knew that too.

Finally, Don raised his head slowly, looked straight at me and agreed that Mushroom's offer was the best.

*

There would be obvious fallout with Warners in light of the Mushroom deal. Although they had made a substantial offer, Mushroom's was even bigger. The current Warners pressing and distribution arrangement was about to expire so I had to carefully consider our options. I could now take those four band-owned albums and go elsewhere, but again it would mean splitting the catalogue, with Warners retaining the product they owned, namely *Cold Chisel, Breakfast at Sweethearts* and *East*. And splitting up the catalogue would almost certainly dilute future sales.

I looked to Warners chair, Brian Harris, to come up with a solution that worked for both of us. I liked Brian; he was a straight shooter, tough but not governed by a massive ego. Brian came back to me with a credible solution: if we granted Warners the rights to the four Cold Chisel–owned albums for an agreed term, when that expired, they would relinquish the ownership of the three albums they controlled. That ownership of all seven albums would then revert to the band. In turn, Cold Chisel would agree to leaving their entire catalogue with Warners for a further agreed period.

As we shook hands, I said, 'Oh, and by the way Brian, this will come with a sizeable advance, right?' He smiled and said, 'I expected that would be the case.'

★

Meanwhile, I was confronted by a *Daily Telegraph* headline: 'Cold Chisel reforms'. Our secret was out. Their 'ace reporter' Dino Scatena had somehow managed to extract from Ian, who was promoting his *Petrolhead* album, a comment that the band had been having a 'quiet play together'. Dino wasn't going to be scooped and he ran the story.

The morning the story appeared, even before I'd showered, I began getting calls from journalists, media outlets, TV stations, radio people, concert promoters, agents—even photographers. I stuck with my well-rehearsed reply: 'They're just rumours—wishful thinking, nothing more.' When I got to the Opera House, Ian was slumped uncomfortably in a corner of the rehearsal room. I felt sorry for him, as some of the guys were genuinely annoyed by his slip-up. Others, however, were relieved that the truth was finally out—as a consequence, it would be much harder for anyone to back out.

The titles of more than 60 songs were now written on the whiteboard in Rehearsal Room 2, which would be whittled down to a still generous 28 by the time we decamped. But exactly what a Cold Chisel album in 1997 should sound like presented a dilemma. It had always been difficult to pigeonhole the band: I believed their strength lay in their ability to integrate a range of rock and pop styles without losing their distinctive sound. There was an underlying concern that they might sound outdated, irrelevant or, horror of all horrors, soft.

I felt that after so many years apart, the band would benefit from having someone independent oversee their record, which led to discussions around the dreaded 'P-word'. Jim saw the merit in bringing someone in, but Steve thought they could produce themselves. Don, Ian and Phil, however, liked the idea of a co-producer.

We started by considering internationals. A producer who immediately came to mind was Dave Jerden, an American who'd worked with The Rolling Stones, Talking Heads, Red Hot Chili Peppers, Alice in Chains, Jane's Addiction and Herbie Hancock. Jerden expressed genuine interest—at least until the opportunity arose for him to do an Offspring album. We then had a similar experience with Kevin Shirley, who'd had great success with the Baby Animals and Silverchair, and who lived nearby in Avalon. Kevin was keen, too, until the opportunity of working on a new Aerosmith record emerged. As for Mark Opitz, despite his great history with Chisel, we ruled him out because the band wanted to work with someone new.

The guys already knew Charles Fisher, having recorded their debut album at his Trafalgar Studios. Charles's production credits included Air Supply, Moving Pictures and Hoodoo Gurus, and he'd recently scored a worldwide smash with Savage Garden. Charles was a song man, brilliant with arrangements, and he agreed to come down to the Opera House to have a listen to the new material. Charles liked what he heard; he even made a few production suggestions. That night, feeling quite excited about the possibility of Charles getting involved, I received a call from Steve asking for his phone number. Steve seemed upbeat about Charles too, and I gave him his number, but inside I began to feel a little uneasy.

The phone rang early the next morning. It was Charles. He told me that he loved the idea of working with Chisel but as a result of Savage Garden's success he'd been inundated with international offers and needed to take advantage of that. I told him I understood but was hugely disappointed. My gut reaction was that after his conversation with Steve, Charles had reached the conclusion that it was too complicated. To be fair, though, Charles later denied that was the case.

To add to my woes, my father passed away after a long struggle with melanoma. He had been an avid sun-lover, coming from an era when everyone sunbaked all day long without worrying about the side effects. He was 85 when his cancer was detected and was too old for surgery. Dad wasn't a religious man but as his final days ticked over, he told me he was quite scared; he didn't know what would happen or where he'd go when he died. His fear was almost childlike. Our father–son dynamic had reversed. I'd dismissed the whole heaven-or-hell scenario early in my life and I struggled for a reassuring answer.

All I could offer was a feeble, 'It'll be okay.'

Being the eldest child, it was my duty to take care of Dad's eulogy. It wasn't easy to write, and I knew it was going to be equally tough delivering it at the chapel, which was packed with family and friends, and people from Dad's film, television and rugby journalism past. I counted seven former Wallaby captains, along with seven former Wallaby coaches. Heads turned when the five members of Cold Chisel turned up in support and took their place in the pews. Radio shock-jock Alan Jones had already given Dad a warm eulogy of his own on his popular morning radio program.

As I stood out front of the gathering, I was fairly confident I could make it through without collapsing in a blubbery heap. Everything was going fine until just shy of the finish line a simple word left a cricket ball–sized lump in my throat. My brief silence was deafening; I didn't dare glance at the crowd. I knew they were with me, but one look would have unlocked the floodgates. I refocused on that A4 cheat sheet in front of me, took a deep breath and managed to struggle through.

★

Cold Chisel's producer problems continued well into October 1997. One idea was to investigate some of the younger guys who were making interesting records. Paul McKercher had worked with The Cruel Sea, Spiderbait and You Am I, and the band decided to give him a crack.

We booked a week in Megaphon Studios, which was located in an old factory in the backstreets of St Peters in Sydney. Ian had recorded his *Petrolhead* record there with Don, and they loved the room. But I sensed trouble as soon as the band's equipment arrived and there were disagreements about where to set things up. Tempers started to fray. Jim wasn't happy, mumbling something about 'amateur hour'. I feared he was close to a meltdown. It was the first strong indication that he was no longer in control of his partying. In fact, I sensed that Jim's partying was in control of him.

Finally, some songs were laid down, but it wasn't an especially positive atmosphere. At the end of the week, some of the guys wanted to continue with Paul; others didn't. It felt like we were getting nowhere.

★

As if I didn't have enough on my plate, with my father dying and the ongoing Chisel hassles, I was about to turn 50. My family and friends told me that we were going to have a party, but I told them that there was just too much shit going on and I didn't have the time or energy. I reached the milestone on Wednesday, 19 November 1997, and after getting presents from Gay and the kids, and having lunch with Robert Hambling and Don, I'd had a pleasant enough day but was glad it was over.

I awoke on the Saturday morning to the news that Michael Hutchence was dead. I was gutted; I'd known Michael since the early days of INXS. How could this have happened? As details emerged of his tragic final hours, I was left with a hollow feeling. The guy had so much talent; he was so young; this shouldn't have happened. As the day dragged on, it was hard not to think about Michael.

'We're going to dinner tonight,' Gay told me. 'That might cheer you up.'

We headed off to Avalon RSL with our close friends Mark and Cas Edwards. As we reached the club, I coincidentally recalled that this was a venue that Chisel and INXS had regularly filled early on in their careers. As I followed Mark up the stairs, I tapped him on the shoulder.

'Where are we going?'

'Oh, the restaurant is upstairs now,' he told me, a bit unconvincingly, as we pushed the door open.

I heard a deafening white noise and looked on, stunned, as a sea of smiling faces—surfers, musos, family, friends—rushed forward, kissing, hugging and backslapping me. How the fuck hadn't I known about this? The Hurricanes were on stage and within minutes they'd fired up and the dance floor was packed.

Somewhere between my second and fifth shots of vodka, one of my surfer mates sidled up to me and asked, 'Are Chisel playing?'

I laughed at the thought and reassured him that The Hurricanes would shake the place up plenty. But then I noticed a piano on the side of the small stage. No way, surely, I thought to myself. Soon after, for the first time in thirteen years, Cold Chisel plugged in and played, running through 'Merry Go Round', 'Roadhouse Blues', 'Bow River', 'Green River', 'Cry Me a River' and a sneak peek of a track from the new album called 'Baby's on Fire'. I couldn't have asked for a better present, and everyone there who understood how historically significant this was went nuts.

Later that night, very tired and more than a bit emotional, I was delivered to my home, courtesy of my surfer mates, in a shopping trolley.

★

The band decided not to continue with Paul McKercher and turned to Rick Will, a Nashville-based engineer/producer who'd worked on Jim's 1993 record *Heat*. The 'Rickster' was a three-time Grammy nominee who'd worked with artists as diverse as Nine Inch Nails, Ziggy Marley and Bobby Brown. Rick loved to create his own unique studio atmosphere: bizarre plastic figurines littered the recording desk, palm trees were dotted around the studio, and a thick incense cloud hung in the air. All that was needed was Queen Laveau, a gris-gris and a dead chicken and we would have had our own voodoo temple.

The band had laid down nineteen tracks with Rick in Q Studios when I received an unexpected call from Rick's manager, Gary Rabin. Gary felt that Rick should have been getting more points on the record than we had initially agreed upon. Gary was a good mate of mine and an equally good hustler, but I told him that no, the deal stayed as we'd originally agreed. And with that, the 'Rickster' sessions were officially over, although he would receive engineering credits for 'Yakuza Girls', 'Water into Wine', 'Pretty Little Thing' and 'He Can't Believe It's Over With You'.

★

In its early days, the band always mixed their studio recordings with live work. Now some of the guys felt that they needed to play live to rejuvenate their old fire in the studio. Ian was the most vocal—he made it known that in order to give his studio playing 'a good kick in the arse', he needed to get on stage in front of an audience.

I could see that it was a good idea, but there were some obvious problems. A big show in any of the major markets would attract a lot of unwanted pressure and scrutiny. If they played badly, it might cast a dark shadow over their reunion. Jim had continued playing live as a solo act in and around the various sessions for the new album, and I put in a call to Michael Long, Jim's personal manager. My idea was for Chisel to play a couple of gigs in rural New South Wales under the guise of a Jimmy Barnes show. Broken Hill, Bourke and Dubbo jumped out as ideal locations, and it was agreed. Secrecy was now paramount.

At midday on Friday, 20 February 1998, two small private planes left Mascot, heading to Broken Hill, the 'Silver City', where the band was to play at the 100-year-old Theatre Royal Hotel. Several hours later, as Chisel shuffled on stage, the response of those in the full house ranged from curiosity to amazement. There were some who were too young for Chisel but loved 'Barnesy', and they focused on him as he strode to centrestage. The older audience members, meanwhile, gaped in disbelief. As the first notes of 'Cheap Wine' rang through the room, I could see people in the crowd mouthing: 'It's fucking Cold Chisel!' The roar was deafening.

We flew from Broken Hill to Bourke for an all-ages show at the aptly named Multi Purpose Centre, which was at the local high school. Indigenous kids stood peeking over the lip of the stage, fixated on what was happening in front of them. The last show was in Dubbo, some 300 ks north-west of Sydney. When the band left the sanctuary of the Shearing Shed Motor Inn for a 5 p.m. soundcheck, a line of eager punters stretched for what seemed like miles around the Garden Hotel. The word was out: Chisel was in town. It was a big night in Dubbo.

★

The three country shows proved that there was a lot of love out there for Cold Chisel, but the band still hadn't settled on a producer for the new album. Tony Cohen was the next name to come up in conversation—Tony had helped out on *Twentieth Century* in 1983 and had worked on the first Tex, Don and Charlie album *Sad But True*. After a fair amount of to-ing and fro-ing, Tony was given the thumbs-up and Chisel entered the Festival studios in Pyrmont to get back to work.

The vibe within the studio was a lot better, a lot more relaxed, after the live shows. Tony seemed to operate in two modes: he either sat quietly at the console watching intently through the glass, or was up on his feet and animated, as though he'd just done a big line of speed. Studio engineer Matt Lovell, fondly known as 'The Love God', was a blessing, the kind of unruffled character who was always there to do whatever was required to keep the train rolling. Festival was good for Jim, too, because he'd recorded there in the past. Even when Jim headed off to Goa in India to deal with some personal issues, recording continued at a steady pace. Upon his return, there was an almost tangible vitality in the studio.

Recording for the album finally concluded at the end of March, and the band then confronted the onerous task of choosing the final album tracks from the 28 they'd recorded. This album needed to be great; 'good' wouldn't cut it. We all understood that. The actual selection process was simple. An A4 sheet of paper was ruled up into six columns, one for each member of the band plus me. The 28 song titles were listed down the left-hand side of the page. Everyone had a vote for their favourite songs. Some songs picked themselves; others were subject to vigorous debate. In the final wash-up, Jim and Steve each had two songs on the album, Ian had one, and the remaining nine were Don's, including the title track, 'The Last Wave of Summer'. There was also a 'hidden' track, 'Once Around the Sun', a co-write of Jim and Phil's.

There were various suggestions as to who should mix the album, and Tony Cohen was under consideration, but I was pushing for an international name. My old mate Kevin Shirley would have been ideal, but he'd just started a new album with The Black Crowes which was likely to drag on for months.

I had been calling international managers representing producers and engineers without much luck. But then I got a call from Shannon O'Shea in LA, proposing we work with John X. John's mixing credits were broad; he'd worked with everyone from David Bowie to The Rolling Stones, and Black Grape to Public Enemy. We agreed to give him a shot.

*

Don, Ian, Robert Hambling and I flew out to LA; Jim would join us in a couple of days. Steve and Phil, however, stayed in Australia because of family matters. Our destination was The Chapel, a studio in Encino in the San Fernando Valley, established by Dave Stewart of the Eurythmics, and at the time owned and operated by Academy Award–winning composer Michael Kamen.

The Chapel was situated behind secure gates; a long, tree-lined driveway led to acres of manicured gardens and dense woodland. The main house had numerous bedrooms upstairs, and a grand piano took pride of place in the downstairs lounge room. Adjacent to a tennis court—with its own grandstand—was a small cabin that resembled a granny flat, housing the studio where The Traveling Wilburys recorded their hit debut album in 1988.

Upon first introduction, John X made a sizeable impression. He arrived decked out in brilliant orange culottes—the puzzled look on Don's face was priceless. This was merely the first of many John X fashion statements: my favourite was a toss-up between the cowhide culottes and a boho summer frock.

The studio was compact, which meant that we spent a lot of time playing tennis on the nearby court. After eight productive days at The Chapel, we headed home to play the results to Steve and Phil. But almost immediately, both of the guys looked concerned. They were not happy with the results—a feeling soon shared by the others—and we were back to square one.

I was just about ready to jump out my office window when Kevin Shirley unexpectedly called me from New York. He had a ten-day window in late June and could mix fifteen tracks for the price of twelve. We agreed on a budget and duly booked Avatar Studios in New York. In the end Kevin mixed eighteen of the twenty tracks, while Tony Cohen mixed 'Pretty Little Thing' and old mate Steve James mixed 'This Time Round' (which appeared on the extended/director's-cut release).

Finally the band had something to show for all the trials and tribulations that they had gone through over the last couple of years. There certainly were times during that period when all of us had questioned whether we would ever get to this stage. Now it was time to get the record out to those who really mattered, the fans, as they would be the litmus test.

19

A BRAVE NEW WORLD

After a fourteen-year hiatus, any new Chisel album needed to be unveiled in a special way. It wasn't like the glory days, when we could simply drop a new record on a radio programmer's desk. We needed to make an impact.

The band had been debating the choice of a single for months, and we eventually went with 'Yakuza Girls', a Don Walker song channelling Jerry Lee Lewis, delivered at break-neck speed, which sang the praises of Asian bar girls. It was certain to excite the fans *and* outrage conservative media and the PC fraternity, which made it the perfect choice. Nothing quite like a bit of 'controversy' to start things off.

The internet, while relatively new, was the buzzword as far as promotion was concerned. We came up with a plan to initially release the new music online; there'd be no hard copy. If fans and radio wanted it, they'd have to download it. Radio wasn't happy with the idea, especially when we revealed our plan to first go online at midnight. Their concern was that they wouldn't have engineers available at that time and they'd miss the morning radio exclusive.

I wasn't going to blow this, so I made a compromise and got a CD to Guy Dobson at Triple M in Sydney. He uploaded it via the internet across the network and we had the breakfast radio market cornered. Within the first twelve hours of launching, we had 228,598 hits on the site and a further 250,000 over the next three weeks. The song was available to be streamed or downloaded, and 108,000 punters did just that. As we'd predicted, some feminist groups and conservative commentators were outraged at the lyrics of 'Yakuza Girls', but fans lapped it up.

Meanwhile in New York, Kevin Shirley continued mixing the songs: next up was the second release from the album, 'The Things I Love in You'. To save time, Kevin uploaded the finished mix via the internet for the band's approval. Due to time-zone differences, we had a 6 a.m. start to hear the fresh mix. Jim was overseas so it was the four Chisels, Robert Hambling, Anthony O'Grady and me who gathered at Soundfirm, a post-production facility in Lindfield on Sydney's North Shore. The download came through at 8 a.m. and, after a couple of suggestions from Don, within a short time we had the final mix of 'The Things I Love in You'. We were all impressed by the magic of the new tech world.

With that done, Kevin got to work on mixing the rest of the album. Everything was rolling along smoothly until I got a call from Steve and Phil.

'We've got some concerns with the mix of the single,' they told me.

I told them, through gritted teeth, that they could both get on the next flight to New York. 'Ian can go as well. I want you guys to sit with Kevin and if you have any problems, tell him what they are.'

Jim was elsewhere in the States and I called him and explained the situation.

'Okay, I'll fly to New York,' he told me. 'Don't worry, it'll be sorted out. Relax.'

I wanted Don to be there, but he was in the middle of a Paul Kelly tour, and I couldn't go as I was up to my eyeballs with the album release and tour plans. But I trusted Kevin; he had good people skills.

Adrienne Overall had photographed album covers for Ian, as well as Midnight Oil, Silverchair, Hoodoo Gurus and Diesel. Don and I met with Adrienne and Robert Hambling one afternoon to throw around some ideas for the cover. Adrienne had a large book on the coffee table opened at a page containing the 1942 painting *Nighthawks* by American artist Edward Hopper. The painting was of a late-night scene at an all-night diner; three patrons sitting at the counter drinking coffee plus a barman/soda jerker. Just as *The Death of Marat* had inspired the *East* album cover, *Nighthawks* did the same for *The Last Wave of Summer*.

With the guys all back in the country, on a chilly winter's night in early August, I pulled into the Caltex service centre at Wyong, a popular stop for anyone heading north. Three plastic tables were set up in the main window, where the band was seated, staring out the window, half-empty plastic cups in front of them. It was reminiscent of the countless roadside diners they had frequented over the years and made for the perfect cover, as captured by Adrienne.

*

For a split second we toyed with the idea of promoting the late 1998 Last Wave of Summer tour ourselves, but due to the problems associated with finishing the record, we agreed to go with an established promoter. Of course Gudinski was super keen but as Mushroom had the record, it presented a potential conflict of interest. My phone ran hot with calls from promoters, merchandisers, sound and lighting companies, support acts, even venue operators—everyone wanted in.

At Dirty Pool, we'd had a very good working relationship with Michael Coppel when we co-promoted international acts. He was my preference, but we had to weigh up offers from virtually all the major promoters. Then things got really interesting when a new promoter, SEL (Sports & Entertainment Ltd), unexpectedly came up with an offer.

James Erskine had formed SEL in 1997 with Tony Cochrane, David Coe and Basil Scaffidi. Their main area of business was sports management, but they'd recently teamed up with theatre producer John Frost to present a successful arena production of *Grease*. James was a straight-talking Englishman, while Tony—the man who had convinced Frank Sinatra to return to Australia in 1988 after Ol' Blue Eyes had sworn to never set foot here again—was wildly enthusiastic. They were two very different characters, but that contrast was appealing. I put aside my natural scepticism—they'd never staged a rock-and-roll tour—and awaited their proposal.

A typical tour proposal was relatively short and straight to the point, with specifics of venues, run, expected gross, bucks, etc. etc., but SEL's response was a bit overwhelming. It contained in-depth market research, pages of back-up information and spreadsheets. It was impressive. And SEL's dollar offer was way more attractive than their closest competitor's, making it an offer that we couldn't refuse.

★

Throughout the Dirty Pool years I'd been in competition with Michael Gudinski, so it felt a bit strange to work with him on *The Last Wave of Summer* album. But he had a strong team: I'd known Warren Costello, who ran Mushroom, for years. He was a good guy, smart and vastly experienced; I knew we'd work well together. Sue McAullay, a friend who I held in very high regard, was head of publicity and promotion. Festival had distributed Mushroom's catalogue for many years, but this was about to change with a move to Sony Music, which was a big plus. Sony Music was a heavyweight and if their boss Denis Handlin believed in the record, I knew he'd do all he could to make it a major success.

As for Gudinski, back in 1983 he'd sold 49 per cent of Mushroom Records to News Corp. Rumours were circulating that Michael was now getting ready to sell the remaining 51 per cent. I raised the topic repeatedly with him, but he flatly denied it. Still, the rumours persisted. When Denis Handlin dropped into Festival to listen to some of the early tracks, I cornered him and asked if he knew whether Michael was selling out. Denis shrugged it off, but I still wondered how much he knew.

Then in August 1998 it was announced that Gudinski had sold his remaining 51 per cent to News Corp. This was a red-flag moment. News Corp owned Festival and it made sense that Mushroom distribution was going to return there at some stage. Obviously, I was concerned about the possible impact on the album. I called Denis, who assured me that Sony had guaranteed distribution of the Chisel record for twelve months after the October release. But when I asked our lawyers for clarification, they advised me that the clause covering distribution within the joint venture agreement was somewhat ambiguous.

It could possibly mean that Sony might have the album for only a few months before it reverted to Festival. This was potentially a disaster: what incentive would Sony have to seriously work the record?

I called Michael, who agreed that this needed to be sorted out promptly, but the soap opera had only just begun. I'd heard rumblings coming out of Sony that Handlin's dynasty was under threat. He'd ruled the company for fourteen years and turned it into one of Australia's most successful labels—and a highly prized Sony International affiliate. But Denis's personal style had upset people and at a conference in Miami there was a 'palace coup'. Denis was ordered to take a break; he was out of the picture for ten weeks. This was not good news for Cold Chisel.

★

'The Things I Love in You' was released towards the end of August, debuting nationally at number 10, but there were issues at radio. While Chisel was a mainstay of FM radio, the response to the new product was less than ecstatic. It was a classic case of 'we like your old stuff better than your new stuff'. Instead of being placed on high rotation, 'The Things' languished in the lower regions of playlists. In September, Mushroom/Sony hosted listening parties around the country to preview the album to media. The overall reaction was good, but I wasn't sure whether this was a response to the music or the fact the band had re-formed. All I could do was hope it was both.

The tour was locked in for an early November start, and we needed somewhere for a warm-up gig. Newcastle had always been a Chisel town and again we employed the ruse of a Jimmy

Barnes show for a gig at Fanny's Nightclub on 2 October. Newcastle's favourite sons, rugby league legends Andrew and Matthew Johns, introduced Chisel and the almost 1000 ecstatic patrons gave the band a thunderous reception.

Six days later, at the Woolloomooloo Bay Hotel in Sydney, Triple M's Richard Stubbs welcomed the Premier of New South Wales to the stage, introducing him as 'Bob "If the van is a-rocking, don't start knocking" Carr'. It was then that Bob announced to the waiting media that Cold Chisel would be releasing a new studio album and undertaking a national concert tour. A week later, *The Last Wave of Summer* debuted at number 1. On the same day, tickets went on sale for the tour— and 9000 were sold in the first fifteen minutes.

Chisel was back.

★

Production values had changed considerably since 1983's Last Stand tour and we needed to adapt. I suggested using designers who were working in the current medium, but Don was adamant that he didn't want the 'big rock-show look'. Instead he was keen to work with people from theatre, whom he felt could come up with a different, more cutting-edge production. I was sceptical; this was rock and roll, after all.

Gavan Swift was a top lighting designer who worked in the theatre, opera and corporate events. Don was an admirer of Gavan's theatre work and felt he could design something unique, something more than the standard rock experience. As we gathered at Steve's apartment in Kings Cross and huddled around a small cardboard replica of the stage set, I thought of the famous Stonehenge scene from *Spinal Tap* and prayed that the result would be different. The design comprised five black steel scaffolds that, when connected, formed a wave-like shape. It not only functioned as a backdrop, but it provided rigging for the sound and lighting.

I knew this wasn't going to be cheap. There was the cost of manufacture and the expense of transporting it from show to show. Production and transport costs were part of our deal with SEL, so I needed to run it by them. As I'd predicted, Tony Cochrane went into a tailspin, but James Erskine was much calmer.

'You can have pink dancing elephants if that's what you want. In the end, you are paying for it!'

I thought, well, good point. After all, the more money we spent, the bigger impact it'd have on the tour's bottom line.

Another additional cost was a small stage set-up to be used in the larger auditoriums. This 'B stage' would be positioned on the floor, at the rear of the venue among the punters, giving the shows a more intimate feel. But this was going to be tricky. Norwest Productions' concert PA was hung on either side of the main stage, broadcasting sound from both the main and the B stage. There would be a slight sound delay when using the B stage, creating an echo, which would be a challenge for the band.

The logical solution was to use in-ear headphones, which would allow a straight feed from the PA, eliminating the delay. It seemed simple enough, but the Chisel guys were old school— raised in beer barns; they fed off the ambience created on stage through floor monitors. Only Jim had experience with 'in-ear' technology, but after a spirited debate, common sense prevailed and they agreed to use the new technology.

Final dress rehearsals took place over a week at Sydney's Fox Studios in early November, using a space designed for film production. Six 44-gallon oil drums were positioned at the front of the stage, and to the rear, amps, drums and keyboards were dwarfed by Gavan Swift's black steel backdrop in the shape of a wave.

The plan was for the oil drums to burst into flames while the band played the finale song of their set, 'The Last Wave of Summer', as a white transparent curtain from above cascaded to the floor silhouetting the band. It sounded spectacular, but the oil drums presented severe safety issues: fire was an unforgiving medium and fire permits would be required for every show. The oil drums, sadly, wouldn't make it past the first show.

Someone suggested that using dancers on a couple of songs would be fun. As often was the case with Chisel, a suggestion made in jest turned into an idea that everyone loved. The blueprint was go-go girls in cages, à la Whisky a Go Go in the late 1960s. Ian's partner Margeaux was given the task of finding the right dancers, which proved to be harder than we thought.

Plenty of contenders could dance—and very seductively— but the art of go-go eluded them. Jim and Jane were friends with choreographer Gary Leeson who was brought in to sort out the problem. The brief was simple: the dancers would strut their stuff during the songs 'Pretty Little Thing' and 'Yakuza Girls'. Two professional drag artists, Amelia Airhead and Tess Tickle, would augment the line-up. It would be a guaranteed jaw-dropper for those in the front rows.

*

The opening night of the tour was set to take place at Carrington Park, the home of the Bathurst Panthers rugby league team. The date was Friday, 13 November. Black Friday. What could possibly go wrong? The Bathurst 500 was being held over that weekend meaning that 170,000 race-mad fans would be in town and ready to party; our promoters were hopeful of attracting a lot of them to the concert. I just hoped we didn't have a repeat of the April 1983 Bathurst Grand Prix riot.

However, the crowd was disappointingly small, just 5000 or so, when the band walked on stage. They were a bit rusty, but the fans loved them. By the time they began 'Yakuza Girls', spurred on by Jim, a couple of the dancers had left the line at the front of the stage and gyrated towards the back, which wasn't part of the plan. Steve looked up from his kit to be met by the sight of a G-stringed dancer astride his bass drum. I glanced towards the side of the stage, where there was a gathering of promoters and media. I noticed a fair share of gaping mouths, nervous grins and chardonnay spillage.

On the flight back to Sydney, Steve shuffled up beside me. He had a look of concern on his face that I had come to know very well, and it could have been about anything: room allocation, song selection or his ongoing debate with Jim—one person thinks he's playing too slow, the other too fast. Steve leaned in close to ensure I could hear him over the drone of the jet's engines. 'Are you sure the dancers are a good idea?' he asked me.

'Don't worry,' I reassured him. 'It's all going to work out. We just have to iron out a few wrinkles.' I looked at my watch—it was past midnight; Black Friday was over.

That Sunday I got a call from Don.

'Have you spoken to Steve?'

My stomach did that bottom-of-the-rollercoaster thing that it had done for 22 years. I knew it meant trouble. Don explained to me that he'd received a call from Steve and his wife Joanne, who felt that the 'strippers'—their words—didn't complement the music. Joanne had used the word 'tacky' before getting stuck into Don. Soon enough I got a call from Steve.

'You were at the meetings when we talked about the dancers,' I told him. 'Why didn't you raise your concerns then?' I explained to him that the dancers were under contract, they'd put aside time to do this. 'It'd be wrong to cancel them at such a late hour,' I said before ending the call.

It was the type of situation I'd been in so many times over the years with Chisel. Just when I thought everything was rolling along smoothly, bang—we'd hit a speed bump. And we were only one show into the tour.

The first indoor shows were at Townsville Entertainment Centre on 16 and 17 November, both sell-outs; 10,500 punters all up, which equated to almost 10 per cent of the local population. The dancers weren't doing these shows, so that problem was on hold for the moment. But as I stood at the mixing desk watching the show, I found that the lighting was so dull I had to squint to see the band. It felt like they were playing through a veil of smog. I spoke with the road crew and their take on it was blunt: the lighting design was the problem.

The band's perspective was that the show went over great, the crowd had loved it and it was a fantastic result. But I knew that from the stage it was impossible to know how the show looked to the audience. It was Gavan's baby, and he insisted that with a few minor tweaks the problem would be easily fixed. When I ran that by the lighting crew, I was met with a firm shaking of heads. 'The design is the problem,' they insisted. By the time we reached Sydney a few days later, the lighting had been redesigned.

★

It had been just one month shy of fifteen years since the band had last played the Sydney Entertainment Centre. The response was huge: diehards had camped out overnight to get the best seats, and more than 25,000 tickets were sold within 24 hours.

Sunday, 22 November was the first of three nights and Jim walked on stage sporting a new bleached-blond hairdo. The show went over great and when the dancers formed a line at the lip of the stage for their curtain call, they dropped their tops—and the stunned audience discovered there were two drag queens in their midst. Afterwards, Jim 'bodyswerved' to a waiting car, leaving the rest of us to dissect the show. Steve left quietly with his family, but I could tell that the dancer issue was far from over.

Soundcheck for the second show was scheduled for late Monday afternoon. The band slowly drifted in and gathered in their dressing rooms. Then suddenly, *whoosh*! A door flew open and in stepped Jim, a phone stuck to his ear. I could tell that the conversation wasn't cordial.

'Steve's not coming to soundcheck,' Jim reported. 'Apparently no one has returned his calls.'

There were blank looks all around until Don spoke. Yes, he had got a message from Steve, but figured it could wait until soundcheck. Everyone looked at me—we all knew what this was about. I found an empty dressing room, called Steve and tried my best to have a civil conversation, fully aware that over 10,000 diehard fans were putting on their best Chisel T-shirts and getting ready to converge on the Entertainment Centre.

Steve finally arrived about an hour before show time, and after a band meeting it was decided that the dancers would take no further part in the Sydney shows. That night on stage it was evident that the aggro that always existed between Steve and Jim was resurfacing. I was relieved that they didn't get into a scrap while playing.

We met the next day at Jim's and, while the discussion began pleasantly enough, it was very clear that Steve wasn't shifting his position: he wanted the dancers gone. Don exploded, insisting that this had nothing to do with the band; it was all about Steve appeasing his wife. There was a momentary silence before Steve returned fire.

'Find yourself another drummer,' he declared and headed out the door.

Jim was the first to respond. 'Well, fuck him, let's get another drummer then.'

I believe Jim was incensed because of the situation with the dancers: he and Jane had been personally involved in getting Gary Leeson, and then the dancers, to participate in the project.

Hiring a new drummer at this stage, of course, was pure fantasy. Cold Chisel was Don, Jim, Ian, Phil and Steve—and everyone knew that. There was only one way this could go and later that day I made the call to Steve.

'The dancers are off the tour.'

★

The next two shows were in Adelaide. This being the band's old hometown, the number of guests who had asked for tickets ran into the hundreds: family, extended family, friends, near-friends, hangers-on—you get the picture. Every ticket given out gratis to a guest was one that didn't earn a cent for the band, and guests expected the best seats in the house—the same seats sought by paying punters. Those close to the guys in the band also wanted backstage passes or, better still, all-access passes.

I had to allocate special staff to handle this. They needed the skills of NATO negotiators to sift through the list, separating those who were genuine friends and family from those who claimed to be distant cousins or long-lost friends of Phil's from kindergarten. In addition to the guest list there was another list of media, competition winners and VIPs. Once again, juggling chainsaws would have been easier, I swear.

As we rolled on to Melbourne for three shows at the Rod Laver Arena, the mood within the band was calmer. I knew very well that there was a pattern with Cold Chisel—there'd be a major drama, a big explosion, then things would settle down and they'd get on with business. In the early days, there had been advantages to travelling together: things would explode in the back of the van and be sorted by the time we reached the gig. But now everyone was travelling separately, so their only real contact was in the dressing room or on stage.

Drugs had been part of the landscape of my life for more than 30 years. I was always a take-it or leave-it type of consumer: if it was on offer, yeah sure, I'd have some, but I didn't seek it out. And I kept away from hard drugs; it seemed like a one-way street to addiction. With Cold Chisel, the drug conversation usually centred around Jim. To my mind, Jim'd had an addiction problem as long as I'd known him. In the early days, it was vodka, which was immensely destructive. If he added speed or coke to the mix, the result was that he became a teeth-grinding demon, not someone you relished being around.

Jim had the constitution of a bull, but by 1998 cracks had started to appear. To be fair, he was always a professional: he would turn up and put in, whether in the studio or on stage, irrespective of what was going on in his world. But during the recording of *Last Wave* it had become obvious that he was sometimes struggling with drugs. On this tour I'd regularly spend time with him right before the show, when his dressing room had been cleared of family, guests and hangers-on.

In that quiet moment, he'd look at me: 'Let's have a line.'

'Why not?' I'd say.

And with that Jim would spill out a gram of powder, which he'd neatly sort into four lines. Then he'd pass me a rolled-up $50 bill. I'd usually manage two railroad tracks—not short journeys, I can attest—and then Jim would take care of the rest, and with a guttural roar he'd head for the stage.

★

A week or so before the show at Burswood Dome in Perth, a rumour began to circulate that two of Western Australia's largest bikie gangs, the Coffin Cheaters and Club Deroes, were fixing to have a showdown at the concert. The local newspapers picked up on the story and gave it the full front-page treatment.

We arrived on 4 December, a day before the show, and I was informed that this rumour now seemed to have some credence. Gary Petterson, our head of security, told me that he had a contact who may be able to find out if the threat was genuine.

Along with Gary and an ex-cop friend of his, we headed out to a suburban pub for a meeting with the leader of the Coffin Cheaters. Gary's friend told us to wait in the car while he went inside. A short time later he reappeared on the pub's steps with a large dude sporting a beard, long hair and a colourful display of body art. They chatted for a while, then shook hands before Gary's mate returned to the car.

'He told me it's just a media beat-up,' he advised us, adding that those attending the gig wouldn't be in club colours. Bikie brawl averted, the show went on and then we travelled back east to Melbourne, Brisbane, Wollongong and Newcastle, before returning to Sydney for two more concerts, wrapping up on 21 December.

At the soundcheck for the second Sydney show, four days before Christmas, I figured I had just 24 hours to get through, hopefully with no more major dramas. At the soundcheck I was told on the quiet that there would be a surprise at the end of the show. I noticed a few of the dancers wandering around backstage; this wasn't unusual because they'd been around at different times during the tour, and some of them were good friends with Jim and Jane. Then I learned that the dancers would be joining the band for the encore.

'Does Steve know about this?' I asked.

Of course not. I took a deep breath and reminded myself that it was okay—this was the last night of the tour.

As the band launched into 'Pretty Little Thing', out they came, the 'outlawed six', cavorting and strutting about the stage. The crowd roared its approval while Steve's focus seemed to be firmly fixed on an unspecified spot on his bass drum. But his steely gaze was interrupted when a blonde dancer in a G-string shook her abundant assets in his direction. The dancers knew what had gone on behind the scenes and were rubbing Steve's face in it, quite literally. They then took their bows and the band kicked into what was the perfect finale for the year and the tour, 'Goodbye (Astrid Goodbye)'.

Afterwards, Jim left the stage and jumped straight into a waiting car parked outside, while Steve sulked in his dressing room and the other three guys breathed a sigh of relief. The Last Wave of Summer was all over.

20

ALL ROADS MUST END

When the dust had finally settled and my blood pressure had come down from the stratosphere, I reflected on the positives. The Last Wave of Summer had been the biggest and most successful tour of 1998—Chisel's twenty-one shows had drawn more than 150,000 punters. Merchandising sales had gone crazy. And the tour had introduced the band to a whole new audience of younger fans—parents had brought their kids and the gigs became cross-generational gatherings. The album, meanwhile, went to number 1 and achieved double-platinum. And sales of the band's back catalogue soared.

Our contract with SEL was for 31 shows, which left the question: what to do about the other ten? SEL wanted to move them to the end of 1999, but I knew this would be a problem. The mood within the Chisel camp had become less than affable and the guys wanted to concentrate on their careers outside of the band. Cold Chisel was not on their radar. I conveyed this to James Erskine and floated an alternative plan if I could get them to play together again: what about markets like New Zealand, Tasmania, Darwin and so on? But he wasn't convinced.

My dilemma was this: I had a band that wasn't at all interested in going back on the road, and a promoter who had a watertight contract—involving serious money—and who expected the deal to be honoured. I needed a prompt resolution. Erskine was a very tough, experienced negotiator and I feared this could get ugly. He and I faced off across a massive boardroom table in the SEL office high above Circular Quay. We bandied around figures, explained our respective positions, and finally after a few tense hours we reached an understanding. Both Chisel and SEL had made a considerable sum of money, and SEL were bound to benefit by having promoted the highest grossing tour of 1998. In the end, Cold Chisel were allowed to walk away from shows they had no interest in playing.

Yet demand for the band continued. Tasmania had missed out on the Chisel experience, and radio stations and newspapers there staged a coordinated on-air campaign to get the band across to the Apple Isle. Every day I received a stream of phone calls and emails, urging, sometimes begging, the band to consider playing there.

I was in two minds: in one way, I could see it as an opportunity to mend some wounds, make some money and sell some records. On the other hand, I needed to get as far away as I could from the craziness for a good while. But I decided to see what the reaction would be from the guys. Jim was busy, he had started a new album—and, as he informed me, 'I don't ever want to play with Steve again.' Don said he could do without the hassle, and Steve, meanwhile, was still smarting from 'Strippergate'. Ian and Phil were cautious but not resistant to the idea. Ever the masochist, I continued to put forward the case for a couple of shows. After much effort and haranguing on my part, I got the guys to agree to two concerts over the 1999 Easter weekend in Hobart.

The shows went surprisingly well, and I could tell that the bitterness that had accompanied much of the tour had faded. At the conclusion, they parted as friends. The bond they'd shared for more than twenty years remained strong.

Anthony O'Grady was also privy to the twists and turns of the Cold Chisel reunion. Totally exhausted and possibly scarred for life, Anthony managed to document the adventure in his terrific book *Cold Chisel: The Pure Stuff,* which was published in 1999.

*

In the wake of the Last Wave tour, I tried, without success, to get the album released in the US and Germany. Most labels questioned why they would release a record if the band wasn't an active unit, which was hard to argue with. But Chisel as a band and Jimmy Barnes the solo act had a small but loyal following in the UK. Jim had toured there a number of times and Chisel was still respected by key industry and media heavy-hitters.

I figured that this, along with the many Aussie and Kiwi expats in the UK, was enough to set up a small run of live shows. I arranged a meeting with the band and ran the idea past them, and much to my surprise they agreed. I called my friend Michael Chugg, asking for help with his UK counterparts. Within a couple of days he phoned me back with the surprising news that Harvey Goldsmith was interested.

I was gobsmacked. Goldsmith was one of the biggest names in promotion in the UK, having worked with everyone and everything from Led Zeppelin to Elton John and Live Aid.

Harvey believed that the band should play at least one night, possibly two, at London's prestigious Royal Albert Hall.

I was thrilled and tried to find dates that would fit with everyone's commitments. That, of course, was a virtually impossible task and over time the idea fizzled out. It made me realise that perhaps it was easier for me to deal with things within my control—like the band's back catalogue.

★

'Hey, it could be fun, not sure what will happen, but rest assured it'll be interesting.' That had been my pitch when I'd first contacted Robert Hambling in 1997, suggesting that he might like to tag along on the *Last Wave of Summer* journey. During the odyssey he shot hundreds of hours of footage. It made for funny, sad, riveting, sometimes disturbing viewing, and without doubt it was the most revealing insight into the beast that was Cold Chisel that I had ever seen. As I write this book, the only people who have seen parts of this footage are Robert, the five guys and me. Whether it ever gets released is totally up to Cold Chisel and Robert. I hope it does.

But Robert did suggest something to me in the aftermath of the Last Wave tour that might just work. He was particularly impressed with the 'B stage' part of the show, the intimacy that the band got to share with the audience.

'This could work as a tour concept,' he told me.

'Got a name for it?' I asked, intrigued.

'"Ringside",' Robert replied.

Inspired in part by the legendary 1968 Elvis Comeback Special, Robert's 'Ringside' concept differed greatly from a conventional concert set-up. The band would be in the centre of the venue, the audience seated all around them. The idea was to stage a few nights in Sydney, which would be filmed and recorded for commercial release, perhaps even for a TV special.

I liked the idea but was still feeling the pain brought on by the Last Wave tour and my disappointment at the failed UK dates. Still, Robert and I talked about Ringside often over a couple of years, workshopping ideas, but that was where it would end. I just wanted to get on with my life. Though I was curious enough to ask Gino to do a full cost analysis. He shot me a stern look and asked, 'Are you sure you want to do this?'

I insisted that he go ahead and a week later he came back to me with some figures, which looked good on paper. But of course a cost analysis didn't factor in the unknown, namely the personal dynamics of the band. By the end of 2002, I'd pitched them the 'Ringside' idea and while most of the guys liked it, Don wasn't completely sold. He was concerned that Chisel might be seen to be aping the 'unplugged' concept. He was also concerned that the band, having built their legend on powerful live performances, might be viewed as going a bit soft. But Don was willing to go along with the rest of the band, who wanted to do it.

I also had to consider some of the problems we'd learned from the B-stage part of the Last Wave shows. The band had used in-ear technology to stay on track, but that was only for a few songs each night. Now we were talking about a full two-hour show. The technology had come a long way, but Chisel, forever the traditionalists, were still reluctant to fully embrace it.

There were other potential problems. The 360-degree set-up needed to be designed to not only provide access for people to be seated, but also allow the band and crew to get to their places. Sound and lighting would need to be hung above the stage. On top of all of this, the stage had to be able to revolve, otherwise some poor punters would be left looking at the band's backsides all night.

I called my old friend Eric Robinson of Jands. I knew that he could sort out this logistical nightmare—and, just as importantly, he had a strong personal relationship with all the Chisel guys. I explained to Eric the problems I'd had with the band and in-ear technology.

'Let me talk to them,' he suggested.

The guys sat in a semicircle, Steve tapping his feet to some imaginary beat, while Eric spelled out in the clearest terms why, if they wanted this to work, they had no other option. Finally, they agreed—and in-ears were go.

*

Renowned artist Martin Sharp had created the iconic poster artwork for the 1982 'Evening with the Circus Animals' shows in Wentworth Park. I felt that the 'Ringside' concept would also suit his style, so I rang Martin and set up a meeting. Robert Hambling and I drove to Wirian, Martin's family home, a heritage-listed mansion situated directly behind Cranbrook School in Bellevue Hill.

Contained within the walls of Wirian was Martin's fascinating world—rooms cluttered with artwork, antique children's toys, books, posters, Tiny Tim memorabilia, even a battered straw hat once owned by fellow artist Margaret Olley. Dominating the front foyer was Martin's large painting of the cover of Cream's 1967 album *Disraeli Gears*. Martin had done the original cover, which interestingly was the actual size of a vinyl album sleeve. He also had co-written the lyrics for one of

Cream's best-known songs, 'Tales of Brave Ulysses'. Martin, who reminded me of the children's TV character Catweazle, loved the 'Ringside' concept and agreed to do the artwork.

I adopted a different approach to marketing the Sydney shows. Rather than use costly television and media advertising, I gambled on a major street-poster campaign throughout the western suburbs, utilising free street press and social media. The total spend was obscenely low in comparison with what we would normally spend on traditional promotion and marketing, and it worked a treat.

On 24 May 2003, the band played a warm-up show at the Function Centre in Orange, a venue that over the years had hosted everyone from Normie Rowe and Billy Thorpe to The Easybeats (playing their final show)—and even Queen Elizabeth II and Prince Philip. On a cold autumn night, 900 payers turned up for a long first gig, the band opening with 'Home and Broken Hearted' and closing, after a marathon 35 songs, with 'Goodbye (Astrid Goodbye)'.

Cobwebs duly blown off, the Newcastle Entertainment Centre had been set up 'in the round' for three days of rehearsals, followed by the first two nights of the six-date Ringside tour. The reaction to the Newcastle shows was amazing so I was confident that the Sydney experience—four nights at the Hordern Pavilion—would be phenomenal. The first show was set for 3 June.

To achieve the best sound and vision, I'd brought together a great team. Steve James, the son of British comic legend Sid James, who had mixed 'This Time Round' on the *Last Wave* director's cut bonus album; I knew he'd be ideal for laying down the live sound feed. Michael 'Jacko' Jackson and his ace team of five camera operators, along with Craig Chapman's

Daily Planet Productions crew, captured the action, overseen by director Robert Hambling.

The concept showcased a more intimate side of Cold Chisel, up close and personal for the first time since their earliest days. The audience got to experience the subtle musical nuances that were often lost within their high-powered performances. Sydney was a resounding success—reviews and audience reaction were over the top, and it was a runaway financial success too, netting a staggering 56 per cent profit. It also provided us with four nights of great material. And no audience member was more than 30 metres away from the band.

As was our custom, each band member, plus Robert Hambling and me, took away a CD from every show to review. The dud performances hit the floor pretty quickly, and then the decision-making fun began. Don had always been assured of a good representation of his songs on any record, while for the others it could be a battle. Robert and I, meanwhile, had the luxury of being able to be totally impartial.

With so many excellent performances to choose from, we knew we had enough for a two-CD set and subsequent DVD— about 30 songs in all. We then brought in Rick Will, who'd been involved with *The Last Wave of Summer*. He presided over the mixing console at Studios 301 in Sydney with his customary assortment of candles, incense, plastic figurines, palm trees and special lighting, transforming it once again into The Rickster's Domain while finalising the *Ringside* album.

*

In September 2003, I met with tour manager Michael Long to discuss the viability of a national Ringside tour. Then I took it to the band and, again, everyone except Don seemed excited. While Don fully acknowledged the success of the Sydney shows, he still had reservations about the show moving away from the true nature of Chisel. I appreciated where he was coming from but believed that the concept presented a whole new version of the band and their music to, potentially, a new audience. Don, to his credit, was willing to take part, but stressed that 'I'm only the piano player'—which was Don-speak for 'I'm not taking the lead role here'.

A national tour was a much bigger challenge than shows in just two cities. Eric Robinson had done such a great job with the initial shows in June that I hired him again for the bigger run. When planning a tour like this I had to take a calculated guess on how many shows I thought we could handle in each market; it was more about gut feeling than precise science. The usual process was to confirm a date, then put a couple on hold hoping demand would be strong. The common logic was to start in Brisbane and travel clockwise around the country to finish in Perth, but that was rarely achievable. You'd often find yourself crisscrossing the country in order to find available venues. This, of course, would eat up precious time and money.

Our run of shows, unfortunately, weaved like a snake across Australia. The tour started in Tamworth in late November, headed north to Brisbane, then went to Perth for two nights. Six days later, two fully laden Kenworth semitrailers pulled into the Adelaide Entertainment Centre, the four drivers having started in Brisbane, a journey of more than 6000 kilometres. Reflecting on my roadie days and the many distances I had travelled, I was glad that time was well behind me.

From Adelaide, our 'circus' headed to Tasmania before Chisel played four sell-outs at the Festival Hall in Melbourne.

The tour finale was three nights in January 2004 at Sydney's Hordern 'Pavlova', where the Ringside journey had commenced eight months earlier. The Ringside concept would generate a 32-track double-CD set that went gold, peaking at number 27 on the charts, as well as a 29-track DVD.

The tour was a success on both a business and personal level—more than 65,000 people bought tickets, and it went off without the usual dramas that had been commonplace in the past.

EPILOGUE

For years, rumours had circulated of massive dollars being offered for Cold Chisel to do major corporate and sporting events. While planning the Last Wave of Summer tour, I'd taken a serious look at sponsorship and learned that the only viable options were beer companies—which, after consideration, we passed on. I guess I've always been an idealist: to my way of thinking, a rock band doesn't need to align themselves with a brand name; they *are* the brand name. Springsteen didn't need it, so why would Cold Chisel? Don, for one, shared my opinion.

In early August 2009, I got a call from Jim's agent, Frank Stivala of Premier Artists, who asked if the band would be interested in a show at the V8 Supercars in Sydney in December. Being more than fully aware of the dynamics of the band— it had been 32 years, after all—I called Don to discuss the idea. He asked about the proposed deal and I sent him some numbers.

A few days later, Don called and asked if I was available for a meeting with the band at Phil's place in Balmain.

307

'What's the meeting about?' I asked, figuring it had something to do with the Supercars proposal. Don, however, told me that the band wanted to make some changes to my role as manager, which came as a surprise. The following day I met with the band, and they told me what Don had made clear: they'd decided to change the terms of my management contract. I indicated this was not acceptable to me.

Thirty-two years was a long time; I'd spent close to half of my life working with Cold Chisel. I understood and accepted that this was about business, and the guys had a right to make business decisions as they saw fit. Whatever I thought about it, it was still their decision to make.

That night, I discussed the matter with Gay. Then I drafted an email to the band, resigning as their manager.

If I'd learned anything from my journey, it was this: life goes on, and what is fundamentally important is that we live each day to the fullest. And, right at that moment, I had the rest of my life to get on with.

*

A year and a half later, on 15 January 2011, my phone rang. It was Don.

'Steve's in hospital,' he told me. 'He's got a brain tumour.'

My mind flashed back to 1993, when Steve had had a benign tumour removed. Don quietly confided that this was worse and that it didn't look good. It was a sobering moment.

Twenty-four hours later, the phone rang in my car. It was Jim. I pulled over to the side of the road.

'He's gone.'

Neither of us knew what to say next. After all those years

of feeling bulletproof, I found it incredibly hard to take it in. I couldn't quite believe that one of us was gone.

I flew to Adelaide for Steve's funeral. It had been more than a year since I'd seen the Chisel guys and we hugged each other warmly. This was no time for animosity. I stood there, staring at that wooden box, struggling to accept that Steve was actually dead.

Sure, Steve could drive you crazy at times, but he was, and still is, like a brother to me. All the guys are. Chisel forever. Forever Chisel.

I kept in social contact with all the guys over the subsequent years, but I never attended any of their live shows. There was no animosity between us. Besides, I felt I had spent half my life with them, and seen them perform so many times, there was no real need, and life moves on. In 2020 they announced another tour. On the quiet I had received word from a couple of the guys that they believed it could be their last-ever tour. As the final shows at Parramatta drew closer, both Don and Jim called me, imploring me to come to the show, so I said I would.

It was an emotional night. I was glad I went. Are we still in contact? Of course we are. It's hard to break that bond.

ACKNOWLEDGEMENTS

I dedicate this book in loving memory of

Mum and Dad	Paul Varley
Deirdre and Bill Neller	Pete Illingworth
Steve Prestwich	Pete Way,
Nick O'Dey	Kim Simmonds
Rob Mackie	Paul Turner
Chris Nairne	Peter Ikin
Gerry G	Steve Hands
Glenn Wheatley	Ray Holder
Anthony O'Grady	Andrew McMillan
Eric Robinson	John Bromell

Thanks to my family, Gay, Shannon, Kelly, Leigh and my six wonderful grandchildren.

My sons-in-law, Ernesto, Greg and Aaron. My sister Vicki who helped with our early family history, my younger brother Ian who in early 1977 pestered me to go and see a little band out of Adelaide, Cold Chisel. My wonderful sister-in-law Tracey, always there to rely on for support.

The Dirty Pool family, John Woodruff, Ray Hearn, Gino Principe, Keith Welsh, Brent Eccles, Jenny Elliott, Richard McDonald and the magnificent girls who manned the fortress so gallantly. Iva Davies and Icehouse. From Preston, Frank Newbold, Eddie Sandham, Laurence Bernard and Ken Maguire.

Robert Hambling and Adrienne Overall for your creative help and treasured friendship.

My surfing mates from Avalon and Palm Beach, Adam, Wato, Rory, Ronny, Dave, Tony, Cliffy, Roy, Welchy, Mick, Finny and many more who gifted me many a wave over the years.

My right-hand women Denise Sharp and Louis Stoven-Bradford.

Dennis, Zoe and Hobbsy, Hendo, Brad, Yanna, Dave and Sharen, Mike, Deb, Vicki, John Frost and Shane O'Connor, and the many more who allowed me to be their friend.

Peter Rix, Tim Prescott, Brian Harris, Phil Mortlock, Roger Langford, Phil Deamer, Mark Opitz and Thomas Heyman.

John Watson and John O' Donnell, who have carried on steering the Chisel ship superbly.

Peter Moss, Mark Pope, Daffy Ferguson, Chris Bastic, Michael Long, and the Chisel crews that went beyond the call to make things work. Dave Blight, John Hoffman, Ray Smith, Lee Conlan, Joe and Peter Konnaris, Glenn A Baker, Tony Mott, Ian Green, Bob King, Greg Noakes, Trevor and Jan Smith, Donald Robertson, Christie Eliezer, Toby Cresswell, Jen Jewel Brown, Deb Fitzsimons, Guy Finlay, Kathy McCabe and Michael Lawrence.

Jane, Margeaux, Firoozeh and Chris for overseeing their wayward charges.

Tony and Kim Hamilton for being the influencers who helped shape my future.

Jeff Apter for your help and guidance in turning my words into a coherent read.

Finally Jim, Don, Steve, Phil and Ian for giving me a go way back in 1977—you changed my life.